World industrial archaeology

KENNETH HUDSON

World industrial archaeology

CAMBRIDGE UNIVERSITY PRESS

CAMBRIDGE

LONDON · NEW YORK · MELBOURNE

Published by the Syndics of the Cambridge University Press
The Pitt Building, Trumpington Street, Cambridge CB2 1RP
Bentley House, 200 Euston Road, London NW1 2DB
32 East 57th Street, New York, NY 10022, USA
296 Beaconsfield Parade, Middle Park, Melbourne 3206, Australia

© Cambridge University Press 1979

First published 1979

Filmset in 'Monophoto' Imprint by Servis Filmsetting Ltd, Manchester

Printed in Great Britain at the University Press, Cambridge

Library of Congress Cataloguing in Publication Data

Hudson, Kenneth.
World industrial archaeology.

(New studies in archaeology)
Bibliography: p.
Includes index.
1. Industrial archaeology. I. Title. II. Series.
T37.H84   609   77-94225

ISBN 0 521 21991 4 hard covers
ISBN 0 521 29330 8 paperback

CONTENTS

Contents

SOURCES OF ILLUSTRATIONS

Illustrations taken directly from journals are given full reference in relevant footnotes.

Der Anschnitt Bochum, 1974, p. 27 (p. 43, middle and bottom)

Belknap Mill Society (p. 173)

Mr W. A. Campbell (p. 214)

© Center in Business History, University of Antwerp (pp. 153, 154)

C. & J. Clark Ltd (p. 178)

© reserved The County Record Office, Stafford. Photo: Peter Rogers (p. 128)

© M. Davies-Shiel, *Bulletin of the Historical Metallurgy Group* (pp. 32, 33, 34)

The Engineer No. 78, 1894, p. 172 (p. 204)

The Faversham Society (p. 228)

photograph courtesy of the Hagley Museum, Greenville, Wilmington, Delaware (pp. 229, 230)

Thomas H. Hair *A series of views of the collieries in . . . Northumberland and Durham. With descriptive sketches . . . by M. Ross* London, 1844 (p. 43, top)

M. Nisser (p. 119)

Historic American Engineering Record National Park Service, Washington D.C. (pp. 21, 93, 94, 95, 137, 138, 141, 208, 209, 210)

John Hume (p. 218)

ICI Fibres Ltd (pp. 182, 183, 185)

Anders Jespersen (pp. 31, 188, 189, 198, 199, 200)

Johnson Line (pp. 221, 222)

Landeskonservator, Rheinland, Bonn (pp. 23, 24, 25, 130, 131, 132, 161, 202)

Robert F. Legget (p. 150)

Kim C. Leslie (pp. 87, 88); Kim C. Leslie 'The Ashburnham Estate Brickworks 1840–1968', *Sussex Industrial History* Winter 1970/71, p. 8, Fig. 3 (p. 90)

Charles Léva (p. 59)

Los Angeles County Museum (p. 51)

Merrimack Valley Textile Museum (p. 16)

copyright Museum Vleeshuis (p. 79)

© National Photography Collection, Ottawa (pp. 157, 158)

Nighswander, Lord, Martin & Kilkelley, Laconia, New Hampshire (p. 175)

William H. Pierson Jr (p. 167)

Preservation Society of Newport County, Newport, R.I. (p. 103)

Radio Times Hulton Picture Library (p. 147)

Claude Rivals (pp. 81, 82, 83, 84)

François Roelants de Vivier 'Bois du Luc: une cité industrielle – een industriewijk' from 'La maison d'hier et d'aujour'hui' *Revue de l'Association royale des Demeures historiques de Belgiques* No. 20, December 1973 (p. 29)

Edward S. Rutsch, Historic Conservation and Interpretation Inc., Newton, New Jersey (p. 140)

Ryhope Engines Trust (pp. 192, 194, 195)

photo Theodore Anton Sande (p. 164)

Gerhard Seib (pp. 44, 46)

The Simon van der Stel Foundation (pp. 168, 169, 170)

Dr N. A. F. Smith (pp. 98, 99)

Smithsonian Institution (p. 166)

photo M. J. H. Southway 'Kingswood Coal' *BIAS Journal* Vol. 4, 1971, pp. 14, 18–19 (pp. 38, 40, 42)

State of California Department of Parks and Recreation (p. 52)

The Steelworks Museum of Surahammar (p. 116)

Stora Kopparberg Bergslags Aktiebolag (pp. 54, 55, 56)

Professor D. G. Tucker (p. 207) Professor D. G. Tucker, *BIAS Journal* Vol. 5, 1971, p. 15, Fig. 1 (p. 203)

C. R. Twidale (pp. 66, 67, 69, 71, 73)

Bergakademie, Freiberg (pp. 48, 49)

Mr Robert M. Vogel, Smithsonian Institution (p. 144)

The aims and academic status of industrial archaeology

There seems to be fairly general agreement that the term 'industrial archaeology' was invented early in the 1950s by Donald Dudley, at that time Director of the Extra-Mural Department of the University of Birmingham, and afterwards Professor of Latin within the same university. Mr Dudley, however, made no claim to be an industrial archaeologist, and did no more than suggest that the academic and practical possibilities of something called industrial archaeology might be worth exploring. The subject's first real impresario was one of Mr Dudley's extra-mural colleagues, Michael Rix, who in 1955 wrote an article for *The Amateur Historian* which gave industrial archaeology, both as a name and as a range of study, to the world. Mr Rix, very wisely, made no attempt to define the subject, but made it clear that the material in which he was primarily interested belonged to the eighteenth and nineteenth centuries, the factories and mills, 'the steam-engines and locomotives that made possible the provision of power, the first metal-framed buildings, cast-iron aqueducts and bridges, the pioneering attempts at railways, locks and canals'. These, he felt, 'represent a fascinating interlocking field of study, whole tracts of which are virtually unexplored'.

Two comments could, with hindsight, be usefully made about Michael Rix's pioneering article. The first is that he made no attempt to suggest what form this 'fascinating interlocking field of study' should take, and the second that he assumed, rightly or wrongly, that industrial archaeology would necessarily be confined to what could be termed, in British circumstances, the period of the Industrial Revolution. Most of the controversy which has surrounded industrial archaeology since the publication of this pioneering article has centred on these two points.

In writing the first book to appear on the subject,[1] I myself refused to accept that industrial archaeology was necessarily and by definition concerned exclusively with the monuments of the Industrial Revolution.

Everything has its birth and its old age and each industry has to be seen and studied against its own time-scale. In the case of the petroleum industry, for instance, the old and rare monuments date from the second half of the 19th

[1] *Industrial Archaeology : an Introduction* John Baker, 1963.

century. For atomic energy and for a number of plastics
and synthetic fibres it is the 1940s that we have to
consider. For iron bridges it is the middle of the 18th
century. It is pointless and ridiculous to try to establish an
arbitrary date which can be used to divide the old from
the recent, the archaeologically approved from the
archaeologically disreputable.

I went on to attempt a definition which I felt would not be unreasonably
restricting to people who might feel drawn towards this new field of
research: 'Industrial archaeology is the discovery, recording and study
of the physical remains of yesterday's industries and communications.'
This seemed to me then, and still does now, to say everything that needs
to be said in the way of a definition, although subsequent experience
suggests that it might have been wise to emphasise the word 'remains'
and to use it frequently in one's writings, as a reminder of the essentially
archaeological character of the work one was doing.

I certainly thought it advisable at that time, sniffing object-
worshippers down wind, to give all possible support to the humanity
and good sense of the founder and first editor of *Antiquity*, O. G. S.
Crawford. 'Archaeology', he once wrote, 'is merely the past tense of
anthropology. It is concerned with past phases of human culture.' I
agreed completely with Crawford's insistence that the basis of culture is
technology and I tried to make my position clear by saying that 'a good
archaeologist must be interested in every aspect of the culture he has
chosen to study – its technology, its social organisation, its political
system. Otherwise, he cannot interpret what he finds, he cannot talk
sense.'

In the third and extensively revised edition of the same work,[2]
published thirteen years later, I suggested that industrial archaeology
in Britain had passed through two stages of development and redefinition and was entering a third. Stage 1, I believed, had ended in about
1960. It had been characterised, I felt, by a notable crusading spirit. 'A
small and curiously assorted body of pioneers devoted a great deal of
time and energy to stirring up the public conscience about the rapid
disappearance of buildings and machinery which document the history
of British industry and technology, especially in the 19th century.'
Some of these pioneers were undoubtedly sentimentalists and some had
little knowledge of the workings of either industry or politics, but they
believed in what they said and they performed an invaluable service in
making the phrase 'industrial archaeology' known. Stage 2, which
covered the Sixties and early Seventies, had three notable features –
'the creation all over Britain of amateur groups pursuing industrial
archaeology as a hobby, the beginnings of a rudimentary National

[2] *Industrial Archaeology: a New Introduction* John Baker, 1976.

Register of Industrial Monuments, and the belated growth of academic interest in the subject', Stage 2 had passed into Stage 3 'at the moment when an increasing number of people begin to take stock of what has been achieved during Stage 1 and Stage 2 and to ask what it all means'. The bits and pieces, I felt, 'must add up to something they must contribute to the understanding of a wider field'. Industrial archaeology had entered into an inevitable period of heartsearching and quarrels. The honeymoon was over.

What began in 1963 as *The Journal of Industrial Archaeology* and ended ten years later as *Industrial Archaeology* was appropriate to industrial archaeology in Stages 1 and 2. This quarterly publication belonged to the subject in what might perhaps be called its describing years, when industrial archaeology still had a novelty value and when its practitioners were devoting themselves fairly wholeheartedly to amassing objects and facts, with little energy or inclination for philosophy. Neither the *Journal* nor *Industrial Archaeology* had much time for the cultural aspects of the subject. They reflected the point of view of people who felt that their work was urgent, because destruction was going on all around them and as much as possible had to be found, recorded and saved before the bonfires, the bulldozers and the scrap-metal merchants swept the remains of the Industrial Revolution out of existence. The psychology was not unlike that of a nation at war: 'We must win the war first and we can argue afterwards as to why it was worth fighting and what we ought to do after peace has arrived.'

When the successor to *Industrial Archaeology*, *Industrial Archaeology Review*, began its career in the autumn of 1976, it was vigorously attacked in a *Times Literary Supplement* review by Philip Riden (14 January 1977). His main reason for thinking little of the new venture was that it reflected what he called 'antiquarianism', that is, the pleasures of the collector, rather than the pleasures of the scholar. Industrial archaeology was, he felt, a shapeless heap, piece piled upon piece without discipline or pattern, a typical and valuable Stage 3 statement and one which quite a number of people might feel inclined to echo. In the course of an illuminating and not always good-tempered exchange of letters which went on for several weeks, Mr Riden was answered by, among others, Dr R. A. Buchanan, who struck a more hopeful note than the review which gave rise to the correspondence.

Industrial archaeology has suffered to some extent from
the fact that much of its material can be and has been used
by neighbouring disciplines – economic and
technological history, post-medieval archaeology,
vernacular architecture and so on – in supporting
hypotheses and in illustrating generalisations. But
industrial archaeology is beginning to perform this more

synthetical role for itself, and forthcoming issues of the *Review* will reflect this development of the subject. (28 January 1977)

There are those who would consider such a statement over-optimistic. What it implies is, first, that industrial archaeology has accumulated a body of knowledge which constitutes at least the core of a subject or discipline; second, that it has developed, or is developing, certain methods of approach, rules of procedure, which are special to itself, and which are understood and followed by its practitioners; and, third, that, with its factual and methodological base secure, it is in a position to encourage outward thinking, that is, exploration of the links between industrial artifacts and the broader cultural development of society. What this might mean has been well described by one of Britain's foremost industrial archaeologists, Neil Cossons, the Director of the Ironbridge Gorge Museum Trust.

After insisting that it is essential, 'in reaching our own definition of the subject not to resort to excessive pontification or the setting of strict and rigid boundaries around something which is so new, so dynamic in character and in such a fluid stage of development'.[3] Mr Cossons goes on to express his own belief that 'industrial archaeology will define its own boundaries, techniques and disciplines, given time',[4] and then explains how he sees the vital matter of outward, contextual thinking.

He considers that the period of the Industrial Revolution 'provides the core area, the mainspring of industrial archaeology', but, he continues,

there is a diffuse penumbra, too, into which the industrial archaeologist, like the archaeologist of any other period, must go to provide a perspective and context for his main area of interest. Industrial archaeology spreads out chronologically, in terms of subject area and in terms of technique well beyond its obvious centre – hence the need for flexible boundaries. Like any other archaeologist (or historian) the industrial archaeologist must have an understanding of the antecedents of his particular area of study. Thus the evolution of wind and water power in the eighteenth and nineteenth centuries can only be fully appreciated in the context of much earlier developments. But to regard industrial archaeology as being concerned with only industrial activity within the last two centuries or so is also to reject the cultural definition. The industrial archaeologist, if he is to have any real

[3]   *The BP Book of Industrial Archaeology*, David and Charles, 1975, p. 16.
[4]   Ibid. p. 16.

understanding of the sites and artefacts of the Industrial Revolution, must look at the landscape in its entirety.[5] Industrial archaeology is in part a landscape study, and the industrial archaeologist cannot restrict himself wholly to the thematic approach. The Industrial Revolution created a new economy, a new landscape, a new way of life. In terms of the lives of all of us, as inhabitants of an industrial nation – the first industrial nation – it is the most relevant period of our past, not only because it is the most recent, but because the specific changes wrought during the last $2\frac{1}{2}$ centuries provide the foundations of our present society and of all other industrial societies throughout the world.[6]

Mr Cossons believes that 'this one word "relevance" provides the key to the widespread growth of interest in industrial archaeology in recent years', and he is not referring, of course, only to Great Britain. The same consideration undoubtedly applies to all industrialised countries in some degree, although the time-span is rather longer in Britain than elsewhere and the quantity of available archaeological material is exceptionally large in relation to the area of the country.

Without disagreeing in the least with Mr Cossons's line of reasoning, one may perhaps be allowed to suggest that the monuments of the Second and Third Industrial Revolutions – the revolutions based on oil in the first instance and on electronics in the second – are just as significant and just as much in need of recording and safeguarding as those of the First. The tower from which the first American astronaut was launched into space in 1962 has recently been demolished, on the grounds that it was 'too expensive to maintain as an historical monument', which, in such a wealthy society, is hardly convincing. If it was right to campaign to save the Euston Arch, one of the most impressive reminders of the early days of railways, it is equally right to protest at the destruction of the spacemen's tower. In my view, not, alas, universally shared, the monuments of nineteenth century railways are no more and no less important than the monuments of twentieth century space-travel.

A second difficulty concerns a considerable proportion, possibly the majority, of the people who have been affected by what Mr Cossons has called 'the widespread growth of interest in industrial archaeology in recent years', the non-academics at the base of the industrial archaeology pyramid, the coolies who have carried out so many of the menial and

[5] Mr Cossons is a geographer by training and background, and the viewpoint which this provides is a valuable corrective to the purely historical and non-visual approach of so many industrial archaeologists.

[6] Ibid. pp. 16–17.

largely unpublicised tasks for the past twenty years. Industrial archaeology, like reading novels, is not simply an academic subject. It has become a matter of great and time-consuming importance to a wide range of people, from lorry drivers to architects and from plumbers to journalists. Industrial archaeology belongs to them just as much as it does to economic historians. They are very likely to become annoyed and rebellious at any suggestion that they should confine their interests to the survivals of the age of coal, iron, canals and railways. They are not preparing themselves to take examinations and not unnaturally want to make discoveries for themselves, not to be kept padding reverently round the same well-trodden pastures. With rare exceptions, these discoveries are now to be made in the places connected with the industries of the twentieth century, not of the nineteenth. The coolies may possibly be antiquarians, although it is difficult to be sure of this, but they expect to get pleasure and satisfaction from what they do in their spare time. If they fail to find this in one direction, they will certainly look in others.

The amateur–professional controversy has to be stated in plain terms. Has industrial archaeology reached the point at which it can afford to regard itself as a wholly professional affair, with no need of its unpaid enthusiasts? If it has, then bodies like the Society for Industrial Archaeology in America and the Association for Industrial Archaeology in Britain are hypocritical shams, ripe for early extinction. If it has not, then the needs and interests of the people who make up the bulk of the membership of these societies – not all the enthusiasts, of course, belong to societies – must be recognised and catered for. What is unpardonable and suicidal is any idea of a first and second level of membership, of officers and other ranks, a situation which is very close to being reached in Britain. The draft of the joint policy statement of the Association for Industrial Archaeology and the Council for British Archaeology, circulated among members of the AIA in Britain at the end of 1976, included a revealing and unfortunate sentence. 'In the study of industrial archaeology,' it said, 'practice has preceded theory, and voluntary enthusiasm has outstripped institutional organisation.' Was man made for the Sabbath, one is tempted to enquire, or the Sabbath for man? Are the spare-time industrial archaeologists to be reproached for their over-enthusiasm? Of course practice has preceded theory, if only for the reason that more people are interested in practice than in theory. The intellectual, the person whose life is dedicated to the objective analysis of facts, theories and attitudes, is a rare animal. But the sentence quoted above is singularly lacking in both grace and gratitude. Industrial archaeology may still be little more than a yard full of bricks from which nothing as recognisable as a house has yet been built, but a great many bricks have been made and carried there by people inspired by 'voluntary enthusiasm' and by little else.

At this point it may be useful to mention the results of a brief questionnaire which I sent to eighteen of Britain's most prominent archaeologists during the summer of 1976, people concerned with the prehistoric, Roman and medieval worlds. They were asked:

1. Do you take Industrial Archaeology seriously?
2. If the answer to (1) is 'No', what would have to be done about Industrial Archaeology in order to make it worthy of serious attention?
3. We have now had 15–20 years of widespread interest in Industrial Archaeology, in this country and elsewhere. Do you think this interest has achieved anything socially, educationally or academically helpful, and, if so, what?

Thirteen of the eighteen replied, an unexpectedly high proportion, and their views may come as a surprise to many people, both inside and outside industrial archaeology.

Of those who replied, eleven said they did take industrial archaeology seriously, and two said they did not. There were, however, certain reservations which are most effectively and fairly presented in the actual words used.

'I admit to feeling that the title [industrial archaeology] is something of a misnomer in some cases, in that it often very properly employs historical rather than archaeological sources.'

'Yes, except when industrial archaeologists start taking themselves too seriously.'

'Yes. In theory archaeological field techniques could usefully be carried out on industrial sites, e.g. on sites inadequately documented.'

'Not personally, except where it is related to ethnology, e.g. the study of modern mills in "backward" areas.'

'Of course I take industrial archaeology seriously, as I take all aspects of archaeology. I think it was a slight mistake to call it industrial archaeology because it is only one aspect of the archaeology of the last 200/300 years, but it clearly made the public interested and this was a good way to do it.'

Three of the thirteen offered suggestions for improving the status of the subject:

'It still seems to lack an academic background, i.e.

integration with modern history, and it still seems to be an "amateur" study, carried out by people who just like it (cf. railway and steam traction enthusiasts). The interest is wide, indeed wider than archaeology, but not to the *same people*, as it should be.'

'There is no clear definition of "industrial archaeology" that distinguishes the subject as a discreet area of study, whilst serving as a useful umbrella term. I think that it is applied rather loosely to areas of study that are in my opinion more accurately described as history of technology, history of industry, local history, social history, etc. The "archaeology" part is now to my mind thoroughly misleading, and improperly defended.'

'It is desperately in need of redefinition and reorganisation. I.A. stands where conventional archaeology stood 100 years ago – largely dilettante antiquarianism, lacking professional and academic standards. In particular, if they are to justify the title "archaeologists", most I.A. enthusiasts, with a very few outstanding exceptions, must submit themselves to the disciplines of conventional archaeology.'

The archaeologists were inspired or provoked to write a good deal in answer to the third question. The achievement of industrial archaeology had, they felt, been remarkable in some ways, less impressive in others. Broadly speaking, it had done very well socially, moderately well educationally and poorly academically.

'*Socially*: as an active or passive leisure pursuit; improving social awareness.
Educationally: availability of and contact with the real thing is inevitably a powerful educational tool.
Academically: as an interdisciplinary area and involving both technical and academic skills, it lacks the cohesiveness of a traditional subject area and therefore has had a slower impact. Useful contributions are being made, but the potential may be restrained by present academic structures and less easy to quantify. Like any "new" subject, it is still breaking the "dilettante barrier".'

'*Socially*: yes, people are more interested in recent things that they can understand, especially machinery and technology.
Educationally: yes, in making people aware of their environment.

Academically: I'm more doubtful. It is particularly deplorable that in Birmingham of all places, I.A. is marginal in our modern history courses.'

'*Socially*: (no comment)
Educationally: it has already provided, in a number of areas which are lacking in interest national monuments of the traditional type, a nucleus of sites and buildings that can be visited by classes and groups and which provide a link with the immediate past of the community and are therefore readily understood.
Academically: it provides the background essential to a proper appreciation of the historical and social development of the country during the Industrial Revolution and, to a lesser extent, of the preceding ages.'

'*Socially*: appreciation of a wasting historical asset and heritage while there is still time to save a great deal.
Educationally: enjoyment and interest of life. There is enormous public interest and response.
Academically: the interest is largely local or, at best, national; not international.'

'*Socially*, *Educationally* and *Academically*. Many people who were born into and live in industrialised areas are becoming less inhibited about proclaiming that the area they live in and the industries associated with those areas do have a past, do have a "history" that people will be interested in, both in an academic and an entertainment/ educative sense.
How much of this has to do with the industrial archaeology movement I am not sure. I think it has more to do with a loss of community identity; rapid changes in life-style, both personal and at work; television – nostalgia makes good television. I think this interest and awareness of our "industrial heritage" would have emerged in the last fifteen years whether it were called "industrial archaeology" or something else.
Whatever the process of evolution of the study has been, it has broken down some of the snob barriers between science and art, history and local history, etc., but there is still a long way to go before most schools and colleges really get to grips with the real concept of industrialisation and how it can be related to local studies and academic work at higher levels.'

'*Socially, Educationally, Academically* In the 1960s a lot of basic research and fieldwork was undertaken in Northern Ireland but for one reason or another it is only now that this is being written up. The resulting Stationery Office publication should have a considerable impact, particularly in the educational field, at all levels. The widespread interest in the subject should crystallise rapidly and with far-reaching results once the official publication sets the limits of the new field and brings it fully into public view.'

'*Socially, Educationally, Academically* I am sure it has done so. I would like to think that it has brought matters archaeological to a wider public than the often feverish devotees of everything earlier than 43 A.D. and nothing much later than 410 A.D.'

'*Socially, Educationally, Academically* Yes, in all these respects, but what is wanted, from my limited knowledge, is more field work – solid survey with excavations.'

'*Socially*: yes, greater awareness by amenity/ preservationist groups, and to a lesser extent the general public of the importance of the industrial heritage. *Educationally*: marginally. I.A. is in some areas a useful basis for local history studies. However, in general, it is badly taught. *Academically*: hardly at all. Archaeology itself is only now coming to terms with its interdisciplinary nature, I.A. not at all. It is still ill-defined and subject to individual whims in its interpretation and application.'

'*Socially, Educationally and Academically* Viewed as an aspect of local history, I think the subject has proved of interest educationally. Divisive elements have tended to lessen the social and academic impact of the subject.'

If one reflects on these comments, two main lines of thought are apparent. The first is a general belief that industrial archaeology, however well or badly practised, has done a great deal to increase public interest in that aspect of history which is referred to as 'our industrial heritage', or 'our industrial past'. The second is that nobody really knows where to place industrial archaeology academically. The chief reason for this bewilderment and suspicion, it may be suggested, is that the wrong criteria are being applied, or, as one of our respondents more delicately put it, 'the potential may be restrained by present academic structures and less easy to quantify'.

One of the principal difficulties with which we are faced is linguistic. It is only during the present century that the word 'archaeology' has become identified with excavation, largely as a result of the remarkable discoveries made in Egypt and Crete by men who had to dig their way into history. As a result of this narrowing of meaning – before 1900 and even later, 'archaeology' was used in the general sense of 'tangible remains of the past' – anyone who claims to be an archaeologist and does not produce evidence of having excavated tends to be regarded as an impostor. What are called, confusingly and somewhat arrogantly, 'archaeological techniques' are for the most part excavation techniques. It is not difficult to identify and list them. They consist, in their logical order, of painstakingly stripping layer after layer of soil and debris from the site; meticulously observing and recording everything revealed by the excavation, in relation to the depth and physical context of whatever is found; subjecting objects to a range of laboratory tests in order to determine their age and composition; relating one's discoveries to the evidence already produced by archaeologists working elsewhere; publishing a description and interpretation of one's work in a form which is intelligible to other scholars and researchers.

In some cases – an early ironworks or pottery are obvious examples – all these techniques may be applicable, but for the most part the industrial archaeologist is necessarily concerned only with the last two. It is, it may be suggested, the fact that the first three do not form part of his world which causes him to be so often written off as a charlatan or dabbler, a person not entitled to the honourable title of 'archaeologist'.

What does not seem to be sufficiently realised or acknowledged is that industrial archaeologists, unlike Stone Age archaeologists, operate in a field in which there is a great deal of written evidence. They amplify and correct the record, but only in very rare instances do they create it. If he had the opportunity, every Bronze Age or Egyptian archaeologist, one supposes, would be delighted to interview the people whose artifacts he has discovered or to read their reminiscences, but the fact that he cannot do this does not, in itself, make him intellectually and academically superior. To the conventional archaeological techniques listed above, the industrial archaeologist can and should add a group of his own. He has an opportunity and duty to study and collect the observations and memories of people who worked on the premises with which he is concerned and who earned a living from the machinery once installed in them. He records, by means of photography, drawings and written descriptions, structures which are still standing, paying careful attention to the materials employed and to the technology involved. He has to familiarise himself with the full range of printed material, from trade catalogues to the reports of Government enquiries, which has a bearing on the site to which he is devoting his attention.

This specialist work is in every way as important and as professional as excavation. It can, like any other form of scholarly work, be done well or badly, but its aim can only be to improve our understanding of the past. This is what archaeology is about. To say, as one of the respondents did, that 'if they are to justify the title "archaeologists", most I.A. enthusiasts must submit themselves to the disciplines of conventional archaeology' is largely meaningless. Industrial archaeology, as I have indicated, demands a special range of disciplines, which overlap with those of 'conventional archaeology', but which are not and cannot be identical with them. The main purpose of the present book is to provide industrial archaeologists in a number of countries with the chance to make this fact clear and to illustrate the contribution they are making to a more comprehensive and more convincing awareness of the recent past. In the process I hope the truth will emerge that the activity of reconstructing working conditions from what remains of a factory is essentially the same as reconstructing the life of a prehistoric community from its rubbish dumps and the foundations and floors of its huts. In both cases, satisfactory results can be obtained only by marrying scientific investigation with a freely and vigorously functioning imagination.

The techniques appropriate to the study

In any field of investigation, the techniques employed are presumably selected and developed in order to meet two criteria: they should contribute towards a better overall understanding of the subject which is being studied and they should make it possible to extract the maximum amount of useful information from the historical raw material which is available. What they should not primarily do, except under very unusual political circumstances, is to demonstrate the manual dexterity of the investigator or his ability to make a particular piece of equipment, scientific formula, or system of organisation work satisfactorily and impressively. Techniques do not exist for themselves. They are for a purpose and before discussing the techniques it is as well to be agreed on the purpose.

What, in the case of industrial history, do we want to know? It is too facile to answer this question by saying that we are aiming at a more complete awareness and understanding of the industrial past. We have to consider what the elements of such an understanding might ideally be. There would seem to be four main headings under which we could usefully classify our needs. Different kinds of historian would probably list these headings in a different order, to indicate the emphasis of their work and the nature of their specialisation, but for our present purpose any concept of priority is irrelevant and unhelpful, since we are considering the complete picture, not individual parts of the composition. We could therefore specify our needs in something like the following form.

First, we have to know as much as possible about the conditions of work at a particular period, and about the attitude of the employers, workers and the general public to those conditions. Second, we require information about what the different parties – workers, owners, managers, financiers, investors – have got out of this or that process, plant or method of working, in the way of income, satisfaction, accidents, ill-health, standards of living. Industry, after all, is for something. It does not exist for its own sake or in a vacuum. Thirdly, we want to understand how the job was done, what the techniques were and how the machinery and equipment was used. Fourthly, we must be able to comprehend, both intellectually and emotionally, the scale of whatever industrial operation is engaging our attention. Finally, we shall do our best to record or recreate the physical environment in which the work was carried out and in which the workers and their families lived.

How much of this is properly the concern of the industrial archaeologist and how much is better looked after by other breeds of historian is a matter for argument and possibly disagreement. At the moment it seems necessary to say only that the total aim of historical enquiry is two-fold, to bring ourselves closer to an understanding of what it was like to be alive at a particular period and, with the hindsight and perspective provided by the passage of time, to assess the significance of past events and achievements. To be of value, industrial archaeology must contribute to the realisation of one or other of these aims and, wherever possible, to both.

It is well to realise, however, that the industrial archaeologist, like the historian in general, may be forced to work within certain political limitations. The conditions of free enquiry which exist in Western Europe and North America are not typical of the world as a whole. In the Western world an accepted and widely used technique nowadays is to collect the reminiscences of veteran workers, in order to discover first hand the details about processes, machines, motivation and working conditions which might otherwise disappear unrecorded. This procedure is not encouraged in the Socialist countries, except under a fairly tight discipline. It is permissible, for instance, to ask an old worker purely technical questions – 'what kind of tool did you use to do that?'; 'when do you remember that machine being first used?'; 'how long did the bricks have to stay in the kiln?' – but not questions about attitudes or working conditions, unless the aim is to collect political ammunition. Once it has been officially decided that the past was bad, or at least selectively bad, and that the present is good, any kind of free-ranging enquiry is obviously full of potential dangers.

It should be mentioned, too, if not emphasised, that in most countries – by no means only the Socialist countries – there are many apparently inoffensive sites and structures which one is not free to photograph. In Britain and the United States, one is at full liberty to photograph almost anything, provided one does so from a point normally accessible to the public, but any attempt to take pictures of factories, bridges, railways, or aerodromes in, say, the German Democratic Republic, the Soviet Union, India or Greece may well result in serious consequences, including imprisonment or expulsion from the country.

In the present book one is writing from a British or American stand-point, which is as near to an historian's ideal as one is likely to get. To say that one is trying to do this or that, and that one should proceed along the following lines makes perfect sense within what is, for good reason, called the Free World. Within the majority of countries, however, it is likely to be regarded as a counsel of perfection at best and as wild, irresponsible day-dreaming at worst.

Having made this clear – and no previous book on industrial archaeology has ever put these blunt truths into print – one can proceed to discuss and examine what appear from their results to be the most fruitful techniques which have been used by industrial archaeologists and to relate them to specific examples and to the broad range of concepts and aims indicated above.

Superficially at least, the most straightforward type of industrial archaeology project consists of the preparation of a descriptive report on what can be seen on a site. In its simplest form, such a description would read:

Thwaite End Coke Ovens SD 494696. Remains of a bank of beehive ovens on east bank of canal.[1]
or
Former Bermondsey Leather Market (early 19th c.) 331796. Western Street, Bermondsey, S.E.1. Three-storey yellow brick and stone building, with giant Doric pilasters and entablature. Warehouses and remains of Brine House behind.[2]

Such a record, although not without its value, is obviously more useful if it is supplemented by some kind of visual material, in the form of photographs or a plan. As it stands, it provides no indication of the size of the building or the ruin, nor of its immediate environment.

A more satisfactory description, giving a brief history of what is on the site and adding details of the surviving buildings, is of the type now adopted as standard by the Historic American Engineering Record. Here is an example from the Inventory of the Lower Merrimack Valley, produced jointly by HAER and the Merrimack Valley Textile Museum in 1976.

Ballardvale Mills   Lawrence
204 Andover Street   19 . 323000 . 472150
Andover

The Ballardvale Woolen Mills were established in 1835 by John Marland, the son of an early Massachusetts woolen manufacturer, on the site of a saw and grist mill on the Shawsheen River. Marland was an ambitious manufacturer, and by 1848 he had erected two large mills,

[1] Owen Ashmore *Industrial Archaeology of Lancashire* David and Charles, 1969, p. 254.
[2] *Industrial Monuments of Greater London* compiled by John Ashdown, Michael Bussell and Paul Carter. Thames Basin Archaeological Observers Group, 1969, p. 49.

powered by water and steam, a sizeable storehouse, and several smaller frame buildings. In 1841 Marland imported English worsted machinery for the purpose of manufacturing delaines, a cloth woven with yarns of worsted and cotton. This was the first instance of American worsted making by power driven machinery, and was apparently not entirely successful. In 1857 Marland went bankrupt, and the mills passed under the control of Josiah P. Bradlee, a Boston merchant who was Marland's chief creditor. Under Bradlee's conservative leadership the company fell back upon the manufacture of flannels composed of a cotton–woolen blend. In 1872 the mills contained 13 sets of cards, 104 broadlooms, and employed 200 hands, making it one of the largest woolen mills of New England. The company went out of business in the 1950s and the buildings have been tenanted ever since. In 1872 power was by water (160 HP) and steam (100 HP). A masonry dam, 200 feet in length, built in 1835, provided about 12 feet of fall. None of the water wheels or engines have survived. The 1835 mill is intact, although the skylights on the pitched roof have been shingled over and the cupola has been removed. The mill is four stories high, brick, 150′ × 45′. The picker house, engine, wheel and boiler house which have been attached to the main mill have been removed. A wool storehouse, built in 1848, is constructed of uncoursed granite rubble and brick. About

Ballardvale Woollen Mills,
c. 1900.

1880 an almost identical storehouse was built across the
street from the 1848 structure. Two large wooden
structures, about 200 feet to the north of the 1835 mill,
which were used for tentering, are intact. In 1842 Marland
built another large mill, the first floor of which consisted
of random coursed granite rubble. The upper two stories
were of wood. The mill had a pitch roof, with skylights
and dormers, which have since been removed. The
wooden parts of the mill have also been covered with
asbestos shingles. The mill and wheelhouse, also dating
from 1842, are largely intact, as well as the attached
boiler-engine house (1842) and dyehouse (1871). (K. E.
Foster, ed. *Lamb's Textile Industries of the United States*
(Boston 1916), vol. II; HHEC; Insurance Survey # 788
'Ballardvale Mills', MVTM)[3] [HHEC = D. Hamilton
Hurd (comp.) *History of Essex County* Philadelphia, 1887,
2 vols.]

This is clearly a much more satisfactory record than the two items
previously quoted. We have the history of the mill's ownership and use;
details of its power supply and machinery; a description of the buildings
as they are today, with an indication of the changes which have occurred
on the site in more recent years; measurements; and a note on the sources
used. An engraving of the mill complex as it was in about 1900 brings
the written description alive and allows us to see the various buildings
in relation to one another.

Having said this, one might usefully point out what we are not told
and what we can only guess at from the information provided. We know
practically nothing about the interior of the mills, the way in which the
space on each floor was divided, the lighting and ventilation, the sanitary
and heating arrangements, the general condition of the premises. We
are left ignorant of the balance of the labour force between men,
women and children, at different periods, of where the workers, the
owner and the management lived, of labour recruitment and labour
relationships during the working life of the mill. We have no idea as to
whether, by comparison with other textile enterprises in the district,
Ballardvale was considered a profitable, well-run, well-maintained mill
or whether it had the reputation of a good or a bad place to work. The
firms which have rented space in the buildings since the 1950s, when
the original company went out of business, are left anonymous.

[3] *The Lower Merrimack Valley: an Inventory of Historic Engineering and Textile Sites.*
Sponsored by Merrimack Valley Textile Museum, North Andover, Massachusetts,
and Historic American Engineering Record, National Park Service, Washington DC.
Directed and edited by Peter M. Molloy. Historic American Engineering Record,
National Park Service, United States Department of the Interior, 1975, pp. 7–8.

This is in no way to accuse either the author or the editor of incompetence. It is simply to show how much more information one requires in order to be able to know and understand the history of the Ballardvale Mills. There is, of course, no end to an historian's possible demands. One kind of historian, for instance, may be interested to know if there were ever any strikes at the mill and, if so, what the causes were. Another may wish for details of the sickness rate among workers there. Without wishing to appear a purist, one could reasonably say that the industrial archaeologist is under no obligation whatever to provide such information. He should, however, be aware that these are important factors in industrial history and he should be on the lookout for any archaeological evidence which might be relevant to them. Do the buildings appear to be unusually badly lit or damp, for instance? Is the ceiling height exceptionally low? Does the stone or brickwork have a heavy coat of soot on it, indicating that the pollution of the area from the factory smoke-stacks was particularly severe? These are archaeological details and the wide-awake, imaginative archaeologist will note them instinctively. If they are not observed and no record is made of them, all trace of them disappears for ever if, as not infrequently happens, the building is burnt down or demolished a short time after the survey has been made.

The circumstances of any archaeological project must to some extent condition the amount and type of information that can be extracted from it. The HAER surveys are carried out with facilities better than anything so far available elsewhere in the world. The Lower Merrimack Valley inventory, for instance, from which the extract concerning the Ballardvale Mills was taken, had the full-time services for several weeks of the curator and administrative staff of the Merrimack Valley Textile Museum, which is quite possibly the best of its kind in the world, together with the help of experts from the Historic American Engineering Record and of paid, experienced researchers and fieldworkers. This situation, which has been repeated several times during the past five years in different areas of the United States, has never occurred at all in Britain, which has a good claim to have pioneered the study of industrial archaeology and which had nearly ten years' start over America. Work in Britain is carried out almost entirely by individuals, usually operating from a university or a museum base, or by local voluntary groups. Very little in the way of supporting funds is available and there are those who would consider the British achievement under these circumstances to be nothing short of miraculous. The industrial archaeology 'professional' in Britain hardly exists, with a mere handful of people in academic posts who are able to devote most of their time to the subject, rather more in museums and perhaps four in various Government institutions. Whatever the situation may be elsewhere, industrial archaeology in Britain is very much a spare-time and amateur affair, and its results and techniques have to be judged against this background. This is not to say, of course, that the work done by amateurs need be sloppy or lacking in system. With archaeology as with golf, the more one practises and the better one's training, the more pleasure and satisfaction one is likely to get from it.

For all but a very few amateurs – the word is used in no derogatory sense – the study of industry, transport and technology is bound to be mainly a branch of local history. Time and money could hardly make it otherwise. Before industrial archaeologists became at all numerous, Britain had a well-established tradition of using and sometimes exploiting the energies of amateur local historians and excavation-archaeologists. By the 1950s, if not earlier, it was fairly generally, if not universally accepted that people working in their spare time could obtain a great deal of useful information which could be digested and eventually published by professional scholars and writers and, in a few cases, by particularly talented and determined amateur researchers themselves. It is indisputable that in Britain, as a result of all this activity and mutual help, both the knowledge gap and the psychological gap between amateurs and professionals were a good deal narrower in 1955 than they had been twenty years earlier, a fact which was particularly important in the specialised field of industrial archaeology, where there was an enormous quantity of nineteenth- and early twentieth-century industrial material in the process of being swept away during the rebuilding and modernisation which was taking place during the post-war period. Without the on-the-spot knowledge and, even more important, the presence and the enthusiasm of local people, it would have been quite impossible to have discovered and recorded this great mass of buildings and machinery at all, before it was scrapped or bull-dozed out of existence. The fact that much was missed and that much of the recording was done inadequately are matters for regret, but only the most vindictive or dog-in-the-manger critics would claim that, if the work could not be carried out to the highest academic standards, it would have been better not to carry it out at all.

But one should never allow proper standards to fall out of sight. There are some very wise words on the point from one of the greatest of our local historians, the veteran W. G. Hoskins. Writing at a time (1959) when industrial archaeology was still very much in its infancy, he insisted that 'there is no excuse for amateur work being bad' and, after noting that the amateur, who is in the game for pleasure, can bring to his labours a zest and a freshness of approach which the over-worked professional can rarely achieve, he explained why the amateur historian should take his hobby seriously and never stop widening his horizon and improving his technique.

Primarily I regard the study of local history and
topography as a hobby that gives a great deal of pleasure
to a great number of people, and I think it wrong to make
it intimidating, to warn them off because they have not the
training of the professional historian. It is a means of
enjoyment and a way of enlarging one's consciousness of
the external world, and even (I am sure) of the internal
world. To acquire an abiding 'sense of the past', to live
with it daily and to understand its values is no small thing
in the world as we find it today. But the better informed
and the more scrupulous the local historian is about the
truth of past life, the more enjoyment he will get from his
chosen hobby. Inaccurate information is not only false; it
is boring and fundamentally unsatisfying.[4]

The point could hardly be better made, but Dr Hoskins is concerned
with the situation in Britain. In other countries, and especially in the
United States, there is quite a different consideration and one of the
greatest importance, to be observed. There is a growing surplus of
trained professionals seeking employment and strongly disinclined to
allow the bread to be snatched from their mouths by amateurs. The
United States attempted to deal with the problem during the Depression
years of the 1930s by hiring unemployed architects and photographers
to produce work for the Historic American Buildings Survey, which
was then in its infancy. The superlatively good drawings and photographs from this period, now safely stored in the Library of Congress,
were done by experts who desperately needed the work. They set both
a standard and a precedent which have been carried over into America's
industrial archaeology period, and many of the beautiful measured
drawings to be found in HABS's cousin, the Historic American
Engineering Record, have been made by architectural and engineering
students and recent graduates who have taken part in officially sponsored
surveys as paid helpers and have been glad of the money. There is also
in America a category of persons known as historical archaeologists,
who are also to be found in some profusion in the labour market. They,
like the more traditional history graduates, also see industrial archaeology
as their preserve.

Given this situation, and funds to provide at least seasonal employment, it would be surprising if the level of recording in American surveys
were not high. The HAER inventories, from which the Ballardvale
entry was taken as an example, are printed direct from HAER record
cards. The reproduction of this particular card shows the edge-
punching which allows the information to be retrieved and sorted
electronically.

4   *Local History in England* Longman, 1959, p. 4.

The cards used for industrial monuments surveys in other countries, notably Britain, France, Denmark, Sweden and West Germany, vary greatly in the quality and quantity of information they contain. Each country tries to learn from another's mistakes and it has been Britain's misfortune, in this, as in many other aspects of the national life, to have been the first in the field. In every Western country apart from the United States, the record cards have been completed piecemeal by volunteers who have sent them in as and when they have felt inclined. The quality is necessarily very uneven, and, looking at the national areas as a whole, there are some patches which are relatively well covered and others which are deserts. It has become clear that there is no substitute for the American method of descending on a fairly compact and cohesive region – the Lower Peninsula of Michigan, the Mohawk–Hudson area, the Lower Merrimack Valley – and, with a well-equipped and varied team of experts, blitzing it with all the financial and technical resources at one's command. The results of the survey can then be brought together, edited and published quickly – facsimile typescript is perfectly adequate for the purpose – so that the work can be in the hands of anyone to whom it will be useful within two years or less of the fieldwork being carried out.

Presented in this way, the material is cumulative in both its effect and its value. In the Lower Merrimack volume, for instance, there are about 300 entries for individual sites, together with a number of well-reproduced pictures and maps, a bibliography and a general introduction describing the industrial development of the region. In five precise,

HAER inventory

factual and readably concise pages we have the rise and fall of the textile and related industries, the archaeology of road, water and rail transport, and the painful adaptations of a nineteenth-century industrial area to the new conditions of the twentieth. Some of the details provided add up to a microcosm of what has taken place over a much wider area, illustrating the not-to-be-forgotten fact that the great advantage which the professional historian or archaeologist has over his amateur colleagues is his ability to see the wood for the trees, to understand the significance of what is under one's nose.

In Amesbury the carriage builders converted their shops into automobile body factories after 1900, enjoying considerable success until the 1920s, when the competition from the auto body makers of the mid-West became too intense. The automobile industry disappeared from Amesbury after 1930, with the exception of one firm which survived as a manufacturer of window channels.[5]

This is local industrial archaeology trimmed, shaped and in a meaningful context. The wide focus of the paragraph just quoted narrows and sharpens into the detailed entries on the Walker Body Company and the Briggs Carriage Company.

It is possible, but as yet unfortunately rare, for this kind of detailed recording to be carried out by government bodies who, especially at the local level, might seem particularly well placed to undertake such work. What has been achieved in the German Federal Republic by the Landeskonservator Rheinland, is an indication of what might be successfully undertaken elsewhere. The work has been undertaken systematically, with the support and staff of the Planning, Historic Monuments and Cultural Departments of the Land Government. Two of the eight volumes which have so far appeared are concerned with the Arbeitersiedlungen – workers' housing estates – built by the Ruhr and Rhineland industrialists during the late nineteenth and early twentieth centuries for their employees. Like all the items in this series, the reports are splendidly produced, with almost all the plans and illustrations one could ask for, except that there are no photographs of the interiors of the houses, a curious oversight which robs the record of much of its potential human quality. The omission is a strange one, as is the failure to provide any dimensions for either the houses as a whole or for the individual rooms. Why, one wonders, were these far from difficult tasks not carried out? Were they felt to be irrelevant or perhaps an intrusion on the privacy of the tenants? In looking through the otherwise excellent reports one feels the lack of this information very badly.

[5] *The Lower Merrimack Valley*, xiii.

It is nearly always the case, with any industrial archaeology report, that the tone and emphasis, what is included and what is left out, depend a great deal on what sort of person or body is responsible for the work. Geographers are likely to stress landscape and environment, economic historians return on investment, technical historians function, architectural historians style and construction, social historians community associations and planners and conservationists what is and might be protected, restored or used for some other purpose. If the report is read by someone for whom it is not primarily intended, what the author would regard as the wrong questions are almost certain to be asked.

The surveys published on behalf of the Landeskonservator Rheinland have been drawn up by people concerned primarily with town planning and with the establishment of conservation areas. The research therefore tended to sift out and discard information not felt to be relevant to this self-imposed discipline and we are presented with entries arranged as follows:[6]

Krupp Estate Altenhof II
Conservation area contains Dwellings for pensioners and invalids from the cast-steel works. An annexe to Altenhof I on the east side of the Kruppscher Waldpark.
Limits of the conservation area Eichenstrasse,

[6]   The translations here and elsewhere in the book are the author's.

Altenhof II. The shaded part represents the conservation area.

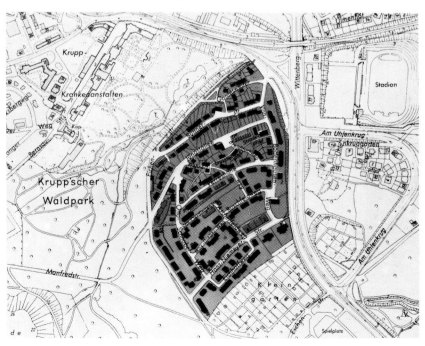

Gebranderstrasse, Hans-Niemeyerstrasse/Eichhoffweg.
History The estate was financed by a grant from Friedrich
Alfred Krupp, made in 1892. Building began in 1893,
under the direction of Robert Schmohl, and between then
and 1914 Altenhof II was extended several times. The
area to the west of the Kruppscher Waldpark, Altenhof I,
was built in two sections, the first in 1893 and 1896 and
the second in 1899–1907. The residential area to the east
of the Park, Altenhof II, was linked in 1907 with the
hospital and convalescent home buildings on the west side
of the Park along Karl-Bersau Strasse (formerly
Agathastrasse). Between 1938 and 1948 the hospital was
enlarged by taking in the old people's home and the
Widows' Home which formed part of Altenhof I.
Characteristics The strongly controlled straight-line
pattern of the early Krupp estates (Westend 1863,
Schederhof 1872–3, Kroneberg 1872 and so on, which no
longer exist) had already been toned down and made less
military in the planning of Altenhof I, which was given
curving streets and a variety of romantic, garden city type
houses. The newer part of Altenhof II follows the
contours of the hill in a carefully thought out and
pleasant manner. The so-called 'cottage system' of
Altenhof I, with individual houses built in the 'old
German', half-timbered style, accommodating from one to
three families, mellows in Altenhof II into houses built in
small terraces. The 'picturesque' façades of Altenhof I
have been simplified into the 1 and 1½ storey plain
rendered walls of Altenhof II.

Plan of typical room
layout.

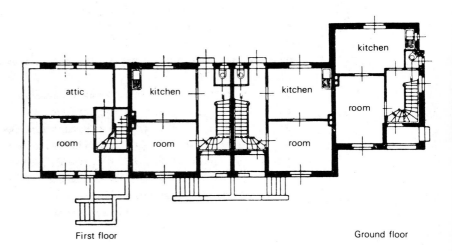

First floor   Ground floor

Condition in 1972 The Altenhof II estate has for the most part survived exactly as it was built. The following houses do not form part of the original buildings, but their designs reproduce very closely those of their neighbours: 136 Büttnerstrasse; 7–17a, 41–45 Jüngstallee; 2 Otto-Schnabel-Weg; 15–21 Verreshöhe; 14 Wehnertweg; 2–8 Hans-Niemeyerstrasse; 19 Eichhoffweg; 9 Von-Oerding-Weg.

The information here is useful and without a doubt accurate, but it is unlikely to satisfy anyone who is interested in the costs and materials of housebuilding, in domestic amenities (how were these houses lit and heated?), or in such social considerations as the rents paid by the tenants and the proportion of their income which this represented. The houses are observed and recorded as the planner sees them, from the outside or from the air. We can see from the photographs and from the plans that the accommodation was seemly and probably comfortable, but not generous – a kitchen, a living room and a lavatory on the ground floor and two bedrooms upstairs, the standard working-class home of the period. There was almost certainly a cellar, too, although we are not shown or told this.

Altenhof: exterior of houses, the ground-floor plan of which is shown on page 24.

But here, as with the Lower Merrimack Valley inventory, the whole is greater than the sum of the parts. However partial or professionally

coloured the individual entries may seem to be, taken together as a group they add up to a valuable picture of the estates which the paternalistic German industrialist was building for his workers during the three-quarters of a century before the First World War. They show in particular how much the coal and steel magnates, led by Alfred Krupp, were influenced by Ebenezer Howard's book, *The Garden City of Tomorrow*, which appeared in 1898, and how their earlier ideas about workers' 'colonies' were modified in accordance with Howard's ideas. They show, too, how the rise in land prices which took place after 1900 persuaded the industrialists that they had to give up their garden-city ideals and enter the less inspiring new world of large multi-storey blocks, which would bring a more satisfactory return from each square metre of ground.

If the techniques employed to meet the particular goal an author sets himself are adequate for that immediate purpose, it is difficult to criticise them on the basis of quite a different set of criteria. Any technique can be evaluated only in relation to its purpose. In the case of an industrial archaeology project, an important part, perhaps the main part, of that purpose may be to arouse public or official support for the conservation of what is on the site. In that case, a report or article will be effective and professional to the extent to which it is able to make clear why the site is important and what its outstanding features are. Putting this another way, we could say that two kinds of report are called for: the first will have a flat, even flow and tone and the second will contain a good deal more light and shade. Both, however, may be of either poor quality or high quality, according to the skill and knowledge of the author.

The American urban and industrial historian, Randolph Langenbach, is much and rightly concerned with the key question: 'Must we destroy our past in order to renew our cities?' He has illustrated this with reference to one of the grandest of all America's industrial creations, the great Amoskeag mills at Manchester, New Hampshire, and in his selection of photographs and language he has gone quite deliberately for the total impression, in order that as many people as possible can understand in what way Amoskeag is important. The technique and the aim are in no way sensationalist. What Langenbach is saying, in effect, is that the total effect, the poetry, is what matters. He quotes Professor Kevin Lynch, of Massachusetts Institute of Technology, in support – 'Many objects which we are accustomed to call beautiful are single purpose things, in which, through long development or the impress of one will, there is an intimate visible linkage from fine detail to total structure'[7] – but he could equally well have used the wise words of the Poet Laureate, Sir John Betjeman, who made known his view, in 1963,

---

[7]   In *Manchester : Downtown Plan* 1967, p. 6.

that 'industrial archaeology is an essentially poetic subject, although there is likely to be no shortage of dull, uncomprehending people like economic historians yapping round its skirts'.[8] The point here is not to foment war between poets and economic historians, but to indicate that there is more than one way of approaching and appreciating the past, whether that past happens to be Victorian industrial structures or Bronze Age megaliths. A strongly developed poetic imagination is, in

[8] Review of Kenneth Hudson, *Industrial Archaeology: an Introduction* in *Geographical Magazine*, June 1963.

Amoskeag, Manchester, New Hampshire.
The Amoskeag Millyard buildings were constructed over a period of 75 years, from 1838 to 1915. At its peak, the millyard complex was the largest in the world, extending along both banks of the Merrimack River for more than a mile. In 1915 it was producing cloth at the rate of 50 miles an hour. By the mid-1960s, the property was in the hands of more than 40 different owners.

Aerial view of the site, showing the surviving housing and factory buildings.

Typical Amoskeag architecture.

any case, no disadvantage to an archaeologist; without it, indeed, he may and does make serious scientific blunders.

But, given his aim, Langenbach will naturally choose suitable words and pictures to illustrate the general thesis. He will say, for instance:

> The few pieces of heavy machinery remaining at
> Amoskeag give an indication of what an enormous and
> important industry the plant once housed. In the interiors
> of the buildings, as well as on the exteriors, quality of
> design and precision of craftsmanship extend to the last
> detail. More than thirty years after the company's demise,
> a visitor can sense the pride its people must have had in
> their work and environment.[9]

and

> Urban renewal plans in Manchester involve providing
> access to certain buildings in the Amoskeag millyard, as
> well as creating parking space where there is none now.
> Both the canal buildings and much of the river façade
> would be demolished, and both canals filled in, destroying
> forever the unity and impact of one of the most powerful
> urban scenes anywhere in the world. Amoskeag can be
> saved only through a drastic redefinition, in human terms,
> of the goals of city development – a redefinition that is
> equally necessary for all American cities.[10]

It would surely be to degrade the archaeologist's function if he is to be regarded as a mere collector of evidence, to be handed over cold and intact to those whose business is to integrate such evidence into a readable and stimulating account of some period in the human past. Few archaeologists would concur in such a limited and uncreative view of their work but it is regrettable if at some times the emphasis on accurate, detailed recording has led to a failure to see the wood for the trees and to writing which is unnecessarily dull and pedestrian.

One of the most thoroughgoing and creative attempts to explore the complex reality of industrial archaeology was made in Belgium in 1975, in the form of an exhibition organised by the National College for Architecture and the Visual Arts, in collaboration with the History of Architecture Department of the University of Florence. Called *The Landscape of Industry*, this lavishly prepared exhibition and its equally sumptuous catalogue-raisonné concentrated on the evidence provided by the North of France, Belgium and the Ruhr and attempted to answer three questions – what do we actually see when we stand in

Harvard Alumni Bulletin 13 April 1968, p. 27.
Ibid. p. 28.

front of one of yesterday's breweries, coal-mines or canal-locks; how do we understand and communicate their position in time, what preceded and prepared the way for them and what came after them; how, 'within the context of a reality which it is difficult to investigate', do we follow 'a disciplinary route of no small complexity, from economic history to geography, from the history of the workers' movement to the history of urbanisation, and from the history of technology to the history of science'. Somehow, it was concluded, 'the physical evidence, those rare but still readable signs on a constantly changing industrial landscape must be given their true significance'.[11] Properly viewed in the landscape and in its historical context, every industrial monument was 'a witness to civilisation'.[12]

So, in its words-and-pictures survey of the former mining village at the Bois-du-Luc colliery, near Houdeng, constructed between 1838 and 1855, the Exhibition was particularly concerned to explore the place of coal-mining in not only the landscape and Belgian history but in the national conscience and psychology. In restoring the 222 houses of the estate, as a project by the National Housing Institute, many obstacles had to be overcome, some subtle, some crudely commercial and political.

In Belgium there is a widespread tendency in political and official circles to advocate the demolition of all buildings whose 'economic cycle' is over. To consider houses (and

[11] *Le Paysage de l'Industrie* Brussels: Editions des Archives et d'Architecture Moderne, 1975, p. 32.
[12] Ibid. p. 35.

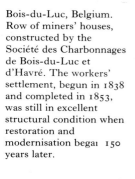

Bois-du-Luc, Belgium. Row of miners' houses, constructed by the Société des Charbonnages de Bois-du-Luc et d'Havré. The workers' settlement, begun in 1838 and completed in 1853, was still in excellent structural condition when restoration and modernisation begaı 150 years later.

by extension the town and urban life) as consumer goods inevitably leads to breaking all visible links with the past, and hence with the future, and to throwing the individual back on his own resources in a universe that is in continuous upheaval. In Belgium as well as in Germany, the inhabitants of workers' housing estates have always preferred the maintenance and re-development of their dwellings to the solutions offered by contemporary town planners.[13]

There are those who would say that *The Landscape of Industry* is not primarily interested in industrial archaeology as such, but with a different subject which might for want of a better phrase be described as environmental archaeology, or perhaps the study of industrial monuments in the landscape. To this, two answers suggest themselves. The first is that now, in 1978, it is very difficult for anyone, industrial archaeologist or not, to avoid thinking in environmental terms. In the early 1920s when the Newcomen Society was founded, possibly, but not today. The second reply is that in indicating a range of possible approaches to industrial archaeology, one is not asking all things of all people. One is simply seeking toleration, mutual understanding and, ideally, co-operation between people of different skills, experience and temperaments.

Some industrial archaeologists have essentially technical minds and their insight into history comes through their understanding of the machinery and tools of the past. One such person is the internationally famous Danish molinologist, Anders Jespersen. Jespersen found no difficulty at all in producing a 100-page account[14] of the Great Laxey waterwheel in the Isle of Man which, apart from a very brief historical introduction, was devoted entirely to the construction and functioning of the wheel, as an engineer had seen it. By means of detailed calculations and discussions with engineering colleagues, he worked out such details as the speed and output of the pumps and was able to find an explanation of a hitherto unsolved problem of great importance to a specialist in waterwheels, 'Why did Robert Casement[15] choose a pitch-backshot wheel for his job, and not an ordinary overshot wheel? The construction is almost identical to that of an overshot wheel and at first sight it seems odd that the water is made to change its direction by 180°, when it could just as well have been allowed to continue its flow without changing its direction.'[16]

[13] Ibid. p. 92.
[14] *The Lady Isabella Waterwheel of the Great Laxey Mining Company, Isle of Man, 1854–1954* Virum, Denmark: published by the author, 1954. For an illustration of the author's method, see page 32.
[15] The engineer responsible for the design and installation.
[16] Ibid. p. 57.

This degree of technicality is to be found – and welcome – in many reports which are clearly within the field of industrial archaeology, although it might be fair to say that they do not exploit all its possibilities. The *Bulletin of the Historical Metallurgy Group* comes closest, perhaps, to the kind of report which is clearly expert and authoritative, which is likely to satisfy at least the more conservative elements of archaeological opinion, but which makes very few concessions to demands that the site

The Great Laxey waterwheel. Page from account by Anders Jespersen.

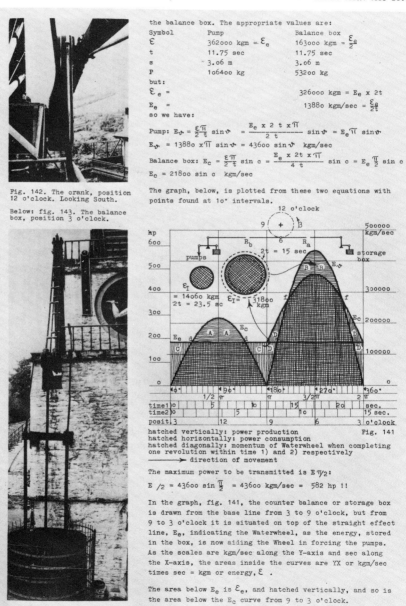

Fig. 142. The crank, position 12 o'clock. Looking South.

Below: fig. 143. The balance box, position 3 o'clock.

the balance box. The appropriate values are:

Symbol	Pump	Balance box
ε	362000 kgm = ε_e	163000 kgm = $\frac{\varepsilon_e}{2}$
t	11.75 sec	11.75 sec
s	3.06 m	3.06 m
P	106400 kg	53200 kg

but:

ε_e = $\qquad$ 326000 kgm = E_e x 2t

E_e = $\qquad$ 13880 kgm/sec = $\frac{\varepsilon_e}{2t}$

so we have:

Pump: $E_{\vartheta} = \frac{\varepsilon \pi}{2 t} \sin \vartheta = \frac{E_e \times 2 t \times \pi}{2 t} \sin \vartheta = E_e \pi \sin \vartheta$

E_{ϑ} = 13880 x π $\sin \vartheta$ = 43600 $\sin \vartheta$ kgm/sec

Balance box: $E_c = \frac{\varepsilon \pi}{2 t} \sin c = \frac{E_e \times 2 t \times \pi}{4 t} \sin c = E_e \frac{\pi}{2} \sin c$

E_c = 21800 $\sin c$ kgm/sec

The graph, below, is plotted from these two equations with points found at 10° intervals.

Fig. 141

hatched vertically: power production
hatched horizontally: power consumption
hatched diagonally: momentum of Waterwheel when completing one revolution within time 1) and 2) respectively
——➤ direction of movement

The maximum power to be transmitted is $E \pi/2$:

$E /2$ = 43600 $\sin \frac{\pi}{2}$ = 43600 kgm/sec = 582 hp !!

In the graph, fig. 141, the counter balance or storage box is drawn from the base line from 3 to 9 o'clock, but from 9 to 3 o'clock it is situated on top of the straight effect line, E_e, indicating the Waterwheel, as the energy, stored in the box, is now aiding the Wheel in forcing the pumps. As the scales are kgm/sec along the Y-axis and sec along the X-axis, the areas inside the curves are YX or kgm/sec times sec = kgm or energy, ε .

The area below E_e is ε_e, and hatched vertically, and so is the area below the E_c curve from 9 to 3 o'clock.

69

should be presented in its social or human context. If Langenbach can be taken as an example of industrial archaeology warm, then the *Bulletin of the Historical Metallurgy Group* is assuredly industrial archaeology cold.

M. Davies-Shiel's report on Stony Hazel High Furnace[17] is representative of the editorial requirements and style of the periodical in which it appears. To the Historical Metallurgy Group, archaeology means first and foremost excavation, with no essential differences of approach or working methods, whether the subject is a seventeenth-century furnace site in Sussex or the metallurgical aspects of Chalcolithic copper working at Timna, Israel. In the case of the Davies-Shiel article, the problem to be solved by excavation was mainly one of chronology, explained by the author in these terms:

Documentary evidence shows that the site was first in private hands, then belonged to the Cunsey Company until at least 1755, when it was made over at a valuable sum to the Duddon Company. Although Harrison, Ainslie & Co. bought up Duddon in 1818, the forge was only made over to a private band of locals in 1822 at a near-nominal amount. It may still have been working in 1833.

If the use of iron ore in the hearth was to obtain partial oxidation of the cast iron, when was that process introduced here? Schubert intimates that, although the method was an English one, it had been forgotten until a Samuel Lucas introduced the method in 1804. The ramp and bin appear to be part of the original fabric of the building complex of 1718. The site calls for further careful excavation to answer these problems.[18]

This is an author in the happy position of being perfectly clear as to the purposes of the study, using accepted archaeological techniques in order to test the initial model, and falling into no temptation to worship

[17] 'Excavation at Stony Hazel High Furnace, Lake District, 1968–1969; an interim report', *Bulletin of the Historical Metallurgy Group*, Vol. 4, No. 1, 1970.

[18] Ibid. p. 22.

Plan of Stony Hazel High Furnace, Lake District, as revealed during excavation.

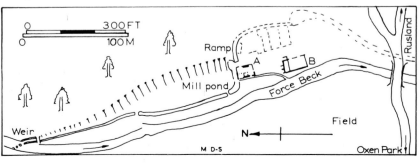

the strange gods of sociology, social history or economic history. It could be suggested that what we have here is either an archaeologist working in the metallurgical field, or a metallurgist working in the historical field, rather than an industrial archaeologist. The difference is an important one. At his most creative, the industrial archaeologist is the person who has constructed a complete historical model which he proceeds to check against the available archaeology. 'This,' he says, 'is what I believe it was like to own a woollen mill and to work in one in Manchester, New Hampshire in 1870. I will now see how I can check or modify this by studying the remains of textile mills, housing, and canals in the area. In the process I may well discover that life and work here in 1870 were different in several respects from what I had originally imagined. The model, in that case, will require adjusting and reshaping.' In the course of his work, such a researcher will consult as wide a range of printed sources as he can, make plans and drawings, take photographs, talk to such people in or formerly in the industry as may have useful first-hand information to communicate. He will do his best to make sure that the record of what he finds and thinks is stored where other people can locate and use it. He will, naturally, try to carry out

Hearth plan in above floor and section on A–A.

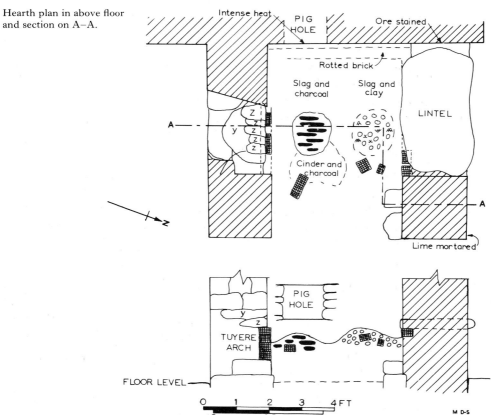

the work as quickly, efficiently and cheaply as he can, and if photogrammetry, for instance, seems to be the only way of making a visual record of a building in the time available, or with the money available, he will apply that technique to what he is doing.

Creative work in the sense in which the word has just been used is, of course, an ideal which is not always realised. As in any branch of archaeology there is much good, solid, reliable work done of more limited scope. It calls on the faculties of careful observation, mistrust of any speculation which does not appear to be firmly rooted in fact, great respect for procedures, for neatness and for accuracy, and conscientious attention to any previous reports of work on the site or similar sites. The results are evident in many of the learned journals and translations of the county archaeological societies. The brilliant paper on Roman or medieval archaeology, illuminated by outstanding intuition and insight, is necessarily rare. Industrial archaeology does no worse and in some respects a good deal better. One should not be deceived into thinking an article is good, simply because it employs the correct scholarly language and is well sprinkled with agreeable-looking plans and drawings of a familiar type.

Plan of building A.

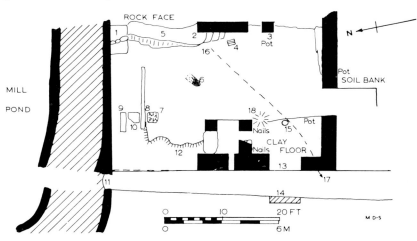

Fig. 2 – Plan of building A

1 Ore bin
2 & 3 Buttresses
4 Remains of wooden box containing finely powdered hematite ore
5 Natural rocky ledge which has been turned into a staircase leading up the bank
6 Broken hammer-head in central floor, used as an intermediate anvil
7 Anvil base sunk vertically into the ground and made of a single large log
8 & 9 Wooden baulks, sunk horizontally into the composite slag-ore floor
10 Exceptionally hard charcoal/slag area

11 & 12 In these areas the dam had previously burst and undermined the hard slagged floor crust, leaving a ragged edge
13 The wheelrace (11–17) varies from 3 feet at the dam to 5 feet width at point 13 where it appears the bellows waterwheel was situated
14 [Not identified in original article.]
15 Deep hole at the end of the waterwheel shaft
16 & 17 Between these two points a drain crosses the floor
18 Pile of pure charcoal apparently dumped ready to put into the hearth

The range of current work

1

The extractive industries

The extractive industries are those which are concerned with digging or pumping minerals and oil from the earth's crust and, in some instances, with processing the resulting materials sufficiently to allow them to be transported more cheaply and efficiently away from the site. Much of the work involved in them is heavy and dangerous, and far enough away from the experience of most people, especially those in the academic world, to necessitate considerable efforts of the imagination, if the working environment of yesterday's miners, quarrymen and oilmen is to be at all satisfactorily re-created from the physical remains of the industry as it used to be. Few branches of industrial archaeology are more in need of support from such reminiscences as one can gather, either orally or in some written form, from the men who were personally involved in the work, since the archaeological evidence can be so meagre – a hole in the ground, a group of ruined cottages, an abandoned and derelict engine-house or railway-siding.

This is particularly so in the case of mining. The miner works, like a mole, underground and when a mine or a gallery ceases to operate, it is sealed off or becomes flooded. Only in rare cases is it possible for an archaeologist to find his underground material for himself. He can look round the pithead buildings and visit the villages and streets where miners used to live, but his evidence of the actual workplace, the point at which the coal and the ore were mined, comes to him at second-hand. Very few of the historians or archaeologists of the coal industry, for example, have ever been down a pit, a most curious state of affairs. Canal archaeologists spend a great deal of their time on and alongside canals and railway archaeologists are inseparable from tracks, cuttings, tunnels and stations but, for one reason or another, those whose professional business is with the past of mining have to allow or prefer to allow their information to filter through to them from the people who actually know or knew about what working in a mine is like.

Sometimes, as at the Mining Museum at Bochum in the Ruhr, one can descend to a very clean and domesticated old mine gallery and arrive at an understanding of how the different kinds of equipment in use at various periods worked and at other places, such as the Miners' Museum at Glace Bay, Nova Scotia, the Anthracite Mine at Weatherly,

Pennsylvania, and the Exhibition Mine at Beckley, West Virginia, it is possible to see men actually carrying out the job. This kind of experience is invaluable, as any visit to a working museum must be, but one hardly needs to emphasise that the visitor is never in any danger. The sections of mines prepared for him have no gas or fire-damp, no sudden roof-falls or inrushes of water, and he has not been required to eat his meals underground, to be covered in coal dust, to develop silicosis or to be physically exhausted after hours of underground toil. But it is certainly better than nothing.

One could also usefully point out that holiday-makers visiting the former gold-rush settlements in Nevada, Colorado and Alaska come to these places for the most part during the summer months, when everything looks and feels at its best, and not in the winter climate which the nineteenth-century gold prospectors had to endure. They do not choose to get frostbite, to go hungry, to murder their fellow prospectors, or to carry great packs of equipment and provisions up mountainsides, simply in order to understand what Victorian gold-mining was all about, and one wonders how many of them – or, for that matter, how many historians and archaeologists really have the feeling, as distinct from the facts, of the job in their bones. Without that feeling, they are

Sketch map of southern part of the Kingswood Coalfield, made by M. J. H. Southway in 1971.

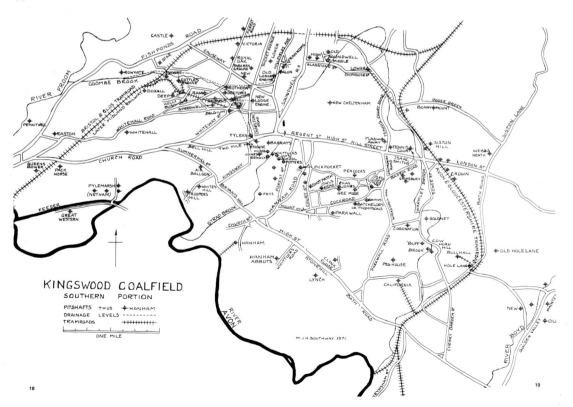

certainly liable to make grievous errors of interpretation, as serious as those committed by the archaeologist who excavates the site of a lake village or a Roman villa without being able to re-create the life that went on there in its functioning days.

These considerations should be borne in mind when studying the following examples of work recently carried out in connexion with the archaeology of what might best be called the earth industries.

The Bristol Coalfield

M. J. H. Southway has been concerned especially with the southern half of the coalfield, the area centred on Kingswood. In three articles published in *BIAS Journal*[1] between 1971 and 1976, the author has combined a study of the documentary evidence for the areas as a whole and for the individual pits with a description of the sites as they are today, with technical information relating to their working and with the memories of old miners. The whole survey is illustrated with maps and photographs and the aim is to present as clear a picture as possible of an industry which has now completely died away in the district, but which was for more than 300 years an important source of wealth and employment in Bristol and a basis for a wide range of other industries – the brass and copper works at Crews Hole alone are reputed at their peak to have bought 2,000 tons of coal a week. The interest, from our present point of view, is to see how effectively Mr Southway has used and welded together his different types of information and what contribution the archaeology can be said to make to his and our ability to understand, both intellectually and emotionally, the development of the industry. It should be mentioned, as a factor in our appreciation of the survey, that the author lives in the middle of the archaeology he is describing and assessing. He is, in other words, soaked in the atmosphere and personalities of the district, as well as in the historical facts belonging to it. For this reason, he is unlikely to make mistakes of scale and proportion. The area and its people are real to him.

Many of the pits have been closed for a century or more and to locate and map them has been a difficult, time-consuming problem. The Kingswood area has been heavily built over and every scrap of evidence, of whatever kind, has had to be searched for and used. This extract illustrates the method.

Player's 1750 plan includes a number of sites of coal workings away from the Levels, and as the scale and positioning are of reasonable accuracy, it is possible to lay

---

[1] Vol. 4, 1971; Vol. 5, 1972; and Vol. 9, 1976. The *Journal*, edited and published each year to a very high standard, is the method adopted by the Bristol Industrial Archaeological Society to give wider circulation to the work carried out by its members.

these, suitably adjusted for scale, on to a modern 6 inch scale O.S. map, marrying up with known sites and projecting the others. Indeed, the late Lands Commission seems to have adopted this method on their own revised O.S. maps.

We can therefore locate *Peacocks* at ST 657732, *Flashaway* at ST 663739 and *Isaac Smiths* at ST 665737, the latter being confirmed in the recent construction of the new Sixth Form Science Room at Kingsfield School, when the foundation concrete turned up later in storm water drains, etc. From these locations, we can project *Josiah Jefferies Work* at ST 661732, *Charles Jones'* at ST 655730 adjacent to the later Gee Moor pits and *Owls Head Works* around ST 652730, completely vanished now.[2]

There is much carefully researched and assembled technical information about the pumping machinery and other equipment installed at the pits at various periods. It is presented to us in this form:

The Hard seam, lost at 96 ft. in the Oxbridge workings, was recaptured at 480 ft. in the adjacent *Frog Lane* shaft sunk in about 1852 at ST 687816. This pit had in fact twin oval shafts 9 ft. × 6 ft. 6 ins. and 660 ft. deep. The southerly shaft was fitted with a Cornish Beam pumping engine made by Bush of Bristol, 85 ins. cylinder dia., 10 ft. stroke, working $6\frac{1}{2}$ strokes per min. There were three 20″ dia. stages, the bottom being a lift pump, and the intermediate and top, force pumps, capacity 129 gals. per stroke. The water was actually raised 615 ft. to a level 45

[2]   *BIAS Journal*, Vol. 4, 1971, p. 16.

Bristol coalfield, Warmley Colliery. This nineteenth-century print shows a group of collieries, with Warmley Church in the background, and emphasises the rural environment of the industry at this period.

ft. below the surface. Steam was supplied at 30 p.s.i. from a battery of four 28 ft. × 7 ft. Lancs. boilers with a fifth 34 ft. × 6 ft.[3]

There are details of the accidents, the floodings, the bankruptcies, the sales, and the mine-owners. The range of material combed for information is very wide – local newspaper files, parish records, sale catalogues, archives of the mining companies, now held in the Bristol Record Office, reminiscences of old miners and, not least, the author's own memories of a long life in the district.

The writer can well remember as a boy seeing the striking pitmen in procession down through Lawrence Hill with their candles in their caps. (The pits were mainly non-fiery.) There was much local hardship, children going to school barefoot for lack of footwear and 'feeding centres' being opened up in local drill halls, etc., to provide a mid-day meal for the school children whose fathers were on strike. Education of the boys in local schools was slanted towards training them for working in the pits, and the writer has a strong recollection of general science lessons devoted to the 'King Hook', a newly invented device to prevent overwind of the cage, a frequent source of disaster. The new invention had a double trigger mechanism to disconnect the cage suspension and lock the cage to the guide rails in the event of overwind. There were also lessons on 'fire-damp', methane or marsh gas, and 'black damp' or 'choke damp', carbon dioxide, together with many descriptions and demonstrations of the Miners' Safety Lamp.[4]

There has been no mining in this area since the 1920s. The people who remember it are getting steadily fewer and most of the physical evidence of its traditional place in the life of Bristol has disappeared. The present inhabitants find it extremely difficult to believe that there were at one time dozens of pits within an area extending about 6 miles south-east and 10 miles north-east of where Temple Meads Station is today. Mr Southway, during years of patient work, has mapped them all; produced what is, in effect, a gazetteer, recorded every scrap of evidence which is still visible, and traced the pattern of ownership from the beginning to the end of the coalfield's useful life. Wherever details of output are available, he has noted them in a way which makes it clear that coal did not mine itself: 'Six hundred men were employed in 1899 and they raised 77,000 tons from *Deep Pit* and 54,000 tons from

3   *BIAS Journal*, Vol. 5, 1972, p. 26.
4   *BIAS Journal*, Vol. 4, 1971, p. 17.

Speedwell during that year, mostly steam coal.'[5] And we are reminded that an output of this order was achieved by men wielding picks and shovels in seams often no more than 2 ft 6 ins. thick.

It is clear that Mr Southway has produced an invaluable historical account of mining in the Bristol coalfield, and that he has achieved that rare success, a total picture of the rise and fall of an industry. What part can industrial archaeology be said to have played in the creation of the total picture? One aspect of this archaeology can hardly be forgotten, although it is not, in the ordinary sense, visible; the whole district is a vast rabbit warren of abandoned mine galleries, which subside from time to time as a reminder of their presence, but there are other items of a more conventional kind, which can feed the historical imagination of those who know what they are looking at – the 'chimney now over-grown with ivy' at Painters Pit; the locomotive shed at Coalpit Heath; the spoil-heaps at Shortwood. Mostly, however, it is a tale of things to be seen until ten or twenty years ago – 'the site of the three closely grouped shafts is now covered by the Technical Development Unit of W. D. and H. O. Wills'; '*Ashton Colliery*, the first shaft of which was at ST 564712, now the site of McDougall's new plant in Ashton Vale Lane' – evidence which Mr Southway himself saw and recorded, but has now disappeared for ever. What are still to be observed in great plenty, however, are the houses of the mining families, the pubs, halls and shops they used, and the non-conformist chapels which drew them on a Sunday. All this is just as relevant archaeologically as anything which remains of the pits and the railways, but until one has the distribution and location of the workings clear in one's mind, a task which Mr Southway has so efficiently and painstakingly performed for us, the

[5] *BIAS Journal*, Vol. 4, 1971, p. 17.

Bristol coalfield, Easton Colliery. Early twentieth-century photograph, precise date uncertain, showing wooden headstocks over the pit, boiler sheds and a waggon with the nameboard, 'Leonard Boult and Co. Ltd. – Easton Colliery'.

significance of the settlement pattern and even of the rise and fall of the ground is unlikely to reveal itself to us.

The last working whim-gin at a West European mine
The development of machinery to wind coal and other minerals and ores up from the pit passed through three stages, before the introduction of steam winding engines – hand windlasses; the early type of powered windlass, known as a gin, in which a horse was attached to a wheel

A whim-gin. Drawing from Thomas Hair's *A series of views of the collieries in . . . Northumberland and Durham* London, 1844.

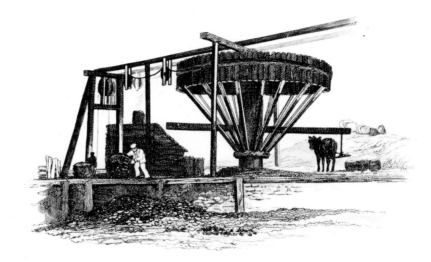

Oberkaufungen: plan showing horse-gin house, shaft and pulley system and part of the overhead unloading platform.

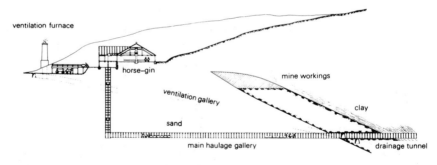

Oberkaufungen, near Kassel: diagram of whim-gin at former Freudenthal brown-coal mine, in relation to the other pit installations.

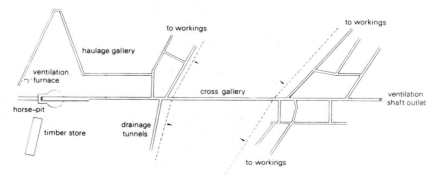

geared to the shaft of the windlass, the rope being wound on the shaft as in the case of the hand-operated machine; and the whim-gin, in which the rope-drum was pivoted vertically, instead of horizontally, and the rope was brought away from the shaft by means of pulleys. This major technological advance in winding machinery allowed the actual winding operation to be removed from the pit mouth, so that operations in the immediate pit area were much less congested. The horse-gin continued in use at smaller collieries in Europe, including Britain, until the end of the nineteenth century.

A gin of this type has survived near Kassel, in the German Federal Republic, on the edge of a new housing estate at Karfungen. It has been fully described by Gerhard Seib.[6] The gin was part of the installation at the former Freudenthal brown-coal mine. The building, 15.5 metres across, enclosing the gin is 14-sided and is joined directly to the half-timbered building covering the pit. The bottom of the vertical shaft of the gin rests on a sandstone base and the top revolves in the centre of the elaborate timbering system of the roof. Fixed to this shaft is a beam, which has an attachment for a pair of horses at one end and a seat for the driver at the other.

The method of operation was as follows. The driver kept his horses moving round and round until the full skip of coal had reached the surface. A bell signal instructed him to stop. The contents of the skip

[6]   Published as 'Der letzte bergmännische Pferdegöpel Westeuropas', in *Der Anschnitt: Zeitschrift für Kunst und Kultur im Bergbau*, Heft 5/6, Bochum, 1974.

Oberkaufungen: exterior of whim-gin building, after restoration.

were then tipped out and the horses were unhitched from the beam and put on again facing in the opposite direction from before. When they went round this time, they pulled up the skip which was hanging from the second pulley, the first skip being automatically lowered back to the bottom of the pit again. Someone who had observed the process in action reported that 'the horses are very well trained. They start off on their own accord when they hear the bell-signal and stop immediately as soon as the skip has reached the surface.'[7]

This particular shaft at the pit was about 28 metres deep. The gin was installed there in 1823 and worked until 1884. It owes its preservation to the fact that it was used for storing straw for its neighbouring and more recent pit, which continued in operation until mining at Kaufungen finally came to an end in 1967. It was officially designated an historic monument in the 1930s. By the 1960s, when the company closed the mine down, it was in poor condition and a restoration project was undertaken, on the initiative of the Cultural Association of Kaufungen and with funds made available by the Kassel local authority, which by this time owned it, and by the Monuments Department of Land Hesse. The building was re-roofed and all the timbering and working parts fully overhauled. Visitors can now see the gin exactly as it was a hundred years ago and in working condition. Unfortunately, there has been a major planning failure, so that, instead of the old buildings being seen in something like their original setting against woodland, new housing has been permitted to come up close to them. The environmental consequences can only be described as disastrous.

For some curious reason, the whim-gin at Kaufungen has received, despite its uniqueness and miraculous survival, remarkably scanty attention from historians and scholars. Very little has been written about it and its importance in the study of mining technology has only recently been realised. Its only rival as a functioning whim-gin, at Jachymov, in Czechoslovakia, has now been dismantled and moved to another site. The Oberkaufungen gin, however, has now been placed in its historical context, as an indispensable example in the typology of pit winding gear which has been worked out in recent years, a story which has its beginnings in the mid-sixteenth century.[8]

Dr Seib's own work in connexion with this site has been essentially that of a synthesiser. He has assembled and presented for the first time the facts concerning the history and technology of the equipment and he has explained, for the benefit of other historians of the mining industry, why this machinery is important and how it has come to be

[7] W. Röhler, 'Der Braunkohlenbegbau bei Oberkaufungen', in F. Mayer, *Oberkaufungen im Wandel der Zeit* Oberkaufungen, 1962.

[8] See H. Schönberg, 'Die technische Entwicklung der Fördergerüste und -türme des Bergbaus', in B. and H. Becher, *Die Architektur der Förder und Wassertürme* Munich, 1971, pp. 250–3, 'Der Göpel'.

preserved and restored. The circumstances of publication are important. The German periodical, *Der Anschnitt*, in which Dr Seib's article appeared, is produced by the Bergbau Museum at Bochum, in the Ruhr. It is a valuable link between industry and industrialists on the one hand and scholars on the other. An article such as this consequently has great tactical and political value, which the Bergbau Museum, established in the centre of Germany's main area of heavy industry, understands instinctively and very well, but which is all too often overlooked elsewhere.

Oberkaufungen: detail of roof-timbering in whim-gin building. (See page 46.)

The Alte Elisabeth silver mine, Freiberg

Like all the Socialist countries, the German Democratic Republic is not content, at least in public, to allow industrial archaeology to proceed under its own steam. The social and political point of such activity has to be emphasised on all possible occasions. An example of the ritual to be observed on these occasions – it is no more than ritual and does not interfere in the slightest with the methodology or scholarship of the work carried out – is to be found in the Preface to the officially sponsored and excellently produced survey of industrial monuments in the DDR.[9] In this Preface the President of the Kulturbund, Professor Max Burghart, writes:

During the past few years, members of the working class have taken the initiative on many occasions to establish a systematic and scientific programme for the conservation and interpretation of technical monuments. Such people are drawn both from the skilled workers in State-owned industrial enterprises and from the staff and students of Technical Universities. The increasingly important role which the working class is playing in our socialist society

[9] *Technische Denkmale in der DDR* Kulturbund der Deutsches Democratischen Republik. Weimar, 1973.

Alte Elisabeth silver mine, Freiberg: showing arrangement and function of the buildings and underground workings and installations.

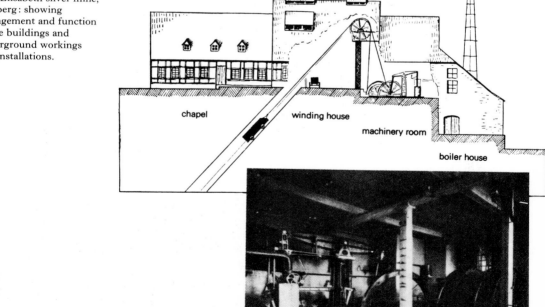

chapel   winding house   machinery room   boiler house guarantees that technical monuments will be given their proper value and that they will be effectively cared for and presented in a way which is to the advantage of the community.[10]

It so happens that the prime mover in industrial archaeology within the DDR has been Dr Otfried Wagenbreth, who lives in Freiberg, where it is natural to take a particular interest in the history of the silver-mining industry, which has been important in the area since medieval times. For centuries, the whole Erzgebirge region, on both sides of what is now the German–Czech border, was Europe's main centre of technical innovation in the mining industry. The early establishment of a Mining Academy at Freiberg bears witness to this. Examples of the techniques and equipment described by Agricola in his book *De Re Metallica* (1546) are still to be found here, side by side with the later developments brought in during the age of steam and electricity.

Dr Wagenbreth's own work has covered both the history and archaeology of the mining district as a whole and the detailed exploration of particular sites. His treatment of the Alte Elisabeth mine at Freiberg will serve as an example. This mine dates from the sixteenth century. Until recently it was used as a demonstration mine for the benefit of students at the Mining Academy and provided an opportunity to see the techniques which had been used in silver mining over a period of nearly four centuries. The equipment still intact includes the 1849 steam-plant, for raising the ore to the surface and for powering the curious system of moving steps which took miners up and down the pit. In the same set of buildings there is the chapel, complete with its little organ, in which miners prayed before going underground to their

[10] Ibid. p. 5.

Buildings at Alte Elisabeth mine, Freiberg. Photograph by Otfried Wagenbreth.

work and again in gratitude after coming safely up again. The gathering in the chapel at the end of the shift also served the practical purpose of checking the number of miners who had returned. Such chapels or, as they were so pleasantly called, 'prayer parlours' (Betstuben), have nearly all disappeared, but the surviving example at Alte Elisabeth carries the visitor and, one hopes, the students as well, back to the atmosphere, the danger and the anxieties of mining a century and more ago. Another such chapel, removed from its original site, can be seen at Freiberg's excellent Town and Mining Museum, but there is no doubt

Alte Elisabeth silver mine: 1849 steam engine by Constantin Pfaff. Photograph by Otfried Wagenbreth.

that much of its emotional value is lost away from the place where it had meaning and purpose.

The preservation of the mine as a public museum and its interpretation in a way which is both scientifically accurate and attractive is largely due to the efforts of Dr Wagenbreth himself. The 1849 beam engine, built by Constantin Pfaff, of Chemnitz, can be made to work now by means of a compressed air system which visitors can set in motion by pressing a button, a concession of which purists might well disapprove.

Dr Wagenbreth's researches and writings into the history of the mine have been divided into three closely interlocking parts.[11] There has been, first, work on the plans, maps and documents in the libraries of the State Archives of Saxony and of the Mining Academy and in the collections of the town museum. This has been accompanied by a close first-hand study of buildings, shafts and machinery of the mine and reinforced by conversations with members of mining families. The mine is no longer operative, so that one cannot, unfortunately, watch men at work. And, a matter of prime importance, Alte Elisabeth has always been kept in the context of the local mining industry, of which it was only one unit. This has been particularly necessary where the drainage of the pit was concerned. Water was got away from the workings by a complicated district-system of channels and tunnels, in which all the pits shared and which used a number of waterwheels and water-column pumps to clear the mines of water. The placing of each individual pit within this network has been one of the most important tasks for industrial archaeologists in the old mining areas of the Erzgebirge. The ditches and tunnels have now all been mapped, with their connexions with streams and rivers indicated. No-one who looks at these maps and who walks round the hilly district looking at the fairly abundant evidence of the system which still survives can fail to be impressed by the ingenuity and patience shown by the old miners and surveyors.

Bodie, California

The ghost towns, in Colorado, Nevada and California, have been visited and described by many travellers and writers, from Mark Twain onwards. One of the most systematic of modern observers and recorders, Muriell Sibell Wolle, has published an account of the journeys she made to ghost towns during the 1940s.[12] In it, she divides ghost towns into four categories:

[11] The method and its results are described in Otfried Wagenbreth, *800 Jahre Freiberger Bergbau*, originally published in the series Freiberger Forschungshefte and reprinted in 1970 by the VEB Verlag für Grundstoffsindustrie.
[12] *The Bonanza Trail* Indianapolis, 1952.

Mining towns that are still alive, like Tombstone, Arizona and Jacksonville, Oregon, which started as mining camps, but are today largely dependent on other industries. They have a permanent population and contain some of the original buildings.

Towns which are partly ghost, such as Telluride, Colorado, and Goldfield, Nevada, where many of the early buildings, both commercial and private, stand unoccupied, although a portion of the town is inhabited and is still carrying on a normal life, the chief industry being mining.

Mining towns which are true ghosts – completely deserted, although buildings still line their streets. Bodie, California, and Gold Road, Arizona, are of this type.

Mining towns which have disappeared and whose sites only remain. Beartown, Montana; Silver Reef, Utah; and Battle, Wyoming, are in this class.

For half a century, between the beginning of the California Gold Rush in 1849 and the opening up of the deposits in Alaska and the Klondike at the end of the 1890s, tens of thousands of restless men, a large proportion of them immigrants, saw gold, and to a lesser extent silver, as their one opportunity to escape from the grind and insecurity of earning a living in more conventional ways. For the remote chance of a fortune, they risked their lives, stayed filthy and foul-smelling for months on end, lost parts of themselves from frostbite, spent years existing in the most primitive conditions and, most important and regrettable of all from the community point of view, established the

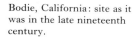

Bodie, California: site as it was in the late nineteenth century.

gambler, reckless of life and impatient of all attempts to control or socialise his activities, as a prestigious type in American life.

Bodie, seven miles south of Bridgeport and close to the California–Nevada border, is now a State Historic Park. About one in 20 of the buildings it had when it was at the peak of its activity now remain. They are maintained in what the Department of Parks and Recreation describes as 'a state of arrested decay', that is, unrestored but prevented from getting any worse. 10,000 people lived there in 1880, when it was notorious for never-ending violence and crime, 65 saloons and a killing a day. It had then, as it has now, a very severe climate. In winter the temperature goes down to 40° below zero, winds reach 100 m.p.h. and the snow, not uncommonly, is 20 feet deep. The wooden houses, such as can still be seen on the site, were not well built – money, craftsmen, time and materials were all in short supply – and a great deal of firewood was required to keep them even tolerably warm. The sawmill on Park Street is one of Bodie's most significant archaeological items.

The history of Bodie and of its individual buildings has been meticulously researched by the State's Department of Parks and Recreation. The details and position of every building are known and, armed with the exceptionally good official guide, today's visitor can walk around Bodie with all the information and encouragement he needs to recreate a mental picture of this 'sea of sin, lashed by tempests of lust and passion' as it used to be. The State authority itself should probably be given most credit for this, for its successful efforts to prevent the remains of Bodie from disappearing altogether and for collating the documentary evidence of Bodie when it was a living, functioning centre. This is an example of a place where there is an excellent supply of industrial archaeology and a great deal of readily available information,

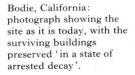

Bodie, California: photograph showing the site as it is today, with the surviving buildings preserved 'in a state of arrested decay'.

but where the archaeologists themselves are shadowy and elusive figures. Bodie has never yet been written up in a way to satisfy scholars, partly, no doubt, because it is too well known from popular legend and partly because the abundant archival and library material has been so thoroughly combed already. Bodie today is a place where the imagination begins at the point where information stops.

Inevitably, much of the town has been burnt down at one time or another. The two biggest fires were in 1892 and 1932 and, paradoxically, Bodie is safer now than at any time since it was first built. The wide open spaces between the existing buildings make it less likely that a fire, once started, will spread very far. It is a curious experience to stand on a plot of ground, map in hand, and to realise that here was the Masonic Lodge, No. 252, F. and A. M.; here was the Bodie Bank, represented now only by its vaults; here was the Casino; and here was the Philadelphia Beer Hall, the most elegant saloon in Bodie, patronised by all classes.

But sufficient remains above ground to appreciate the style and scale of life that the town offered – the Schoolhouse, originally the Bon Ton Lodging House; the Miners' Union Hall, the centre of much of Bodie's social life; Chinatown; and the Town Jail, from which only one person is known to have escaped. There are also on the edge of the town four cemeteries – Ward's Cemetery, the Masonic Cemetery, the Miners' Union Cemetery and the Chinese Cemetery. Murderers and others not generally accepted as respectable were buried outside the cemetery fences and with nothing to mark their graves.

Some, but tantalisingly insufficient evidence remains of the mining activities which were the whole reason for Bodie's existence. Chief among these is the hydro-electric station and power station, which have an interesting history. In the earliest years, the ore-crushing mills supplied by the 30 local mines were driven by steam engines, the boilers being wood-fuelled. Wood soon became scarce and expensive and in 1889 Tom Legget, the superintendent of the Standard Mining Company, decided to test his theory that electricity could be transmitted over wires for a considerable distance, an experiment which had never previously been made. Legget built a hydro-electric plant 13 miles from Bodie, on Green Creek near Bridgeport, to develop 13 h.p. and 6,600 volts. The poles – some of them still stand – were erected in a dead straight line, because there were doubts at the time as to whether electricity could turn corners. The system worked perfectly well and Bodie had the distinction of having installed the first electric motor in the world to operate over long-distance power-lines. The Standard Mine, too, was one of the first, if not the first to use an electric hoist.

Bodie is also famous for having perfected the cyanide process of extracting gold from the ore. This process allowed mine tailings, previously unprofitable, to be worked for gold. The cyanide plant itself, the largest in the United States, has gone, but it is commemorated indirectly by the house of Lester E. Bell, the manager-in-charge. His son, Lester L. Bell, became an assayer for Bodie's mining companies and his son in turn, Bob Bell, was born in Bodie – a rare distinction nowadays – and worked in the mines. Bob Bell lives on the site and for a number of years he has worked on the restoration and, as it is termed, stabilisation of the buildings in the town on behalf of the California Department of Parks and Recreation. Bodie is not without its traditions and threads of continuity.

The Stora Kopparberg mine, Falun

The Falun coppermine in Dalarna is the most famous mine in Sweden and possibly in the whole of Europe. Now owned and operated by the Stora Kopparberg Company, it was first worked in the eleventh century and ore was being exported by the twelfth. Production dropped in the early sixteenth century, but new and more easily accessible deposits were discovered in the 1570s and after that the output from the mine rose rapidly. By the middle of the seventeenth century Stora Kopparberg, the Great Copper Mountain, was producing most of the copper used in Europe. During the same period the Swedish state financed its wars from the sales of copper. The abundance of copper in Sweden had other political and commercial consequences, including the habit of using copper instead of silver for coinage. The policy was prudent, rather than convenient, since a copper coin weighed a hundred times as much as a silver coin of the same value. A transaction of any size

Stora Kopparberg mine, Falun, as it appeared in 1687.

A, C, D, G Winding houses
B Aqueduct
E Ore crushing mill
F Old miners' meeting house
H 35 fathom pit
I Tub haulage machine
K New miners' meeting house
L Winding house for 70 fathom pit
M 127 fathom pit
N Hoist

consequently involved the use of waggons to transport the payment and this appalling nuisance led to the introduction of paper money in 1656, Sweden being, for good reason, the first European country to decide on such an innovation. One can hardly say that the seventeenth-century coins and banknotes to be found in Swedish museums are part of the archaeology of the copper industry, but, for those in possession of the

The rope-drum at Stora Kopparberg (1805).

facts, they are a powerful reminder of the extraordinary way in which copper dominated the Swedish economy at one time. With the decrease in Stora Kopparberg's output during the eighteenth century, Swedish copper began to lose its importance on world markets, despite strenuous efforts on the part of the Government to stimulate production and to increase exports. Iron then gradually took the place of copper in the Swedish economy. By 1800 the value of the copper produced was only a seventh of the value of the iron. During the nineteenth century the operations at the Falune mine changed their character completely. The mine produced an interesting range of ores and these were processed to yield sulphuric acid, red ochre, silver and a certain amount of gold, as well as copper. Copper was last produced at Falun in 1895.

Today, the Stora Kopparberg Company has industrial interests, chiefly in iron, timber, woodpulp and engineering, throughout Sweden. Its prosperity, combined with the traditional interest taken by Swedish industrial concerns in cultural matters, has led to the commissioning and production of a most thoroughgoing and beautifully produced company history,[13] one of the few such works of which it can be truthfully said that no expense was spared.

Until very recently, the mine buildings at Falun were constructed mainly of wood and their survival rate has consequently not been high. A further hazard has been the continuous widening of the Great Pit – in order to go deeper, one was compelled to go wider – which inevitably meant that the buildings around the edge were being constantly demolished and replaced on a more suitable site. One can see, merely by standing on the edge of the pit and looking down to the bottom as it is

[13]   Sten Lindroth *Gruvbrytning och Kopparhantering vid Storakopparberget* 2 vols., Uppsala: Almqvist and Wiksell, 1975.

Stora Kopparberg mine, Falun. The Great Pit, bottom right, as it is today. The aerial photograph also shows the modern town and the lake which formed part of the mine's system of water transport.

today, that the problem of raising ore to the surface and keeping the workings clear of rubbish must have been a formidable task before the days of power-operated hoisting machinery. Part of the problem was caused by the collapse in 1687 of the walls between the three largest quarries, which created the Great Pit. A number of the most profitable galleries were filled with earth and rubble, and the workings had to be reorganised. For many years, nearly all the ore that was raised was obtained by sorting out the huge masses of material that had resulted from the 1687 disaster and others of a similar nature. With the methods then available, there could have been no slower or less productive form of mining, and one has only to gaze at the pit with the historical facts in mind in order to understand very well the despair which faced the company for much of the eighteenth century, and the eagerness with which technical ideas were taken up.

The excellent company museum, close to the Great Pit, makes it possible to study the technical developments in their proper context. One can, for example, see models of the remarkable hoists designed by the great Swedish inventor and engineer, Christopher Polhem, who worked as Machine Director at Falun from 1700 to 1716. Polhem was responsible for founding a school for mining engineers at Falun, together with an engineering research institute, a 'laboratorium mechanicum'. One can fairly say that all the innovations which took place at Falun – and, as the Museum shows, there were many – were the product of sheer necessity. The Stora Kopparberg motto might well have been, 'Innovate or perish', and the constructions and techniques worked out there during the eighteenth and nineteenth centuries made Falun one of Europe's great places of pilgrimage during this period.

The Museum itself is a symbol of the remarkable degree of social responsibility and public spirit which Swedish industrialists have always shown. No other country in Western Europe has given evidence of such enlightened self-interest on the part of its industrial enterprises. The contrast with France, where the historical consciousness of the major employers is probably the lowest in Europe, is very marked. The main building of the Museum, formerly the Mine Office, was erected between 1771 and 1785. Early in the nineteenth century, the administration of the Stora Kopparberg Company was moved to the centre of the town, and the old building fell into a bad state of repair. By the 1960s, as a result of the extension of the mine, it was perched precariously on the edge of the pit and had been damaged by subsidence. In 1964–6 it was moved to a safer site not too far away. Because of decay and damage, not all the original building could be used in the reconstruction, but the roof, bell-tower, doors and many of the furnishings are original. The remainder has been faithfully restored on the basis of old drawings and descriptions.

One might sum up the Stora Kopparberg achievement, which is by any standards remarkable, by saying that the various elements one needs in order to acquire a full understanding of the industry are all present here – the mine itself; a number of its old buildings, including eighteenth- and nineteenth-century houses; a good museum and archive; a first-class company history; and an opportunity to visit part of the modern mining operation in order to be able to relate the past with the present. It is difficult to see what more could have been expected of any industrial concern. If industrial archaeology has to have industrial patronage this is how to do it, at least under the conditions of a capitalist economy.

Le Grand-Hornu

In 1968 Professor Marinette Bruwier and two of her colleagues at the University of Mons published what was, for Belgium, a pioneering article on the new subject of industrial archaeology. It was concerned with one of the most spectacular sites in all Europe, the workshop-complex and company town at Le Grand-Hornu, near Mons, and it appeared, significantly, not in an academic publication, but in *Industrie*,[14] the monthly journal of what was then called the Fédération des Industries Belges and has since, moving with the times, become the Fédération des Entreprises de Belgique.

Le Grand-Hornu is in that area of Belgium known as the Borinage, where the conditions in the coal-mining industry were notorious during the nineteenth century, especially after the publicity given to them by Emile Zola, in his highly successful novel, *Germinal*. It was at that time one of the poorest and most harshly exploited parts of industrial Europe. Coal-mining came to an end here in 1951 and in 1966, just before Professor Bruwier's article was published, an Ordonnance du Roi was issued, ordering the removal of all evidence of coal-mining in the Borinage, partly on aesthetic grounds, but even more because the industry was reckoned to give rise to memories which were better for-gotten. The article attempted to show that some, at least, of these industrial monuments were an important part of the national heritage and deserved to be kept and even cherished. One should point out, perhaps, that the article would almost certainly never have been published at all, if the Fédération's Head of Publications had not happened to be a man with a doctorate in archaeology, who took a keen personal interest in these matters[15] and who was influential in political and industrial circles. The combination is very rare and has proved to be

14 Issue for January 1968. The article, by Marinette Bruwier, Anne Meurant and Christiane Pierard, was reprinted, in a translation by Kenneth Hudson, in *Industrial Archaeology*, Vol. 6, No. 4, November 1969.

15 Dr Georges van den Abeelen's own masterly survey of the industrial archaeology of Belgium appeared in *Industrie* in February 1972.

of great benefit to industrial archaeology in Belgium, as indeed would have been the case anywhere.

In writing her article, Professor Bruwier had a two-fold task. She had to marshal a large mass of historical evidence and present it in a way which would match her own academic standards, and she had to convince influential opinion in Belgium, where the conservation of industrial monuments is still in its infancy, that Le Grand-Hornu was worth saving from the bulldozers. There can have been few more crucial statements within the short history of industrial archaeology to date and the fact that Le Grand-Hornu still exists testifies to its success.

During the second half of the eighteenth century, the Borinage was reckoned to be a technically advanced area, so far as coal-mining was concerned. In particular, it invested in an exceptionally large number of steam engines. This was partly because gravity-drainage of the pits was more difficult to arrange here and partly because deeper than

Le Grand Hornu: aerial picture showing former workshop complex before restoration, surrounding central courtyard, and streets of workers' houses.

average seams were being worked. Between 1750 and 1810 an important coal trade was built up with the North of France and with other parts of Belgium, so important that the Borinage engaged hardly at all in any other kind of economic activity. Among the coal-traders at the turn of the century was Henri de Gorge. He prudently married Eugénie Legrand, of Lille, who belonged to a rich family of wholesale merchants and whose dowry was appropriately impressive. With the dowry as a valuable addition to his working capital, de Gorge entered the mining industry, sank a number of pits at Hornu, prospered enormously and died of cholera in 1832, when he was 58. By then, he had established an integrated industrial empire, with large engineering and machine-building workshops as well as the mining and marketing of coal and a horse-drawn railway, the first of its kind in Belgium, to link his pits to the Mons Canal. He had also planned and built a new town for his workpeople, a cité ouvrière, with amenities which were remarkable for the time. There were 425 houses, providing accommodation for 2,500 people. There were baths, meeting rooms, a dance-hall, a school and, eventually, a hospital staffed by nurses. It was paternalism at its early nineteenth-century best and, by making it possible to recruit workers of high quality, it was certainly to the interest of Henri de Gorge.

The archaeology, then, consists of the town and the workshops. The evidence of the mines themselves has been obliterated. The workshops, designed by the noted French architect, Bruno Renard, were of exceptional architectural quality. They were built around an elliptical courtyard, 140 metres in length and 80 in breadth; and included a foundry, an assembly shop, stores and an administration block. The ends of the ellipse consisted of a roofed arcade, which was used for storing iron, oil and patterns, and for garaging the fire-engine. The southern entrance to the courtyard is in the form of a quadrilateral, joined onto the ellipse. It was designed to provide stabling and further storage space.

The workshops, which manufactured steam engines, as well as a wide range of mining machinery, began operating in 1831, only a year before de Gorge died. In the middle of the ellipse is a cast-iron statue of him, erected by his family, which continued the business, in 1855. Some parts of it have since disappeared, but it is known that iron representations of a miner's lamp and tools and of machine-gears were at one time to be seen at the feet of de Gorge.

Planned industrial towns were rare before 1850. Le Grand-Hornu was built over the site of the mine, but there seems to have been no serious subsidence. The streets are wide and perfectly straight, with the width increasing as one approaches a cross-road. Green open spaces formed an important part of the plan. Chief among them was the Place Verte, which contained a bandstand where the town band gave concerts twice a week during the summer. There was a second square, facing the de Gorge family residence, which was a substantial affair, forming part of the total composition. After Henri de Gorge died, his heirs gave up the house to the manager of the Company and built a much larger mansion in a large garden behind the office block.

The workers' houses vary a little in size, but are nearly all to the same design. Built in terraces, on two floors, with a cellar, each has six rooms, a garden and a coal shed. There was an oven and a well for every ten houses. The records kept in the State Archives in Mons show that the houses were inhabited by families containing from six to ten people and often by a lodger as well. The parents and the older children worked in the mine or the workshops, and the company had the right to take possession of the house if the head of the household was dismissed, which no doubt helped to maintain industrial discipline.

As Marinette Bruwier wrote in 1968:

> The history of technology is still in its infancy. It is certain, nevertheless, that an architectural creation such as Le Grand-Hornu will find a significant place in any future assessment of nineteenth-century achievement. Its interest is as much for the economic and social historian as for someone whose main concern is with architecture or technology. One very rarely comes across a nineteenth-century industrial complex as complete as Le Grand-Hornu which has survived without radical renovation. A study in depth of this remarkable example of architecture and town planning might well be the first important piece of research within the field of industrial archaeology to be carried out in Belgium.

This 'study in depth' has not, alas, taken place yet. Professor Bruwier herself has been swallowed up by academic administration, as Dean of the Faculty of Arts, and no-one else has yet appeared to carry out the detailed research which the project demands. In particular, no attempt has been made so far to collect the memories of the last generation of people who worked in the company workshops and mine, an historical investment which will have to be made very soon, if it is to be made at all.

What has, however, been achieved is the preservation of the site. Without this, there would have been little for future archaeologists to study. Many of the former tenants of the cité ouvrière have bought their houses and modernised them, not always in the way one might have hoped. The great workshop complex itself was bought at the eleventh hour by a successful architect, Henri Guchez, who was born in the town and is strongly attached to it. Guchez has spent a fortune on putting the buildings to rights and in installing his large architectural practice there. The former stable-block has been transformed into a centre for art exhibitions and, facing it across the courtyard, a building once used as a sugar factory has been carefully restored in preparation for its eventual use as a museum of industry and technology, which Belgium so far lacks. The project to which Bruno Renard and his patron devoted so much imagination has been saved for posterity and for industrial archaeologists but not, it is sad to note, by the efforts of the State.

Le Grand-Hornu is not, as yet, a European place of pilgrimage for tourists, but for those who are interested in the industrial past, and in attempts to preserve its more significant monuments, it has a great deal to offer, both in the grandeur and scale of its conception and in the skilful way in which paternalism took the sharp edges off profit-making, at a time when such a policy was far from fashionable.

2

Food and drink

Of the numerous varieties of archaeology which now exist – under-water archaeology, marine or maritime archaeology, urban archaeology, rural archaeology, railway archaeology, aviation archaeology are a few of them – there is, as yet, nothing calling itself agricultural archaeology. The gap is a curious one, partly in view of the apparently unstoppable tendency of people with specialist interests to coalesce into groups and to establish societies and periodicals, and partly because the material to be studied is so abundant. There is, of course, an academically respectable subject known as agricultural history, with a number of national societies linking together those people who have a special interest in it and editing journals in which members can publish the results of their researches. The British Agricultural History Society is such a body and its journal, *The Agricultural History Review*, has been appearing since 1953, printing solid articles and reviewing books. The *Review* is typical of the best of such journals. Its contents cover a wide field, dealing both with the core and the fringes of agriculture in an authoritative and scholarly manner, but rarely venturing into anything which could reasonably be called agricultural archaeology. Like its contemporaries overseas it is essentially a library and archive-based periodical. The titles of the contributions to Volume 23, 1975, Part I are representative of those which have appeared during the present decade:

'Tenure, Tenant Right and Agricultural Progress in
Lindsey, 1780–1850'
'The Development of Market Gardening in Bedfordshire,
1799–1939'
'The Cattle Trade and Agrarian Change on the Eve of the
Railway Age'
'The Progress of the Early Threshing Machine'
'Some Farming Customs and Practices in the late 1860s:
the Case of St. Quinton v Lett'

The *Review* cannot fairly be accused of conservatism. Its articles cover a wide range and occasionally approach the adventurous and exotic – 'Changes in the Supply of Wild Rabbits, 1790–1910' and 'The Three-Field System of Sixteenth Century Lithuania' are examples.

But it keeps, for the most part, well away from archaeology,[1] that is, from papers which are based on a study of the surviving physical remains of this or that system or process or economy. Most of the authors do not give the impression of having spent a great deal of time looking round farms and the countryside. This may be either because the editor is offered very few papers written by people whose approach to agricultural history is based on archaeological interests, or because the quality and importance of the non-archaeological papers happens, year by year, to be superior.

The industrial archaeologists do not, so far as one can judge, from books, periodicals or conferences, have any particular prejudice against agriculture or food processing, although there has been a lot of argument as to whether farming, that is, the actual production of food in its raw state, is fully entitled to the name 'industry'. The National Farmers Union has no such misgivings, and refers loudly and on all possible occasions to 'the British agricultural industry'. Certainly, whatever may be happening in the fields themselves, a modern pig or poultry farm can be considered a factory in every sense of the term, and certain types of intensive horticulture can safely be brought under the same heading. This particular book at least finds no difficulty in including agriculture in its list of industries and considers that an archaeological attitude of mind can be very helpful in arriving at a better under-standing of agricultural history from the mid-eighteenth century onwards.

'Food' or 'food production' involves much more, of course, than merely running a farm. It covers the processing of raw foodstuffs, in order to make them palatable and saleable; packaging, distributing and selling them; and providing the farmer – the term is used comprehen-sively to include every kind of person growing or rearing material for ultimate human consumption – with the supplies and equipment he needs in order to carry out his business. The archaeology of food embraces all these and, for this reason, represents one of the biggest and richest fields to which the industrial archaeologist can devote his attention. The examples which follow are intended to illustrate this range and to indicate what kind of results can be expected from an archaeology centred enquiry.

[1] There are a number of articles in which the author drops a clue that he has in fact actually seen what he has been writing about, even though he has not ventured into description at any point or strayed across the archaeological line. An example of this is provided by Keith Sutton, 'A French Agricultural Canal – the Canal de la Sauldre and the Nineteenth Century Improvement of the Sologne', Vol. 21, 1973, Part I, which ends: 'In modern France the value of areas like the Sologne can probably be better measured in amenity rather than agricultural terms. In this respect a relict agricultural canal without the normal accompaniment of industrial eyesores can still represent a valuable resource for the French countryside.' This suggests, but does not prove, that the author had taken a look at the Canal for himself.

Since reference has already been made to the scarcity of agricultural archaeology reports in *The Agricultural History Review*, it seems no more than an act of justice to consider first two such articles which have in fact appeared recently in the *Review* and to enquire to what extent they provide information and insight which could have been obtained in no other way. One deals with Northumberland and the other with South Australia.

Wheelhouses in Northumberland

A wheelhouse was the building sheltering the horse-propelled wheel which drove a threshing machine and other kinds of barn machinery. Dr J. A. Hellen, a geographer, it should be observed, not an historian, made a special study of them during 1969 and 1970, and has published the results of his enquiry both locally[2] and for national and international circulation in *The Agricultural History Review*.[3]

The first effective threshing machine anywhere in the world was installed by George Meikle at Kilbogie in Clackmannanshire in 1786. Threshers spread quickly from the Scottish corn-growing counties to those of north-east England, mainly on the larger farms, that is, farms which maintained two or more plough teams. The threshing machinery was driven by windmills and waterwheels, as well as by horse-wheels, and on the larger farms by steam engines from about 1840 onwards. In many cases, the wheelhouse was kept for other purposes after the wheel had been removed.

Before beginning his detailed investigations, Dr Hellen noted: 'Although there appears to be some local interest in wheelhouses, as evidenced by local history societies, countryside magazines, and newspapers, no specific work on their geographical distribution at the county scale is known to the author.' His work was carried out in two stages.

In Stage One,

all possible wheelhouse sites, whether round, polygonal or square in plan, were identified from close study of all the 25-inch O.S. sheets for Northumberland, the second edition (1896–8), surveyed in 1858 and revised in 1894 being used. In practice every rural building in Northumberland's 2018 square miles was scrutinised from the plans and a provisional inventory of sites drawn up.

Stage Two consisted of field work, carried out by students. Every one

[2] 'Some provisional notes on wheelhouses and their distribution in Northumberland', *Journal of the Geographical Society, University of Newcastle upon Tyne*, Vol. 18, 1970.

[3] Vol. 20, 1972, Part II. 'Agricultural Innovation and Detectable Landscape Margins: the Case of Wheelhouses in Northumberland.'

of the 575 sites identified from the O.S. sheets was visited.

Standard data sheets giving details of architectural and site characteristics were compiled for each wheelhouse site and the majority of surviving buildings were photographed. In many cases it was possible to identify a demolished wheelhouse from the remains of foundations or roof timbers, as well as the opening in the barn wall through which the lying shaft had passed. In other cases farmers or farm workers were able to specify when demolition had obliterated a wheelhouse – locally known

Distribution of wheelhouses in Northumberland, as plotted during a survey made in 1969–70.

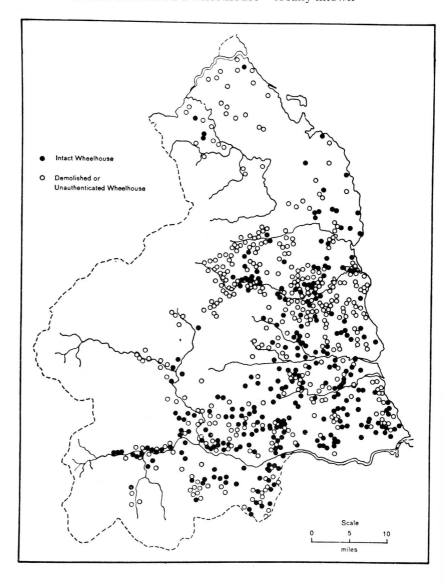

as gin gan – or how often repairs or re-roofing had been necessary. It is felt that very few intact wheelhouses were overlooked, although it would be surprising, in view of the number of personnel involved, if some errors had not materialised.

On the 575 sites, 276 wheelhouses were found intact and 299 had been demolished or remained unauthenticated. When the distribution map of the wheelhouses was compared with other maps constructed to show good and marginal land within the county, it became evident that there were many wheelhouses in areas which are today considered

Distribution of wheelhouses in Northumberland in relation to marginal land.

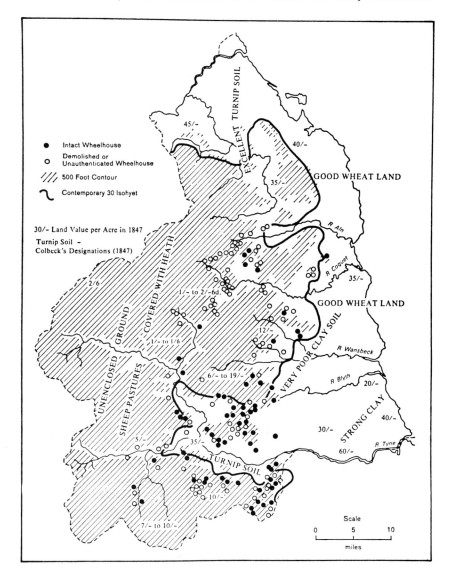

marginal from a farming point of view and which are in some instances nothing more than heath. This was taken as evidence of the extent to which high cereal prices during the 1840s and 1850s had induced farmers to extend their grain acreage on to soils and up to altitudes which represented the furthest possible limits for arable cultivation. This was borne out by the official returns. The land under tillage in Northumberland fell from 327,165 acres in 1866 to 133,771 acres in 1939. Since then, a policy of subsidies and price supports has pushed the marginal line for cultivation further back towards the point reached in 1866. But, even with modern techniques and knowledge, the 1866 line is still a long way beyond what was regarded as possible in the early 1970s. In Dr Hellen's words, 'around 175 of these farm sites are located in what are today highly marginal to semi-marginal agricultural areas'.

Dr Hellen was pioneering, but there can be no doubt that his work did indeed produce evidence not previously available. The results of this survey suggested other lines of enquiry which could be profitably followed. Much more information is required about the dates when the wheelhouses were built. This is most likely to be obtained from a detailed study of surviving farm and estate records and accounts. It would also be helpful to know more about the economy of at least some of the farms which evidently produced grain in the middle of last century and which have never considered it worthwhile to do so again. But the information with which Dr Hellen's survey has already provided us is invaluable for showing us the changing pattern of land-use in the area or, as he himself has put it, 'an apparently insignificant farm building can assume a useful role in explaining something of the process of historic agricultural innovation as well as fluctuations in the boundaries between unstable forms of land-use and the circumstances which caused them to become stranded as incongruous relics.'

It could also be suggested that a diligent search might also discover, in the files of local newspapers or in county or agricultural society archives, the views of farmers and farm workers themselves on something which must have caused profound changes in their way of life. The ploughing up of moorland to grow corn is a sufficiently daunting enterprise, given modern equipment and techniques; in the 1840s it must have been an experience to remember.

The evidence of strip fields in South Australia

The European settlement of the region running inland from what is now called Adelaide dates from the 1830s. In 1960 research workers concerned with problems of soil erosion in the Mount Lofty Ranges noticed what were clearly traces of the narrow field-sections known as 'lands', which had characterised European agriculture for centuries. The new settlers had evidently brought the system with them to

South Australia.
Distribution of 'lands'.

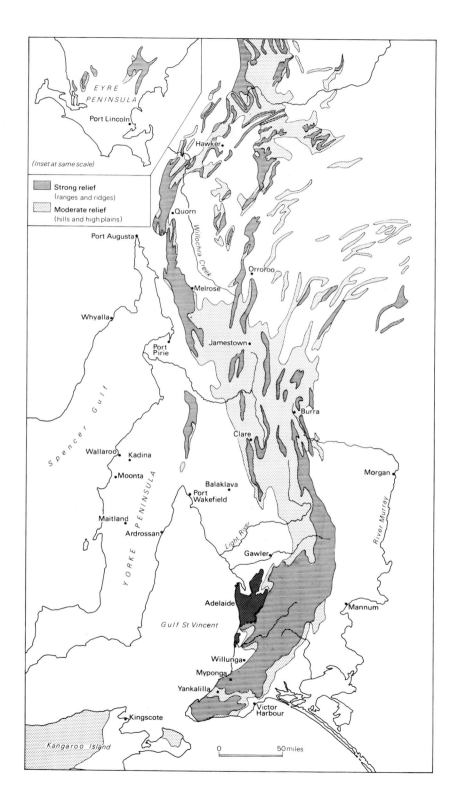

Australia and evidence of it has remained on long-abandoned farms in the new colony.

'Lands' are produced by first throwing up a ridge across the field with a plough and then by turning successive furrows against the ridge. This process can be continued as long as one wishes, but at any point the 'land' will be marked by open furrows at its extremities. When the 'lands' on either side of the first have been completed, the open furrows dividing each pair will, of course, be two furrows wide. In the old open-field system which was normal before enclosures, adjacent lands would often belong to two different people, so that the open furrows or ditches remained in the same position year after year, acting as boundary-marks between the two holdings. Otherwise, the new ridges are turned into the old open-furrows, so that the field is kept reasonably level. Sometimes, however, the open-furrows were perpetuated, to assist with drainage.

In Australia, what can still be seen of the old lands, after wind and water erosion and modern cultivations have done their best to remove all traces of them, makes clear that ploughing was always carried out up and down the slope, never following the contours. With the type of plough then in use, this was easier for the ploughman, but, given the heavy rainfall sometimes experienced in the Mount Lofty region, it encouraged the erosion of the ground and, from this point of view, was bad farming practice. The evidence of the lands needs, however, to be set beside what one already knows from documentary sources, that cereal-growing in the Adelaide area was comparatively short-lived. During the late 1850s and the 1860s, the Mount Lofty Ranges, together with the adjacent plains, supplied not only South Australia but also Victoria and other parts of the country with wheat. Between 1860 and 1890, the more easily cleared, drier and flatter areas of the mid-north became South Australia's major wheat-producing region. In the 1920s and 1930s, cereal growing also declined in the Eyre Peninsula, and here, as around Mount Lofty, many of the fields reverted to pasture, which has preserved the pattern of the old lands.

In a detailed, comprehensive article published in 1972,[4] C. R. Twidale brought together all the evidence regarding strip-fields in South Australia, linking it with the facts about climate and soils, and with the general history of the settlement. The author has also talked to people who remembered this form of cultivation being used, or who had heard about it from friends or relations. In the course of these enquiries, he discovered, with some surprise, that single-share ploughs were in common use until well into the present century, despite the shortage of manpower in Australia. The reason for this was partly, no

[4] '"Lands" or Relict Strip Fields in South Australia', *Agricultural History Review*, Vol. 20, 1972, Part 1.

doubt, because single-share implements were cheaper, but it also has to be remembered that 'the team of animals – whether horses, bullocks or donkeys – required for it was smaller than for the larger machine. The lesser demands of such smaller teams on insecure water supplies assisted the retention of the single-share plough until the advent and widespread use of machines powered by the internal combustion engine.' To an Australian geographer or historian, accustomed to heat and drought, this kind of reasoning comes more naturally than to someone accustomed to conditions in North-West Europe, where one does not tend to think first of the shortage of water as the explanation for technical oddities.

What is particularly useful about Mr Twidale's work is the way in which he brings all his information – documentary, archaeological, human – to bear in order to dispose of previous hypotheses and to establish the story on more solid foundations.

Map showing the Mount Lofty and Flinders Ranges of South Australia.

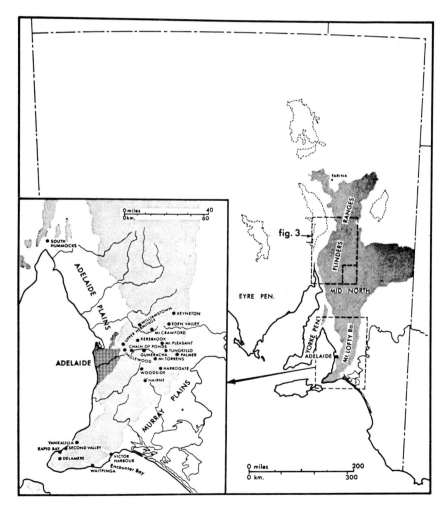

Previous hypothesis That the survival of such clearly marked evidence, under Australian climatic conditions, proves that the same ridges and furrows were deliberately perpetuated year after year and that the farmers must have had a good reason for doing this.

Demolition of hypothesis 'Local evidence does not support this contention. Interviews with farmers who have ploughed lands and who followed the procedures taught them by their fathers and grandfathers suggest that the South Australian lands were not permanently located, in the sense that the lands were laid out for all time. Some farmers used the previous year's furrows as tops and ploughed into them, thus shifting the precise position of the depressions.'

Previous hypothesis That ridges and furrows were formed to improve land drainage.

Demolition of hypothesis 'In the Mt. Lofty Ranges, most lands are preserved on appreciable slopes, and many are ploughed in well-drained sandy soils. Likewise in the Flinders Ranges, the scarp foot situations which seem favoured for wheat growing and where lands are commonly preserved, are well drained. Only in local basins of interior drainage is there occasional flooding. In any case, water shortage rather than surplus is the problem in these arid and semi-arid climates.'

Previous hypothesis That a land represents a day's labour for the ploughman.

Demolition of hypothesis 'This hypothesis is also held in some parts of South Australia, yet it is manifestly invalid, at any rate so far as South Australia is concerned. For if the suggestion were correct there should be a relationship between the site environment on the one hand and size of land on the other. Thus lands ploughed on light sandy soils and on flats or gentle slopes should be more extensive than those made on heavy clay soils and on steep gradients. In both the Flinders and Mt. Lofty Ranges, there is no apparent correlation between size and the factors mentioned.'

Why, then, did this ancient European system persist under the very different conditions of Australia? After looking carefully at all the evidence and, a step unfortunately not taken by all historians and archaeologists, using his common sense, Mr Twidale comes to two conclusions, both of which seem entirely reasonable. First, the wider the land – the widest possible land is the extreme width of the field – the greater amount of empty running on the headlands. Since the early settlers could not afford to waste time in this way, they kept the lands fairly narrow. Second, the farmer was usually dependent on the labour of himself and his family, and since, in South Australia, it was essential to catch the first rains if the seed was to germinate and get away to a good start, work had to be carried out as quickly as possible. The farmer with only a single-furrow horse-drawn plough could not cover the ground fast enough to risk ploughing the whole field first and then sowing it afterwards. By that time the rain might have passed and the ground dried out again. So 'what he may have been forced to do was to plough a relatively narrow strip – a land – and then either proceed to the next while his family sowed the first ploughed strip or sow his first land himself before going on to plough the next. Thus, he may have ensured that some at least of his field was sown and stood some chance of yielding a crop.'

This kind of deductive reasoning is of precisely the same order as archaeologists have employed in pondering the evidence provided by the field systems and agricultural methods of prehistoric times. Unlike Mr Twidale, however, they are unable to have conversations with people who have actually farmed in this way. If they had, their conclusions might well be different. The main point of this discussion about lands in South Australia, however, is to emphasise that industrial archaeology or, if one chooses to be purist, agricultural archaeology, does not require buildings or the ruins of buildings. All that matters is that the evidence shall have been man-made, and plough-markings are certainly that.

Narrow 'lands' on undulating hillside near Harrogate, South Australia, providing evidence of early European settlement in the area.

Corn Flakes at Battle Creek, Michigan

During the last quarter of the nineteenth century many rich, self-made men in America became abnormally concerned with their health, on the probable grounds that, having made a lot of money, they wanted to remain alive to enjoy it as long as possible. Not surprisingly, there were people, inside and outside the medical profession, who were anxious to sell the rich recipes for living longer. And since what the rich do today many other people are likely to do tomorrow, the health-mongers found their market always expanding, often in a spectacular fashion.

This, assisted by eccentric religious beliefs, provided the mainspring for the phenomenally rapid growth of the breakfast cereal industry in the United States. The first such product, Graham Crackers, were ahead of their time. Launched in 1829, they were the invention of a temperance lecturer, Sylvester Graham, whose aim and promise was to save souls by saving the stomach first. There was a hiatus until after the Civil War, when America was blessed with Granula (1863), the predecessor of Grape Nuts, Shredded Wheat (1893) and Puffed Wheat (1902). With hindsight, however, the historian can see that the key date was 1866, when the Seventh Day Adventists established the Western Health Reform Institute at Battle Creek, Michigan, subsequently rechristened the Battle Creek Sanitarium. Ten years later, Dr John Harvey Kellogg was appointed Superintendent. Among his patients was Charles W. Post, who became aware of the commercial possibilities as well as the physical benefits of 'health foods' during his stay at Battle Creek, and in 1897 founded the Postum Cereal Company, from which the mighty General Foods Corporation eventually sprang.

Dr Kellogg's brother, W. K. Kellogg, was the Sanitarium's business manager from 1879 until 1906. They were both well aware that many of the patients at the Sanitarium owed their poor state of health to the fact, not unknown among rich people before and since, that they ate too much and an important part of Dr Kellogg's cure was to put them on a strict diet and, even more, to persuade them to like it. The first was comparatively simple, the second a great deal more difficult, mainly because the new, light diet was not as attractive as the one it replaced. In particular, the patients tended to feel hungry at breakfast time, which suggested to the Kelloggs, and not to them alone, that there could be a market for some new form of breakfast food which tasted and looked agreeable, but which was in no sense rich or heavy.

During his long years at the Battle Creek Sanitarium, between 1879 and 1906, W. K. Kellogg, with his brother's assistance, discovered the process known as 'tempering the grains', which meant, in practice, treating animal food – maize – in such a way as to make it highly palatable and desirable in the eyes of human beings. This meant, basically, that the grain had to be rolled and cooked into thin, crisp flakes. To do this, Kellogg set up the Battle Creek Toasted Corn Flake Company in 1906, having previously bought the machinery and formula – which competed with his own – of the Korn Krisp Company, and the Bartlett Avenue plant of the Hygienic Food Company. The premises in Bartlett Avenue were unfortunately totally destroyed in a disastrous fire in 1907. Had they survived, they would have been an item of food-processing archaeology of the first magnitude of importance. As it was, Kellogg built himself a much superior new factory in Porter Street in 1908. This remained the world centre of Corn Flakes, with exports going to many countries, until 1924, when another huge fire obliged the Kellogg Company to start all over again. Its present vast complex on Porter Street has been mercifully spared further disasters, and remains, much visited and continuously prosperous, as a symbol of the concern for hygiene in the factory preparation of foodstuffs which the Americans developed and in due course installed all over the Western world. Kellogg did not originate the theory that, in the food business at least, never-ending attention to cleanliness and staff welfare were of immense benefit to sales – H. J. Heinz had beaten him to it by several years – but he did as much as anybody to foster it and to add the kind of refinements which were necessary to keep it up-to-date. The enormous breakfast cereal industry is the supreme example of twentieth-century consumerism, with the demand created and sustained wholly by advertising and with the price bearing no relation to the intrinsic value of the goods.

Any physical remains of the early days of such an industry must therefore be of archaeological interest, although what they can tell us in addition to what we already know from other sources is a matter for discussion. Three buildings originally attached to the 1908 Kellogg factory survived the fire of 1924: two structures known as the Horse Barns[5] and two more described in the Company's site plans as machine building and repair shops. They remained insignificant and unnoticed until a team working on behalf of the Historic American Engineering Record carried out a thorough survey of the area in the mid-1970s,[6] and took the old Kellogg buildings in its stride. The description of them given in the printed report is brief and strictly factual, accompanied neither by plans nor by photographs, although both of these exist in the Record's archival collection.

After a very short introduction, saying little more than that the Kelloggs worked at the Sanitarium and that two fires destroyed

[5] For the benefit of non-American readers, it should perhaps be mentioned that 'barn' is still used in the old, general Anglo-Saxon sense of 'shelter'. One can therefore speak, for example, of a 'trolley-barn', i.e. a tram depot or tram garage.

[6] Published as *The Lower Peninsula of Michigan : an Inventory of Historic Engineering and Industrial Sites* ed. Diane B. Abbott, Washington, DC: Historic American Engineering Record, United States Department of the Interior, 1976.

Factory 1 and Factory 2, we are provided with these entries:

The Horse Barns   'The Horse Barns are the oldest
remaining structures on this site. Both are two-story
frame structures. The barn dating from 1916 is 50 feet
square, has a gabled roof and sheet metal siding,
probably not original. The newer structure (built in 1920)
measures 50 feet by 80 feet, has a flat roof and shingle
siding, probably installed in the 1930s. Both buildings are
now used for storage.'[7]
Kellogg Maintenance Shops   'These two buildings,
located at the rear of the Kellogg Company's immense
Porter Street complex, have always been described in the
Company's site plans as "machine building and repair
shops" and this was probably their function during the
early years of the Kellogg Company. They now stand
vacant and are occasionally used for storage. The
northernmost of the two structures, which are about three
feet apart, is a wooden-framed, one-story building, with an
arched roof supported by wooden Pratt "Rainbo"
trusses. It is 125 feet long and 40 feet wide. The second
building, also wood-framed and one story high, has a
gabled roof and measures 100 feet long and 40 feet wide.'[8]

There are a number of points to notice in connexion with this, and
indeed all, the reports published by the Historic American Engineering
Record. The first is that, on a majority of the sites investigated, HAER
is carrying out pioneering work. It is collecting, assembling and
presenting a coherent body of information for the first time. Secondly,
like all other research bodies, HAER never has enough time, money or
people to do a perfect job in comfort. It accomplishes wonders, but it has
to set its face against anything that could be regarded as a frill or a
luxury. And the third point one should remember is that some HAER
surveys are able to draw on more resources than others. This is particularly marked on the publication side. *The Mohawk–Hudson Area
Survey*, for instance, published in 1973, is a sumptuous, generously
illustrated volume, by comparison with the more spartan and more
compressed *North Carolina* of 1975. The published reports, however,
are not necessarily a fair guide to the total mass of material accumulated
by the field workers, which is filed and accessible in the Library of
Congress.

In the case of Kellogg buildings there is a special problem, in that
there is no satisfactory history of the Company. The buildings and the

[7] Ibid. p. 25.
[8] Ibid. p. 26.

site cannot, for this reason, be placed within the kind of economic and technical context which one would like to have. The officially inspired histories of the Kellogg Company which have appeared from time to time have been either idolatrous or of the Romance of Great Businesses type, presenting only a very partial and slanted picture of what took place and saying virtually nothing about the technical processes, which are mistakenly regarded as secret, about costs, quantities and profits or about staffing, wages and expertise. Kelloggs, like most other large international businesses, have regarded only a small part of their history as public property. This puts an impossible load on the industrial archaeologist, who is required at one and the same time to survey, interpret and integrate what he finds. In the circumstances, the HAER teams adopt the only possible course, to describe and record what they see and to publish this as quickly as possible, so that the results may be widely and easily accessible.

One should not, even so, underrate the value of the evidence provided by such superficially unimportant examples as the two items of Kelloggiana to which reference has been made above. From the facts supplied by HAER, we can deduce, for example, that in its early days the Kellogg Company built as cheaply as possible; that this may well have been a major cause of the two disastrous fires; that, even as late as the 1920s, Kelloggs, a prosperous, growing international concern, was using a lot of horses; and that, since 1924, the need to expand has not been great enough to justify demolishing these old ancillary buildings and putting up something more productive and profitable on the site. When one knows that, from the Twenties onwards, Kellogg policy was to invest and manufacture abroad rather than to export from the United States, the various pieces of the jigsaw begin to fit together.

The Brewers' House, Antwerp

Within the beer-drinking countries, few types of industrial archaeology site are more numerous or more widespread than breweries. Until the formation of the mammoth brewing groups of the twentieth century, every town of any size in north-west Europe had its brewery and small-scale brewing was a normal activity of many taverns, inns and large households as well. For this reason, brewing archaeology has suffered particularly badly from the mergers and closures of the past 30 years especially. Breweries are difficult to convert to other purposes and, especially when the site is valuable, demolition is extremely likely once brewing has ceased to be carried out on the premises. Casualties have consequently been both sad and numerous and, unfortunately, recording has frequently, perhaps normally, been very inadequate before the old buildings were pulled down.

In Britain, the most serious loss has undoubtedly been the historic

Stag Brewery, between Victoria Station and Buckingham Palace. The brewery was certainly established in the 1630s and may well have been operating earlier. Enormously expanded during the eighteenth and nineteenth centuries, it was eventually demolished in 1959 and the site sold for road and office development. A large rampant statue of a stag and 'The Stag' public house are now the only reminders of what was for three centuries a major industrial enterprise and one of the biggest brewing centres in the world. Unfortunately, the Stag Brewery was demolished before industrial archaeology, as an enthusiasm and a set of techniques, really got under way in Britain and before there was even the limited amount of conscience about the destruction of historical industrial buildings and equipment which exists today.[9] The even larger and more famous Guinness brewery, at St James's Gate, Dublin, was reduced in size during the late Sixties and early Seventies, and it is encouraging to note how much more care and discrimination was used at the later date to photograph, record and, in some cases, preserve significant material. Most of what has been preserved at St James's Gate is comparatively small and portable and capable of inclusion in the Company's excellent museum, and there is little doubt that the bulk of what future generations are going to see of pre-merger brewing will be in museums of one kind or another. The most interesting and useful of these museum displays take the form of a complete craft-brewery transferred to the museum. This method allows the visitor both to look at and understand the equipment used by the old hand-labour breweries and also to get a feeling of the scale of the operations which were carried out. Such exhibits are to be found at, for instance, the Brewing Museum in Stockholm; the open-air museum, Den Gamle By, at Århus, Denmark; the open-air museum at Arnhem, in the Netherlands; at Bokrijk in Belgium – another open-air museum; and in the Technical Museum, Vienna.

The Brewers' House or Water House in Adriaan Brouwerstraat, Antwerp, is exceptional, in that the building itself has been preserved on its original site. It now forms part of the city's museums. A two-storeyed gabled building, in a back street near the harbour district, it was built in 1554 by Gilbert van Schoonbeke to draw water for the 16 breweries he had set up in the same street. To begin with the water was taken from the town moat, but in 1635, after the moat had become

[9] It is interesting to observe that practically none of the important histories concerned with the brewing industry is what one might call archaeology-conscious. Written by scholars whose interests are primarily economic or biographical, they have appeared for the most part before the archaeological approach had begun to add a new dimension and a new viewpoint to industrial history. One thinks, for example, of Patrick Lynch and John Vaizey, *Guinness's Brewery in the Irish Economy* Cambridge University Press, 1960; Henford Jones, *The Red Barrel : a History of Watney Mann* John Murray, 1963; and Peter Mathias, *The Brewing Industry in England* Cambridge University Press, 1959.

seriously polluted, it came from the Herental Canal, which had been dug to provide Antwerp with a supply of fresh drinking water from the moorland outside. The water was led first into a cistern in the cellar and from here it was transferred up to a smaller cistern by means of a scoop-elevator powered by horses operating a treadmill. From the upper cistern it was distributed through a system of lead pipes to the various breweries along the street. There was a fixed payment per barrel of beer, one-sixth going to van Schoonbeke and the rest to the Emperor. After van Schoonbeke's death, the City of Antwerp brought both the waterworks and the breweries, providing a supply to other nearby

Water-raising machinery in the Brewers' House, Antwerp.

buildings as well as to the breweries. The waterworks continued to operate until the 1930s, although at the end of last century a gas engine replaced the treadmill, to be supplanted in its turn by an electric motor just before the First World War.

A Brewers Guild was formed in 1581 and a room in the house, the Brouwerskamer, became their meeting hall. Sumptuously furnished and decorated in the baroque style during the seventeenth century, it has been preserved in excellent condition, complete with its monumental fireplace, gilt leather hangings, large chandelier and paintings. The original treadmill, which must have been often repaired, is still in position, but the stables for three horses are a reconstruction. It is known that the horses worked in shifts, day and night. The treadmill was connected to a large wooden cog wheel, which worked the scoop system. This consisted of 40 iron scoops fixed to a pair of cables leading down into the reservoir in the cellar and then round a drum on the top floor, where the scoops discharged the water into the upper cistern.

The machinery was much modified during the nineteenth century. Parts, such as the cog wheel, which had previously been made of wood, were refashioned in iron and in the 1850s the scoop-elevator was supplemented by six pumps, which were also worked by horses. The visitor now sees the room very much as it must have looked in mid-Victorian times. The environment of the Brewers' House is greatly changed, however, as the canal, the Brouwersvliet, has been filled in and the surrounding buildings are decayed and unimpressive. As a piece of archaeology, even so, the Brewers' House performs two kinds of function very well: it illustrates the kind of engineering achievement which was possible 400 years ago, when inventiveness was supported by the money and determination of a powerful public figure, and it is evidence of the social and cultural importance of one of the city's major guilds. The modern visitor has to use his imagination to recreate the complete system centred on the Brewers' House – the canal, the 16 breweries along the street, the water mains which joined them up to the cistern, the horses working round the clock by the light of a lantern, the extraordinary blend of technology and grandeur which the building represents, a blend which makes proper sense only when we remember that, in the seventeenth century as today, brewers did very well for themselves and were accustomed both to having the best the age could offer, in industrial efficiency and in personal comfort.

The windmill-assisted salt industry of the Ile de Noirmoutier

The Ile de Noirmoutier, as the map shows, is on the Atlantic coast of France, on the edge of the Vendée. The inhabitants have earned their living at different times by growing corn, potatoes and early vegetables, as well as by fishing and cultivating oysters. They have also, for several centuries, operated salt-marshes. The marshes are in the centre of the island. They are below the sea-level and are protected against inundation by dykes. At one time, there was an important salt industry in this part of France – the Vendée, the Ile de Ré and the Ile de Noirmoutier – with a considerable export trade to northern Europe, but during the past 150 years it has largely died away in the face of competition from the huge salt mines in eastern France, and to a lesser extent from the sea-salt industry along the French Mediterranean coast. Sufficient remains, however, to provide the most valuable of all archaeological evidence, techniques and equipment which can still be seen in operation, but which almost certainly have little further life ahead of them.

The working of the salt-marshes on the Ile de Noirmoutier has been carefully studied by Claude Rivals, whose main interest is in windmills.[10] In its corn-growing days, the island had dozens of windmills, of the tower type. They are all now disused. A quite different type of windmill is still working, however. These tiny mills, 13 feet high and with a sail-spread of only 3 feet, are used to speed up the evaporation of the brine. The method of working is very simple. As with all salt marshes, the

[10] The result of his work is summarised in a paper presented to the Second International Symposium on Molinology in Denmark in 1969 and printed in its *Transactions*, ed. Anders Jespersen, Brede, 1971.

Ile de Noirmoutier, in relation to river and sea transport facilities.

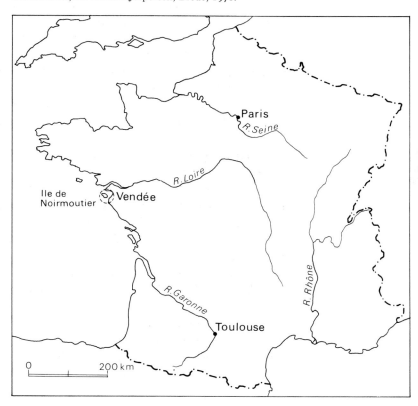

sea-water is led from one salt-pan to another as the water gradually evaporates. When it has reached the last pans, where the salt will ultimately be gathered, the windmills are used to pump off most of the remaining water, so that the wind and the sun can evaporate what remains more quickly. This is reckoned to save a month, which means that the Noirmoutier saltmaker can finish the season not far behind his more fortunate rival in the hot sun of the Mediterranean. Once the water has gone, the salt is raked to the side of the pan and then thrown up into heaps on the dividing baulks, to dry out completely and then to be taken away to the store.

At that point the windmills have no further work to do until the following year. They are taken to pieces, removed from the rough wooden trestles on which they are fixed during the salt-making months of the year – April to September – and put away in a shed. The construction shown in the diagram could hardly be more simple, but it is perfectly effective and has stood the test of time. Almost exactly similar midget windmills are known to have been used at Lymington, on the English south coast, but no trace whatever of them remains. The English industrial archaeologist, studying the history and layout of the Lymington salt-pans, is therefore able to fill a gap in his knowledge and experience by studying the complete, living job as it is still carried out on the Ile de Noirmoutier.

Ile de Noirmoutier: location of mills on the island.

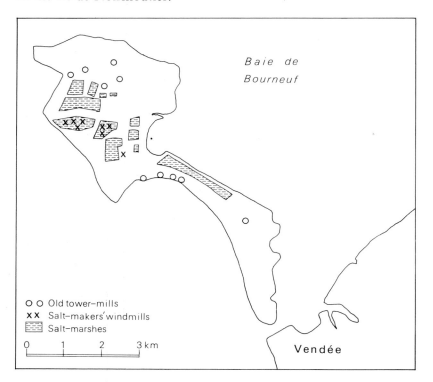

The examples given in this chapter illustrate the special problems faced by anyone who wishes to concentrate to any extent on the archaeology of the food and drink industries. Chief among them is the fact that developing and constantly improving ideas of hygiene make it difficult and in some cases quite impossible to continue to work in the buildings which have served for generations or with the same kind of equipment. Food processing machinery of any kind has a short life nowadays and it is very rare to preserve, or to think worth preserving, what was in common use only 20 or 30 years ago. The regulations concerning food processing became steadily stricter each decade, and what was good enough in 1939 is, in many cases, no longer legal today. When this fact is combined with two others of almost equal significance, the trend towards larger and larger units of production and the movement of the food and drink industries away from a city's industrial districts to more pleasant and more salubrious areas in the suburbs or the open countryside, one can see that the chances of any food producing unit of the early part of this century having survived more or less intact must border on the miraculous.

We therefore have the paradox that the older stages of one of the food

Salt-maker raking salt from pan, with one of the miniature windmills in the background.

industries, when the work was carried out by craft methods, are much more likely to be represented both by buildings and by working equipment than the more recent stages, when industrial techniques have been employed. Put in more precise terms, a Dutch agricultural museum will contain the wooden vessels and hand tools used in cheese-making a century ago, but not the power-driven, scientifically controlled equipment of forty and fifty years ago, which was mostly too large and inconvenient for a museum to be able to accept, and which has been therefore scrapped and replaced as soon as anything better became available. This does not mean, however, that an empty building or one long since converted to other uses is irrelevant, unhelpful or not worth studying. All countries in north-west Europe contained at one time, for example, a considerable number of small railside depots which were used for collecting milk from farms in the immediate area and for load-

Diagram showing construction of salt-maker's windmill.

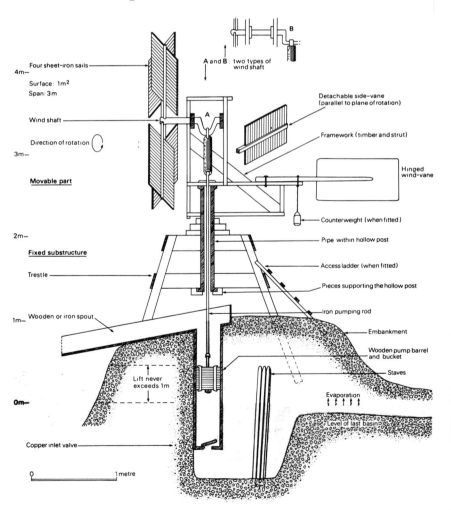

ing it into rail tanker wagons for bulk transport to large cities. Most of these depots were closed down during the 1950s and 1960s, as road-tankers took over from rail-tankers and as bulk collection of milk from the farm became more common. The new system required fewer and larger processing centres, and in strategically different places. The milk map, one might say, has changed radically. But most of the old depots are still there, being used for a wide range of different industrial purposes, the railway which gave them birth having itself disappeared. An important task for the industrial archaeologist is to locate them, photograph them, map them and generally assess them, relating them to the new centres which have taken their place. And so with breweries, wineries, banana-ripening depots, mills, bakeries, slaughter-houses and all the other processing plants relevant to food and drink. Where the building is, why it was put there and how big it was are considerations quite as important as what it was. Where a building or a complex of buildings has continued to be used for its original purpose, it is important and interesting to observe, in as much detail as possible, what changes and adaptations have had to be made over the years in order to keep it in business. The author knows of no instance in any country in which a study of this kind, covering buildings, machinery, fittings, amenities and environment has been made. The gap is a serious one. We have no completely documented factory histories of this kind, an extraordinary lack, when one considers the ever-growing size of the academic research industry.[11]

[11] Farm buildings have, for some reason, fared rather better in this respect. For examples, see Nigel Harvey, *A History of Farm Buildings in England and Wales*, David and Charles, 1970. No such book or approach yet exists for industrial concerns.

3

Construction: purpose, design and materials

The frontiers of the archaeology of building and civil engineering are not easy to draw. In one sense, the archaeology of construction is the history of architecture, written in terms of those buildings which are still there to be seen. In another, it is the history of the materials and techniques which made a particular building possible. Every building is necessarily a museum dedicated both to the person who designed it and to the practical men who had the skills to interpret and realise the design, and to produce the bricks, steel, glass and other materials required to turn a set of drawings into something that could be used.

It is highly regrettable that these two aspects of a building should have been considered separately for so long, and that there should have been such a sporadic and inadequate dialogue between those experts, the art and architectural historians, whose prime concern is with the appearance of a building, and those, the engineers and craftsmen, who have the duty of making and assembling its components and of creating a final product which will satisfy the customer. The great and indeed essential virtue of industrial archaeology is its integrating role. It provides a forum where the different parties can meet and a language which can be used with some hope of mutual understanding. But it can achieve this only by keeping one question, 'What exactly was this structure designed to do?' continuously and clearly in the centre of the discussion. If one knows what the original client's needs and wishes were, it is a relatively simple matter to set about the task of investigating how and how well the architect and constructor met those requirements, and to make comparisons with other attempts to meet a similar kind of demand. Unless one knows what the aim was and what limitations were imposed, one is in no position to judge a building's merits. For this reason, the techniques of industrial archaeology, properly and imaginatively employed, can be of great assistance to art historians and not in any way a hindrance or an irrelevance. Equally, the industrial archaeologist or technical historian who has failed to cultivate his aesthetic sensibility is all too likely to see a building as nothing more than a complex kit of bits and pieces which has been turned into a more or less functioning machine.

These considerations apply to any kind of structure, to the Woolworth skyscraper as much as to a suspension bridge, a cooling tower, a farm cottage or a swimming bath. To understand it and to measure its success, one must know a great deal about it; the experience which lay behind it; the technical problems which had to be solved; the prejudices of the public, the architect and the client; the money that was available; the market for building labour at the time; the possibility of experimenting with new materials and techniques. It is also extremely important to know how the structure behaved since it was completed, what the people who used it thought about it – a miserably neglected aspect of architectural history – and what subsequent modifications have been needed to put faults right or to bring it up-to-date.

This chapter will examine four examples of what for the moment can be loosely termed construction-history in order to see how the general principles set out above can be applied to a range of different specialisations within the field. It seems sensible to consider materials first and completed structures afterwards. It is perhaps useful to mention that almost any industrial archaeology site can be studied under two or more different headings. A railway bridge is part of the history of transport, the history of engineering and the history of construction; a cotton-mill belongs to the history of textiles, the history of fire-proofing and the history of steam-engines.

Making sense of a brickworks

In the late 1960s Kim C. Leslie made a thorough survey of the Ashburnham Estate brickworks, in Sussex. He investigated the documentary evidence, watched the various processes in operation and talked to men who had been doing this work all their lives. The results of his researches

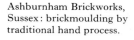

Ashburnham Brickworks, Sussex: brickmoulding by traditional hand process.

were published in 1970.[1] The Ashburnham brickworks, Mr Leslie
pointed out, was

a survival of a method of production rarely, if ever, seen
today. Brickmaking was by hand, by methods that have
passed from generation to generation. Perhaps more
unusual than this was the fact that the bricks were burnt in
an open kiln fired with wood. Until 1961, when tiles were
last made at the yard, a pug mill for grinding the clay was
driven by a horse. This mill is the last recorded instance
of a stationary horse engine (a horse gin) to have worked in
Sussex. In other words, until its recent closure, the
Ashburnham brickworks continued to demonstrate the
state of brickmaking as it was before the brickmaking
revolution of the nineteenth century. Indeed the methods
and equipment employed at Ashburnham have remarkable
resemblances to those evident in some of the earliest
known illustrations and descriptions of the industry.

This amounts to saying that the site was of outstanding importance and
that the research on it was carried out at the last possible moment, while
all the evidence was still there to be gathered.

Mr Leslie's paper falls into three parts: a summary of the history of
the works, a description of the equipment and manufacturing processes,
and an account of the products, the three being skilfully welded together
to form a report which answers all the questions which any reasonable
person might be likely to ask.

[1] *Sussex Industrial History*. Winter 1970–1. Chichester: Phillimore, 1970.

Ashburnham Brickworks:
moulded bricks being
wheeled away for drying
before firing. It will be
noticed that the moulder's
shed, typical of all the
buildings on this site, other
than the kiln, is of a very
flimsy nature, so that few
above-ground remains
were likely to survive for
long once the works had
closed.

There had been a tileworks at Ashburnham since at least 1362. Brickmaking came later, probably in the eighteenth or early nineteenth century, although exactly when is not known. The works was moved to a different part of the Estate in 1840, just before the marriage of the fourth Earl of Ashburnham. According to oral tradition, which may well be reliable, this was because the Earl 'feared to offend his new bride with an unsightly industrial appearance at the entrance to the Park'. Until the mid-1850s, the yard was producing mainly for the estate itself, but from then until its final closure, commercial sales were important. The biggest single job it ever undertook was the complete refacing of the mansion, Ashburnham Park, which took place between 1846 and 1855.

Outside customers during the second half of the nineteenth century were mostly within a radius of 12 miles from the works. A wide variety of both bricks and tiles was offered at this time, as well as drainage pipes and flower pots. During the present century the range was gradually pruned, until in the 1960s only building and paving bricks were being produced. Research into the Estate account books makes it clear that the brickworks was never a profitable investment. It was always thought of primarily as a service industry to the estate, commercial sales being merely an agreeable extra, which helped to keep the men in steady employment and the plant in regular use. Production was in any case too low to make the brickworks commercially viable. The total capacity of the two kilns was only 40,000 bricks, and the fact that the whole manufacturing process from beginning to end was carried out in the open meant a curtailment of operations during bad weather.

The best tribute to the skill of the men employed at Ashburnham is the fact that they produced a consistently high quality of brick with very primitive equipment. Mr Leslie watched them carrying out the whole job – preparing and mixing the clay ('loam') and sand, moulding, drying and burning the bricks – and set down in great detail exactly what he saw. Here is an example of his method.

The day before brickmaking, in the morning enough loam for one day's making was pulled down from the weathering heap with a half-mattock, and thoroughly turned over. Water was then added, being at hand from the brick-making area from a man-made conduit leading from Forge Pond: the bucket was lowered into the well at the end of the conduit using a water hook, similar to a shepherd's crook. Water and loam were mixed with a shovel, the procedure being called 'packing down a soak', the soak being the total amount of loam worked at any one time. Left until the afternoon, covered if the weather was particularly dry, the wet soak was then further worked into a plastic consistency, using a turning iron (like a skeleton

Diagram of Scotch kilns in
use at Ashburnham.

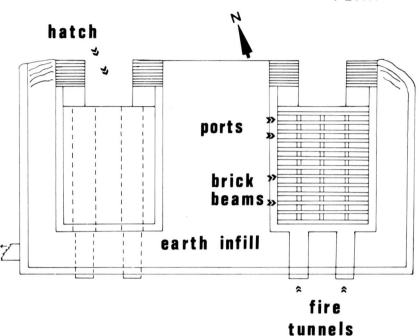

KILNS - TOP & FLOOR

PLAN

hatch

N

ports

brick
beams

earth infill

fire
tunnels

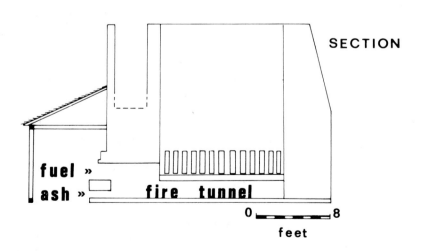

SECTION

fuel »
ash »

fire tunnel

0 ⊨▬▬▬▬ 8

feet

spade). This was called 'turning in'. A half-mattock
pounded the loam smooth, removing the lumps, known as
nubs. This was 'hummocking'. By now it had been worked
into a smooth and easily worked mass, and was known as
pug. Covered and left, it was ready for brickmaking next
day. The secret of the operation was to know precisely
how much water to add so that the pug would be neither
too dry and stiff, nor too wet and soft. If the pug was too
soft, the brick would suffer by slumping, causing it to lose
its shape as soon as the mould was removed.

A description such as this relies partly on Mr Leslie's powers of
observation and on his eye for significant detail, but also on the conversations he had with the workmen. 'What', we can imagine him asking,
'is this called? Why exactly are you doing that? What would happen if
you were to add too much or too little water?' Combining looking with
asking, Mr Leslie leads us through the whole sequence of operations
required to produce the finished brick. It is doubtful if the very
complicated firing process in particular has ever been set out in writing
with such painstaking attention to detail.

Ashburnham-made bricks always had a high reputation, 'the best
bricks in the world', in the words of the men who made them. To test
this, Mr Leslie had a sample scientifically tested at the Redland brick
factory at Horsham. The verdict[2] was that they were of excellent quality,
with an attractive texture and colour. It is an interesting commentary on
technical progress that 'a yard working with such archaic methods could
produce bricks to standards absolutely comparable to those from works
employing the most up-to-date techniques'. The Redland Brick
Laboratory, however, is only one kind of laboratory. The other, equally
significant, is formed of the buildings on the Ashburnham Estate and
elsewhere in the district which used the bricks and subjected them to the
effects of time and weather. They, together with the claypits and the
grass-grown vestiges of the kilns, sheds and heaps, constitute the
archaeology of the Ashburnham Estate Brickworks.

Cast-iron storehouse (1859) at Watervliet Arsenal, New York
According to the Historic American Engineering Record[3]

The Mohawk–Hudson Area Survey was conducted during
the summer of 1969, using the techniques of industrial
archaeology to produce a historical record of a selected

[2]   Based on British Standards Institution testing (BS 3921).
[3]   *A Report of the Mohawk–Hudson Area Survey*: a Selective Recording Survey of the
Industrial Archeology of the Mohawk and Hudson River Valleys in the Vicinity of
Troy, New York, June–September 1969. ed. Robert M. Vogel, Washington:
Smithsonian Institution Press, 1973.

group of nineteenth century engineering structures. For
the most part the survey concentrated its attentions in the
vicinity of Troy, New York, on the Hudson River 150
miles above New York City. Funding and staff support
was furnished by the Historic American Buildings Survey
for the sake of determining the feasibility of purely
engineering surveys, but the survey was conducted and
organised by the Historic American Engineering Record
(HAER).

The use of the phrase 'purely engineering surveys' is interesting.
What is meant, as a reading of the Report makes clear, is, firstly, that the
structures which were studied were selected primarily for their
importance in the history of engineering and building construction and,
second, that the team was concerned mainly to record the structures as
structures, not as elements of a complete, rounded item of social or
industrial history. This approach was explicitly stated by emphasising
the view of both HAER and the editor that industrial archaeology is an
identifiable, clear-cut activity. 'The industrial archaeologist,' says the
Report, making its position quite clear, 'as do all others in the various
branches of archaeology, studies man's past achievements on the basis
of physical, rather than written remains. The concern here is expressly
with the remains of technology, engineering and industry: the products
of the industrial era.' The results of the survey are presented in a way
that follows this general principle fairly closely, but not so closely as to
justify the rash, puritanical claim that what has been carried out is a
'purely engineering' investigation. It is difficult to imagine, in fact,
what a 'purely engineering' study of a building might be, since one can
hardly think of the building outside its functional context. If one is to
strip away everything that is not 'engineering', one ceases to think and
write sense. And, since the various reports in this book make both
excellent sense and good reading, it is hardly surprising to find that they
contain much useful information which has no immediate connexion
with engineering at all. It could not be otherwise. Even a Puritan, one
might say, has to eat. He cannot live by prayer alone.

In passing, one might comment on the unnecessarily narrow definition of 'physical remains' which is widely, if not generally adopted. It
is perfectly true, as this report says, that one can distinguish between
'physical' and 'written' remains, and it is equally true that archaeology's
great contribution to the understanding of history lies in the discovery
and interpretation of physical remains. But the physical remains of a
factory, store or workshop include both the surviving buildings and
equipment and the surviving workers. A person does not have to be a
corpse or a skeleton in order to qualify for the archaeological label,

'remains'. If he represents and reflects a departed industrial order, he is just as much 'industrial remains' as an antiquated machine is, and his conversation and memories can be equated with the film, especially a sound film, of an old piece of machinery in action. Once this is accepted, the industrial archaeology Puritan can face the Lord each day with a clear conscience, and at the same time collect survey material documenting both inanimate objects and living people. Both are remains, in the sense that history has passed over their heads and left them behind as industrial monuments.

In this particular instance, HAER had it both ways. The team of architects, photographers and engineers concentrated on the task of measuring, drawing and taking pictures of the structures and a group of historians was engaged to accumulate the historical documentation which was necessary as background material. 'Each,' the Report tells us, 'was assigned a group of the finally selected structures, related largely to his own specialised interests, with instructions to prepare a historical account from research in available primary and secondary sources'. Given the financial resources available, this was certainly the most sensible and effective way of going about the job. A heterogeneous body of experts can tackle the different aspects of the historical whole in ways specially suited to their experience and talents and a skilful editor can weld all the contributions together into a single story. The account of the Watervliet Arsenal does precisely this, with all the advantages of plenty of space, good paper and a large number of excellent illustrations. The

Example of HAER drawings, prepared on standard sheets for filing: exterior of cast-iron storehouse at Watervliet Arsenal, New York.

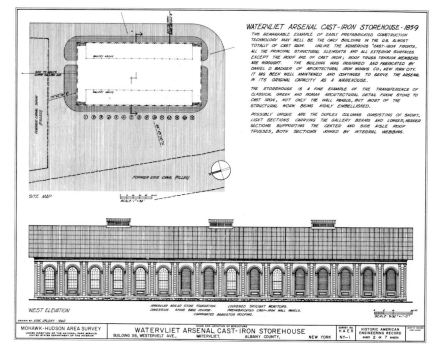

HAER group not so much solved as by-passed the problem facing most industrial archaeologists – how to carry out a satisfactory survey and write a report of real value, complete in all its dimensions, when all that is available is the time and labour of one or two hard-pressed people. Even with the resources at its command, HAER, it should be noted, was able to deal with only a very small number of the sites in the Mohawk–Hudson region. 'A continuation of the Mohawk–Hudson Area Survey could,' the Report pointed out both encouragingly and sadly, 'go on almost indefinitely.' But what was actually studied and published indicates a method and an approach which have been proved extremely valuable in planning and carrying out subsequent work, not only in the United States. The section on Watervliet Arsenal is typical of the contents of the volume as a whole.[4] After providing basic information as to the exact location of the building, the date of completion, its present owner and use, the Report gives its significance – 'May be the only remaining all-iron building still used for its original purpose. It is also an early example of prefabricated construction, all of its parts having been constructed by the Architectural Iron Works in New York and shipped up the Hudson for erection on the site.'

The Arsenal was established in 1813, on the west bank of the Hudson

[4]   The Watervliet section was edited and written by Selma Thomas. The historical
      material was supplied by Carole Huberman, Charles Peterson, Lewis Rubinstein and
      Robert M. Vogel, and the architectural information was prepared by David Bouse,
      Charles A. Parrott III, and Richard J. Pollak.

Detailing on HAER
drawing.

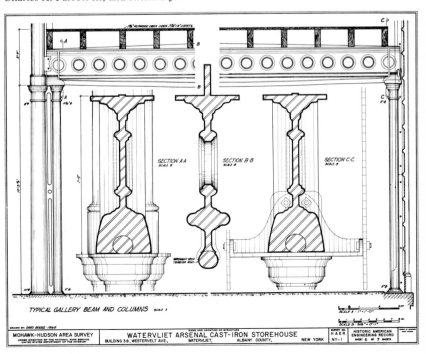

River. From the beginning, it was subject to flooding and in 1857 the decision was taken to build a large single-storeyed storehouse above flood-level, mainly to accommodate new gun-carriages awaiting shipment. It had to be both fire-proof and 'ornamental', and eventually the contract was given to the Architectural Iron Works. The Report gives considerable detail of the controversy concerning the kind of building required and the exact site on which it should be located. It was put up and ready for use in six months and it has functioned completely satisfactorily ever since. It still functions as a storehouse, although 6,000 sq. ft of the building have now been converted into an ordnance museum.

The Report deviates from the straight line of a 'purely engineering survey' at three points. The first two, already indicated, are the history of the Arsenal in the account of the arguments about the kind of building required; the second is the biographical material about the two principal figures in the story, Major Alfred Mordecai, who was in charge of the Arsenal, and Daniel Badger, founder and owner of the Architectural Iron Works. The biographical material is strictly relevant, with no straying into anything of a purely personal, family nature. It is important to know, for instance, that Major Mordecai had had an engineering background at West Point and that he had been sent to Europe to study technical developments there. These had included a study of iron structures, especially at railway stations. Badger, on the other hand, was a self-taught man. After early experience as a contractor,

Detailing on HAER drawing.

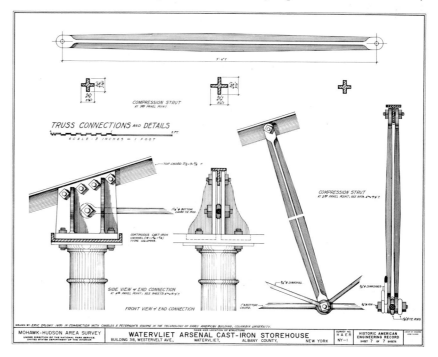

he achieved success with rolling iron shutters for protecting the new wide windows in shops. He built his foundry in New York in 1846 and the business flourished until 1870. It was based on a mass-production method and used a range of standard structural components. Badger was a pioneer of pre-fabricated construction. His 1865 catalogue announced that during the previous 20 years the Company had 'erected a great number of iron buildings in all the principal cities and towns throughout our country, of a great variety of styles, designed by the best architects'. The greatest undertaking had been to supply the iron-work for Vanderbilt's original Grand Central Station (1869–71) in New York, but there were a number of others, such as the 800 ft long Manhattan Market, which approached Grand Central in importance.

The architectural description of the storehouse is very detailed, covering materials, measurements and structural systems. The following extract illustrates the method:

Wall construction: Cast-iron panels connected by flathead, countersunk machine screws through flanged and lipped surfaces, only the countersunk heads appearing on the exterior. The paired cast-iron pilasters, $\frac{1}{2}$-inch thick, are part of load-bearing channels that provide stiffening for the walls and support one end of the gallery roof trusses on the side walls. Corner pilasters are built up box columns. The fenestrated panels and the rusticated detail between the pilasters, both generally $\frac{5}{16}$ inch thick are non-loadbearing.

We are told about the roof covering, skylights, flooring, lighting, ventilation, doors, 'notable hardware' and wall finishes. Special care is taken to mention anything which represents a change from the original form of the building, such as 'corrugated asbestos replaces the original covering' and 'The building was painted light gray in 1969, similar to its original color. By 1971 the exterior had been repainted buff.'

A point not specifically mentioned by the editors, but none the less very apparent to anyone reading the Report, is that each of the sites selected for study has its own natural drama, its peaks of interest built into it. It is exciting to understand how the conservatism of authorities is overcome, how experiments are made and succeed, how specialists can come to work together and to respect one another's expertise. It is unnecessary and gratuitous to introduce bogus interest; a well thought out building has plenty of interest in its own right, provided one is given all the essential facts, well presented. The HAER Report proves this without trying, although one is well aware that the members of the research team had enthusiasm, as well as knowledge and skill to help them.

Early Spanish dams

Industrial archaeology has yet to strike roots in Spain, yet here, as in Italy and Portugal, there is a great deal of material which, beyond all question, is ripe for the full attention of the industrial archaeologists – textile manufacturing, ports and harbours, wine production, food processing of all kinds, railways, to name only a few parts of the field. It is difficult to decide exactly why the Latin countries should be reluctant to agree that they have any kind of industrial past. The two chief reasons are probably the superabundance of Greek, Roman and medieval archaeology around the Mediterranean, which tends to overwhelm everything dating from a later period; and the absence of industrial areas with the associations of the Ruhr, Lille or Sheffield. But the strength and continuity of tradition within the field of technology in countries such as Spain should be more than enough to encourage the establishment of an industrial archaeology movement, to locate, study and conserve what remains from the past. The great Spanish dams are an excellent example of this, formidable in their design and construction, and an inspiration to the civil engineers of today. Ironically, they have been studied in the greatest detail, not by Spanish historians or archaeologists, but by a British engineer, Norman Smith, of Imperial College, London. His authoritative article, 'Early Spanish Dams', published in 1969,[5] looks at the series of dams which led to the building, in 1747, of the prototype of all modern buttress dams, near Almendralejo, in Badajoz; and which have provided twentieth-century engineers with the experience and the confidence to create the even larger and more impressive structures which are possible with today's materials and equipment. The two most remarkable Roman dams in Spain are to be found in the area of Mérida, near the Portuguese frontier. They were originally built to provide a water supply, but they have since been used for irrigation purposes. The Proserfina dam is 1,400 ft. long and 40 ft. high, the smaller Cornalvo dam 650 ft. long and 65 ft. high. Both have complex masonry and concrete walls and buttresses, and contain a considerable quantity of earth fill.

During the thirteenth century, Christian engineers in Spain continued the tradition of great reservoir dams, but combined it with a more recent tradition, the irrigation techniques introduced by the Moslems from the beginning of the eighth century onwards. One of the dams of this period which has survived is at Almonacid de la Cuba, near Belchite in Aragon. It is a massive, straight masonry wall, blocking a deep gorge. When he inspected it in the late 1940s, Dr Smith noticed that the height had been raised at some time in the past, in an effort to

5   In *Endeavour*, a review of the progress of science, published by Imperial Chemical Industries, Vol. xxviii, January 1969. Dr Smith is Leverhulme Research Fellow in the History of Technology at Imperial College.

The six great Spanish
dams.

Profiles of the six dams
(Almonacid, Alicante,
Eiche, Relleu, Almansa,
Almendralejo).

Elche

Relleu

Almendralejo

overcome the silting-up which had taken place. In its original form, it must, he believed, have been about 70 ft. high and 250 ft. wide at the top. Increasing the height had worked for a time, but eventually the silt won the battle and nowadays what was the reservoir is completely filled with soil and under cultivation.

150 years after Almonacid, at the end of the fourteenth century, the technically very important Almansa dam was built in the province of Albacete. Subsequently raised in height, it is curved, not straight, although its thickness, 30 ft. at the crest and 50 ft. at the base, would have made it strong enough to resist the pressure of the water even without the extra strength provided by the curve. During the next two centuries, Spanish engineers continued to experiment with curved dams and to refine their techniques. The dam at Alicante, built between 1579 and 1594 across the Monegre River, is an immense structure, 140 ft. long, 65 ft. thick at the top and 115 ft. thick at the base. It has been estimated that it contains over a million and a quarter cubic feet of masonry and mortar, which time has solidified into a single mass in a remarkable way. One has good reason to try to imagine what the Alicante dam meant in terms of human labour and with the primitive transport and engineering equipment available. Where, one asks, did this great army of workmen live during the construction of the dam? How were they recruited and trained? How were they fed? What was the casualty rate? In print, Dr Smith himself neither puts nor answers these questions, but it is difficult to believe that they were not in his mind as he stood looking at the dam and as he was writing about it.

The Spaniards continued to build curved dams in the seventeenth century, but by this time their engineers had learnt that, by including arches in the designs, it was possible to reduce the thickness and therefore the cost considerably. Elche dam is 76 ft. high, but only 30 ft. thick at the crest and 40 ft. at the base. Relleu dam is very high, 105 ft., but it is a mere 17 ft. thick, which would have seemed impossibly daring a century earlier. It is important to realise that these engineers did not have even the most elementary of structural calculations to guide them; they relied entirely on experience and on a feeling for the materials and the site. But, however cautiously they proceeded – the early structures were, much thicker than was necessary – some degree of risk was unavoidable. Alicante was more than twice as high as any dam previously built in Spain, and until the end of the nineteenth century it remained the highest dam in the world. The four dams mentioned above show how dams, like the columns of cathedrals, were steadily becoming more slender as the engineers gained confidence. At Relleu, Dr Smith points out, the height-to-thickness ratio is more than 6, a figure which had never before been achieved. 'The trend towards higher "slenderness ratios" which the four dams exhibit,' he says, 'is an interesting example of what one might call structural evolution; that is to say, the tendency to develop the theoretical ideal in the absence of analytical methods of design.'

Relleu and Alicante were built in deep, narrow gorges. The others are long dams. All, however, have the advantage of the same kind of site, a hard, strong limestone to support the dam at foundation level and against the sides of the valley. They were all designed for irrigation purposes and only the first, at Almonacid, has been seriously affected by silt. This is not accidental. The later engineers solved the problem by building what are known as 'scouring tunnels', large, straight tunnels at the base of the dam, at approximately the point where the original stream flowed. The way in which the tunnels are operated is effective, but dangerous. 'The mouths of these galleries are kept closed by means of sets of thick wooden beams held in grooves in the masonry. At intervals of several years workmen enter the tunnels and remove the beams. Then, from the tops of the dams, the silt beds below are stirred up with long iron bars and as soon as the deposits are loosened the water pressure from a full reservoir is sufficient to drive the bulk of the sediment through the galleries.' This method is effective, but it has one disadvantage; the whole contents of the reservoir have to be used to flush out the silt. At Alicante, the scouring gallery is tapered towards the outlet, showing that the engineers understood the principle of the diffuser or draught tube.

The technique for drawing off the water needed for irrigation purposes is also interesting. At Almansa, the method is simply to have a low level tunnel controlled by an iron sluice gate. Alicante, Relleu and Elche have a more complicated arrangement. The outlet tunnel is connected at the reservoir end with a vertical well, which has a series of openings at different levels to allow sufficient water to enter the well, no matter how much silt has accumulated. At Alicante, there is sufficient thickness to allow the well to be built into the dam itself, but at Elche and Relleu, where the structure is much thinner, the wells are in extensions projecting into the reservoir.

All the dams have a core of rubble set in mortar and are faced with large blocks of cut stone. Dr Smith thinks it probable that the facing was placed in position first and that the rubble was poured into this stone shell as the work proceeded. The cost of construction and the task of finding the labour force were the responsibility of the communities which would eventually benefit from the irrigation. Sadly, and remarkably, we know nothing of the engineers who planned and supervised these great works. They are anonymous.

The Spaniards continued to be pre-eminent in dam-building right through the eighteenth century. In 1747 they built the prototype of all modern buttress dams, at Almendralejo, in Badajoz. Given the dimensions of the dam – 400 ft. long, 72 ft. high, 40 ft. thick at the base and 32 ft. thick at the top – the buttresses were not strictly necessary, but the engineers were taking no chances. It is important in the history of civil engineering for another reason, however. It was built for milling, with the machinery installed within the body of the dam. There is no previous record of such an arrangement, so that Almendralejo can claim to be both the earliest buttress dam and the earliest hydro-power dam. All traces of the milling machinery have disappeared and the dam, heightened, is now used for water supply.

At the beginning of the nineteenth century the Spanish engineers seem, for some reason, to have lost their skill and flair where the building of big dams was concerned. In 1802, the foundations of the 164 ft. high Puentes dam, built on wooden piles driven into sand and gravel, gave way. The dam collapsed and 600 people in the town of Lorca were drowned. A little earlier, in 1799, a dam on the Guadarrama River, planned to reach a height of 305 ft., was washed away by floods. During the nineteenth century, pre-eminence in dam-building passed from the Spaniards to the French, who applied mathematical calculations in a way the Spaniards had never done. But the French engineers responsible for such dams as Furens and Ternay owed a great deal to the study they made of the earlier dams in Spain, and the great Spanish achievement, the gravity dam with curvature, was widely adopted all over the world. 'It is intriguing,' Dr Smith reminds us, 'that the mighty Hoover Dam is descended from Spanish works of the sixteenth and seventeenth centuries'.

Dr Smith's work is important from a number of points of view. On the one hand, he is doing what, strictly speaking, the Spaniards should be doing for themselves, that is, he is applying the British tradition of industrial archaeology to non-British material and in this way encouraging another country to consider the value of sites within its own boundaries. Second, he is pursuing a difficult but immensely useful type of research, leading to what one might perhaps call continuous or cumulative industrial archaeology, in which the sites to be studied are spread over a fairly long period of time, but given coherence by being all within the same country and the same branch of technology. Third, he has demonstrated how essential it is to actually inspect these structures for oneself, on the site and in the context of the district they were built to serve. And, lastly, his work reminds us that the historically minded, socially minded engineer is a person desperately needed if the full potential of industrial archaeology is to be realised.

'Château-sur-Mer', Newport, Rhode Island

After the Civil War and until the entry of the United States into the First World War, Americans who had made fortunes from industry, finance and commerce built themselves, at immense cost, Loire Valley châteaux and Renaissance and baroque palaces and mansions which were finely constructed architectural mongrels. Their favourite locations were New York City and New York State, San Francisco and the fashionable New England coastal resorts. The style with the highest prestige was really no style at all, a vigorous, self-confident, aggressive medley of several identifiable styles blended into something distinctively American. The mix included French Renaissance, English Tudor, Gothic and American Colonial, with Italian and Japanese features to add excitement and extra distinction. The American Victorian and Edwardian palaces made much play with baronial halls and massive staircases. Mrs William Astor's house on 34th Street, New York, had a ballroom to accommodate 400 people. The Vanderbilts were great mansion builders, with an Italian Renaissance palace at Hyde Park, New York, an even bigger place, 'Biltmore', at Asheville, North Carolina, and two huge residences at Newport, Rhode Island, in one of the most remarkable clusters of millionaires' properties to be found anywhere in the world. One of these houses, 'The Breakers', has 70 rooms and was built in the 1890s as a summer residence for Cornelius Vanderbilt. 'Marble House' (1890–2) nearby was built for William K. Vanderbilt. Other colossal properties at Newport include 'The Elms', completed in 1901 for Edward J. Berwind, the Philadelphia coal magnate, and 'Château-sur-Mer', built in 1852, much earlier than most of its neighbours, for William S. Wetmore, who had made a fortune in the China trade. It was greatly extended and improved by his son in 1872.

'Château-sur-Mer', Newport, Rhode Island.

The Historic American Buildings Survey took 'Château-sur-Mer' in its stride, during a survey made in the early 1970s.[6] Rhode Island has certainly not been neglected by American architectural historians and HABS had a great deal of previous work to draw on.[7] The Rhode Island Historical Society, the Preservation Society of Newport County and the Rhode Island Historical Preservation Commission have also been very active. But there are fashions in preservation, as in all other kinds of collecting and cherishing, and, as HABS pointed out: 'The time is ripe for studies of those later periods and styles that so far have not been popular with the historians.' 'Château-sur-Mer', more particularly in in its improved form, is an excellent example of a style which has only in recent years begun to receive the academic attention it deserves.

But, it should be emphasised, the architectural historian and the industrial archaeologist have very different attitudes towards 'Château-sur-Mer', and indeed towards any kind of housing. Industrial archaeologists are only marginally concerned with what is called, not altogether happily, 'style'. What, after all, is 'Château-sur-Mer'? What is the visitor or the scholar really faced with as he stands in front of it and walks round inside? He is in contact, one might say, with several kinds of history, which could be summarised as the history of practical skills, the history of materials, the history of wealth and its sources, the history of social privilege, the history of the taste and ambitions of rich people and, lastly and probably least important, the history of what the architectural historians call style, which is little more than the icing on the cake. Unfortunately, very few industrial archaeologists have shown much interest in mansions and palaces, so that the kind of illumination and understanding which their special approach could provide in these cases has still to come. At the moment, it seems worth saying with some

6   *Rhode Island Catalog* compiled by Osmund Overby, edited by John C. Poppeliers, HABS, 1972.
7   The main works are listed on pp. 1–8 of the *Rhode Island Catalog*.

Château-sur-Mer: elevations of plans of porter's lodge and entrance arch.

1 Arch
2 Porch
3 Living room
4 Dining room
5 Kitchen
6 Bedroom
7 Dressing room

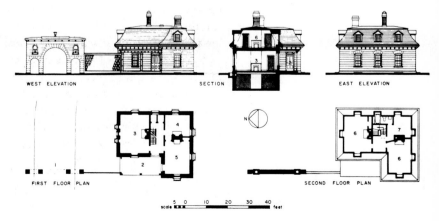

force that there is something very one-sided and ridiculous about a branch of archaeology which is keenly and actively interested in the places where money was made, in the capitalists' workshops, so to speak, and in the houses inhabited by members of the working class, but which has so far shown itself relatively indifferent to the places where industrial profits were spent, including the residences of the rich. If the study of these mansions is abandoned to the architectural historian, the result, as experience has shown, will be a very incomplete picture indeed. The industrial archaeologist and the architectural historian simply do not have the same kind of eyes and aims, although in fairness one should admit that there are signs of change among both architectural and art historians, where a new generation is beginning to show impatience with the tradition of studying buildings outside the contexts of social and political organisation on the one hand and of technical development and innovation on the other.

Having said this, one may usefully quote what the Historic American Buildings Survey, which is not staffed by industrial archaeologists, has to say about 'Château-sur-Mer'.

'Château-sur-Mer', Wetmore House, Bellevue Ave., between Shepard and Leroy Aves. Historic house museum. Granite, regular coursed ashlar, irregular L-shape about 100′ by 100′, two-and-a-half stories plus intermediate and attic floors, mansard roofs with pavillions and towers, plan arranged around skylit central hall open through three stories with richly decorated formal rooms on the first floor, comfortable private suites on the second floor, bedrooms on the third floor. Built 1851–1852; Seth Bradford, architect. Enlarged and extensively remodeled 1869–1873, c. 1890; Richard Morris Hunt, architect.

Plan of the 'Château-sur-Mer' estate, c. 1917.

317

1 Entrance arch
2 Porter's lodge
3 Château
4 Chinese gate
5 Palm house
6 Grapery
7 Formal gardens
8 Stables
9 Barn
10 Tool house
11 Vegetable garden
12 Location of present rose garden
13 Clothes yard
14 North gate
15 South gate

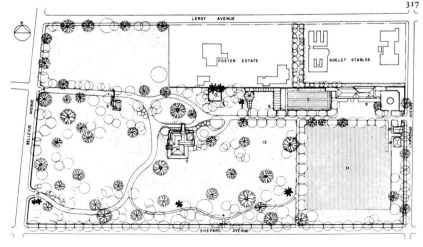

Dining room and library decoration c. 1875; Luigi
Frullini, designer. Additions and alterations, 1914; John
Russell Pope, architect.

The catalogue then goes on to list the drawings and photographs
which form part of its dossier on 'Château-sur-Mer' and which can be
inspected by students.

All this is straight architectural history, which HABS has always
seen its task to be. It is concerned with 'the cataloguing and preservation
of historic structures'. The Society of Architectural Historians, however, has carried the exploration of 'Château-sur-Mer' considerably
further and over a much wider field. The American Society for Industrial
Archaeology, a lively and well-run organisation and much more tolerant
and broadminded than its equivalent in other countries, has not so far
tackled buildings like 'Château-sur-Mer'. One awaits the day when it
does with great interest.

In 1970[8] the Society of Architectural Historians devoted 27 pages of
its handsomely produced *Journal* to a study of 'Château-sur-Mer'.
This was in two parts, the first called 'The Transformation of "Château-
sur-Mer"' and the second, 'The Outbuildings and Grounds of
"Château-sur-Mer"'. The second part, somewhat surprisingly but
very charmingly, contains much interesting material about the family
which built the house. Biography is evidently regarded as secondary
stuff, and to be put on the same level as outbuildings. The historian and

[8] Vol. XXIX, No. 4, December 1970, pp. 291–317.

Plan of the new stables at
'Château-sur-Mer'
forming part of the
Wetmore extensions.

1 Tool house
2 Harness room
3 Carriage room
4 Wash room
5 Dressing room
6 Feed room
7 Stalls
8 Stable yard
9 Water basin
10 Storage
11 Work shop
12 Kitchen
13 Living room
14 Groom's bedrooms
15 Clock works
16 Feed bins
17 Hay loft
18 Water tank

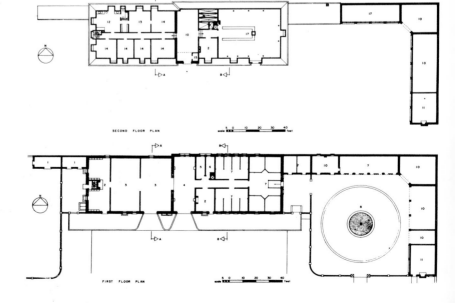

archaeologist, none the less, may well prefer to read the two parts in the reverse order to that in which they are printed. The present author certainly found this method of proceeding more fruitful.

William Shepard Wetmore, we are told, was born in 1801. After leaving Cheshire Academy, Connecticut, he went to work in a shipping firm run by two of his uncles. He was sent on trading trips round the world, during one of which his ship was wrecked off Valparaiso. Once on land, Wetmore took employment in Valparaiso with the firm of Richard Alsop and eventually went into partnership with them.

'Château-sur-Mer': sectional drawings, showing arrangement of interior.

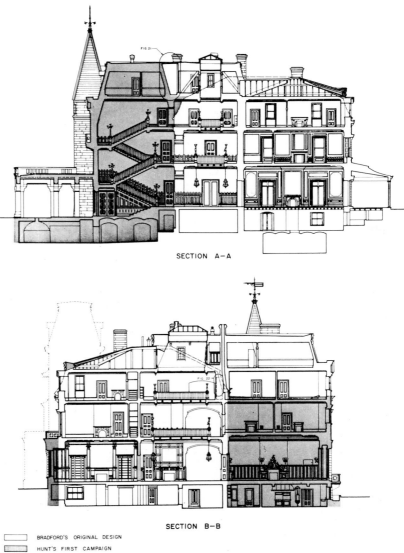

SECTION A—A

SECTION B—B

☐ BRADFORD'S ORIGINAL DESIGN

▨ HUNT'S FIRST CAMPAIGN

☐ HUNT'S SECOND CAMPAIGN

In 1829 Mr. Wetmore retired from the firm of Alsop, Wetmore and Cryder, with what represented an ample fortune for those times, and in 1833 traveled to Canton, China, where he took over a partnership with Dunn and Company and associated himself with the firm's junior partner, Joseph Archer. The firm prospered, becoming one of the largest houses in the East Indies.

Helped by these details, we are beginning to see the owner of 'Château-sur-Mer' as a real person and we are becoming interested in him. Mr Wetmore married twice, once in 1837 and for a second time in 1843.

A year after his second marriage, William Shepard Wetmore formed the house of Wetmore and Cryder. It succeeded so well that he withdrew a substantial interest from this venture when he retired from the firm in 1847, adding considerably to his already ample fortune. He then took up an association with the leading businessmen in New York City, but soon sought complete retirement and moved his family to Newport, where he acquired some fifteen acres and where, in 1851–1852, he built 'Château-sur-Mer'.

William Wetmore entertained on a considerable scale at his new home – a Fête Champêtre for 3000 in 1857 being among the more ambitious undertakings. Some of the guests came by boat and more than 40 yachts were anchored in Newport Harbour for the purpose. The host unfortunately had only a few years in which to enjoy his marine retreat; he died in 1862 and his second son, George Peabody Wetmore, succeeded to the estate. George Wetmore had a legal training and served as a member of the U.S. Senate for many years. He died in 1921, and his two sons in 1917 and 1925. The care of the estate then passed to his two daughters, who never married. Both died during the 1960s and at that point 'Château-sur-Mer' passed out of the keeping of the Wetmore family and into that of the Preservation Society of Newport County.

It is a not untypical rich man's story, a fortune made in commerce, a short retirement, a son who inherited and improved the property and who became an important figure in public life, a family which died out in the third generation, leaving a mansion as a monument to a style of life which had long since become antiquated.

In the first part of the *Journal* article concerning the transformation of the house by George Peabody Wetmore, Winslow Ames remarks on the 'ruggedness and almost crushing scale' of the house. This seems a little hard. Stonebuilt and solid are equally applicable and more complimentary adjectives and, in any case, nobody but a fool would build a house on America's Atlantic coast that was not 'rugged'. The remodelling certainly cost a lot of money; the interiors of the library and dining room were reported to have required $60,000 each, at a time when it was possible to live in a lodging house for $2 a week. The arrangements were generally regarded as appropriate for the time and for a man in Wetmore's position, not in any way ostentatious. The service system was certainly elaborate, but it was based on numerous servants at low wages. Another echo of the social customs of the period was to be found in the washing and lavatory arrangements. 'Upstairs there were five bathrooms for ten bedrooms – lavish by European standards, not by American – four dressing rooms, a day nursery and a sitting room. Every bedroom suite had a washstand, but the smaller bedrooms had no washstand. On the ground floor, the only lavatory was the one off the billiard room, for the convenience of male guests. Women had to go upstairs.'

'Château-sur-Mer', constructed of the best materials, furnished and decorated expensively, and with plumbing and other practical amenities as good as anything available at the time, stands as a symbol of an upper-class generation which was immensely sure of itself and which asked above all of a house that it should be respected by one's friends and social equals. It represents a class trying to express itself. This particular house was the creation of a family which probably had taste which was well above the average for its class. It certainly announced to the world that its owners had a great deal of money, but it also made clear, in its decor and furnishings, that they were not vulgar.

What is very significant and marks Winslow Ames's article as belonging firmly, despite its late date, to the traditional architectural historian's world is the fact that this long, detailed and generously illustrated article has nothing of any consequence to say, and no pictures whatever, of either the bathrooms, lavatories, servants' bedrooms or of those areas of the house where the work was done, the kitchens, sculleries, pantries, laundry and the rest. This is the essential difference between the way in which the industrial archaeologist and the architectural historian describe structures. The architectural historian identifies himself with the owners, goes in through the front door and remains within those parts of the house where the master and mistress were to be found. The industrial archaeologist, on the other hand, is just as likely to enter by means of the back door and to be so fascinated by the kitchen and the boiler room that he will have to be reminded to leave sufficient time to take a brief look at the drawing room and the best bedroom.

4

Metal processing

The problem of deciding, for any particular country or region, when the extraction and smelting of metallic ores and the subsequent founding or forging can be said to have emerged from the craft stage and to have become 'industrial' is extremely difficult. Is a forge with two men and a boy a branch of handicraft or can it be reckoned part of an industry? If three employees are too few to allow the forge to qualify for the industrial label, are six enough or does it have to be sixty? More important, does it matter?

Very sensibly, in the present author's opinion, the British-based Historical Metallurgy Group, which has an international reputation for the quality of the articles published in its *Bulletin*, has no worries about including in the same issue reports on prehistoric, Roman, sixteenth century and Victorian ironworking sites. It sees the working of metals as a continuous historical process, in which each generation learns from its predecessor and improves to some extent on its methods, and the phrase 'industrial archaeology' is never used in either its publications or its conference papers, leaving members of the Group free to pursue their researches without any nagging worry as to whether they are studying an industry or a craft. They are concerned with technology, which has no need to preoccupy itself with such theological questions.

If, however, one is to talk and write about the working of metals within the framework and disciplines of what we have decided to call industrial archaeology, it does no harm to enquire if some kind of time limit is possible and desirable. It is therefore assumed here that the sixteenth century is the beginning of the modern or industrial period in ironworking. This is for two reasons: the blast-furnace was by then in fairly widespread use, at least in Europe, and water-power was being applied by many, if not most, ironworkers to drive their bellows and hammers. These developments were very unevenly spread over the different countries of the world, but in the sixteenth century they existed and they were increasingly adopted with each decade that passed.

Those who link industrial archaeology firmly to what they are content to call the Industrial Revolution are unlikely to accept a sixteenth-century starting point for any industry, on the grounds that before the eighteenth century the market was too restricted and working units too small to make the term 'industry' reasonable or helpful. Since, however, the same people are very likely to find reasons for excluding many, if not all, twentieth century factories from the Industrial Archaeology (the capital letters are important) canon, one does not need to take their objections very seriously. They represent the rules of a club, rather than any particular logic.

The key question is of an altogether different kind; are there any essential differences of historical and archaeological approach towards a metal-working site of, say, the sixteenth century on the one hand and of the nineteenth or twentieth centuries on the other? The answer must be that there are not. One can only examine what the site contains in the way of evidence, record one's findings and relate them to any information which is available from other sources. There is no other way of proceeding and the antiquity or youthfulness of the site is of no consequence. There are, of course, complicating factors. A small rural ironworks, forgotten in woodland, may be more convenient and possibly more pleasant to investigate than a much modified and enlarged steelworks in Pittsburgh or Essen, and the documentary evidence relating to an ironworks of 1860 may be much more abundant than for one of 1660. But this is a matter of good fortune, not of method. Equally, a water-driven forge, pleasantly situated by the side of a country stream, may well be a far more agreeable place in which to conduct one's researches than Oberhausen or Sheffield. The first type of site may have a greater romantic or tourist appeal than the second. As far as industrial archaeology is concerned, however, these are completely irrelevant considerations.

A discussion of half-a-dozen examples will help to illustrate these general points.

A nineteenth-century blast furnace at Ridsdale, Northumberland

In Northumberland, as in most counties of Britain, the history of iron-making goes back to the fourth and fifth centuries, but in this particular region blast-furnaces lasted for exactly a century, from 1800 to the 1890s. The cost of working the local ores was high, because of the thin seams and the great thickness of the overburden which had to be removed before the ore was reached. There were nine furnaces altogether, at Wylam, Haltwistle, Wallsend, Bedlington, Ridsdale, Hareshaw, Brinkburn and Elsdale.[1]

Recent archaeological work undertaken at Ridsdale indicates the methods employed by a prominent member of the Historical Metallurgy

For a summary of what is known about these workings, see R. F. Tylecote, 'Recent Research on Nineteenth Century Northumbrian Blast Furnace Sites', *Industrial Archaeology*, Vol. 8, No. 4, November 1971.

Group, Dr R. F. Tylecote, of the University of Newcastle, and an authority on metallurgical problems in archaeology.[2]

Two blast furnaces existed at Ridsdale in 1836 and another was added in 1839. All three remained in working order until the works was closed in 1857. The only building remaining on the site in 1970 was the house for the two blowing engines. It was in poor condition and liable to collapse at any time, so the decision was taken to make a complete record of it. A ground plan was constructed and the elevations of the building were recorded by means of photogrammetry, which is, as Dr Tylecote says, 'a particularly useful method of recording ruined buildings which are too dangerous to climb on to measure in the usual way'.

As the map shows, the quarries which provided the furnace with its ore and limestone lie about half a mile from the furnace, with what remains of a row of kilns another half-mile from the quarries. Dr Tylecote at this point engages in some useful detective work.

A stone at the end of one of the kilns bears the date '1876' and it is clear that these are not the original kilns marked on the 1863 O.S. map, but must have been rebuilt by W. G. Armstrong for the furnaces at Elswick. It is clear from the line of old rail track serving the kilns that these were for roasting ore and not limestone. The rail track looks as though it had an earlier alignment which is probably that shown in the 1863 map. It was probably

2 Ibid. pp. 349–58.

Engine house at Ridsdale, Northumberland, viewed from west.

realigned and raised to a higher level when the new kilns
were built in 1876. These kilns are of an unusual type,
with a common horizontal flue at the back, no doubt
originally terminating in a tall chimney. The discharge
side of the kilns was served by a low-level road and finally
a railway; opposite are heaps of waste shale with some
nodules of ore.

That paragraph describes and interprets what the archaeologist
actually sees on the site. He then proceeds to link his observations with
what is known from the documentary evidence and in this way to
provide a complete and convincing reconstruction of what remains of
this part of the plant.

It was originally built to serve the Ridsdale furnaces with
calcined ore and went out of use in the 1860s. When
W. G. Armstrong took over the site in 1864, he developed
the ore workings to supply his Elswick furnaces and sent
the ore by rail to the area of the earlier kilns, which he
rebuilt to supply his Elswick furnaces in 1876. The
Hexham and North Tyne Railway had been opened in

Map of Ridsdale site.

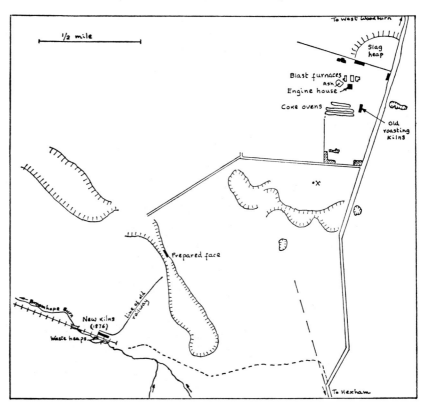

1862, making rail connection with Newcastle possible. These kilns must have closed down by 1896 when the Elswick furnaces ceased working. It is also possible that the kilns went out of use much earlier, since we know that Spanish ore was being used at Elswick in 1880. The blast furnace limestone is not usually calcined, but the kilns could have been used for agricultural purposes.

This is industrial archaeology of a highly efficient, classical kind. There is no thought or mention of workers, living conditions, wages or profits. All that concerns Dr Tylecote is a pair of simple questions: 'What do these ruins and foundations mean? What exactly went on here and why?' In his attempts to provide answers to these questions, he very naturally took a careful look at the ironore quarries and analysed the material he found there. The quarry face was cleaned up with the help of a bulldozer, provided by Vickers Armstrong, and this revealed that the nodular carbonate (siderite) containing the iron was in very

North elevation of Ridsdale engine house, drawn from data obtained by photogrammetry.

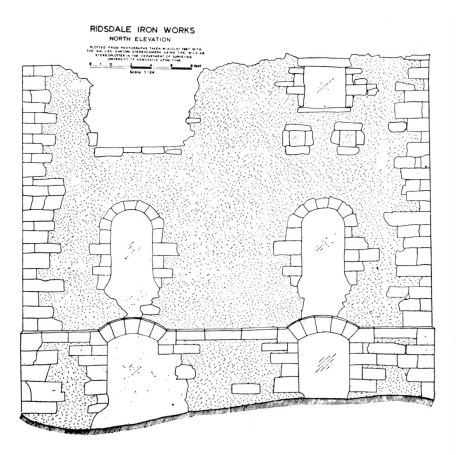

narrow bands, totalling no more than 6 feet over a total quarry face of 30 feet. There was, however, a shell band, well defined, of continuous stone. This could have been used as a limestone flux in the furnaces and probably was. The one quarry could therefore have produced both the materials required for smelting iron, a very fortunate state of affairs, not often found.

Surahammar ironworks, Sweden

The Swedes have a term, 'bruk', which is not easy to translate, if the full flavour is to be retained. 'Industrial settlement' is as near as one can get. A bruk was a self-contained industrial village, usually owned by a single family, with workshops, workers' housing, proprietor's house and all the ancillary institutions – farms, saw mill and corn mill, blacksmith and church – which a self-contained community required and which would allow it to function even during the hardest of winters. Some of the bruks, in Sweden and in Finland, have buildings which are

Location of Surahammar in relation to other iron-working centres in the Bergslagen region of Sweden. The lakes and rivers provided the industry with its means of transport.

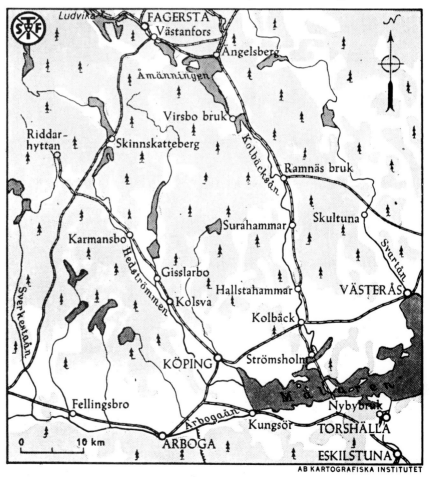

AB KARTOGRAFISKA INSTITUTET

architecturally very impressive. Lövsta bruk and Forsman bruk, both in Uppland, are particularly fine.

Most of the bruks were concerned with iron-making and they have usually suffered one of two fates. Either, as at Lövsta, operations have long ceased and most of the old industrial buildings have been demolished, leaving only the manor house, the workers' cottages, the church and the park, or, as at Edsken, in Gästrikland, or Munkfors, in Värmland, the bruk has kept pace with technical change, so that modern factory buildings can be seen more or less side by side with the remnants of the old works. Surahammar, in Västmanland has had the second kind of history. Ironworking has been carried on here and in the region since the first half of the seventeenth century. The works remained small until the 1840s, when two puddling furnaces and a rolling mill were built. During the nineteenth century Surahammar became well known for the manufacture of railway material, especially wheels and axles, and then, towards 1900, began to expand and diversify. A new steelworks has been built by the side of the old forge and the company, Surahammar Bruks Aktiebolag, now forms part of a large electrical and engineering group, and concentrates on making castings, forgings and plates for the heavy electrical industry.

The original forge has not only survived, but is preserved and cherished as part of the Company museum, complete with its water-wheels, tilt-hammer, reducing rolls and Lancashire re-heating furnaces.

Plan of museum at Surahammar bruk.

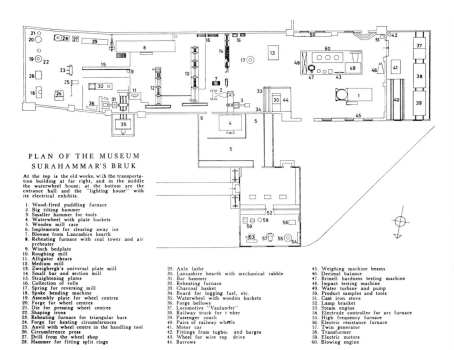

PLAN OF THE MUSEUM
SURAHAMMAR'S BRUK

At the top is the old works, with the transporta-
tion building at far right, and in the middle
the waterwheel house; at the bottom are the
entrance hall and the "lighting house" with
its electrical exhibits.

1. Wood-fired puddling furnace
2. Big tilting hammer
3. Smaller hammer for tools
4. Waterwheel with plate buckets
5. Wooden mill race
6. Implements for clearing away ice
7. Blooms from Lancashire hearth
8. Reheating furnace with coal tower and air preheater
9. Winch bedplate
10. Roughing mill
11. Alligator shears
12. Medium mill
13. Zweigbergk's universal plate mill
14. Small bar and section mill
15. Straightening plates
16. Collection of rolls
17. Spring for reversing mill
18. Spoke bending machine
19. Assembly plate for wheel centres
20. Forge for wheel centres
21. Die for pressing wheel centres
22. Shaping irons
23. Reheating furnace for triangular bars
24. Anvil with wheel centre in the handling tool
25. Circumference press
26. Circumference press
27. Drill from the wheel shop
28. Hammer for fitting split rings

29. Axle lathe
30. Lancashire hearth with mechanical rabble
31. Bar hammer
32. Reheating furnace
33. Charcoal basket
34. Board for logging fuel, etc.
35. Waterwheel with wooden buckets
36. Forge bellows
37. Locomotive "Vaulunder"
38. Railway truck for timber
39. Passenger coach
40. Pairs of railway wheels
41. Motor car
42. Fittings from tugboat and barges
43. Wheel for wire rope drive
44. Barrows

45. Weighing machine beams
46. Decimal balance
47. Brinell hardness testing machine
48. Impact testing machine
49. Water turbine and pump
50. Product samples and tools
51. Cast iron stove
52. Lamp bracket
53. Steam engine
54. Electrode controller for arc furnace
55. High frequency furnace
56. Electric resistance furnace
57. Twin generator
58. Transformer
59. Electric motors
60. Blowing engine

It is on the edge of the country and the meadows and woods running right up to the river and the old forge remind us that, for much of its history, iron-working in Sweden has been a very rural affair, located where there was a usable river to provide the motive power for the hammer, rolls and other machinery.

The present owners of the site have gone to considerable trouble to preserve the evidence of its history. Apart from the forge museum,

Survivals of wooden bruk housing in Surahammar.

Aerial picture, showing the two phases of workers' houses which succeeded the early wooden buildings at Surahammar.

there is an excellent archive and a series of well produced booklets giving the history of the works, the town and the company. In this case, the industrial archaeologists who have been most actively concerned with the remains of yesterday have been the company itself. There are some disadvantages in this, glad as one is bound to be when any industrial organisation takes such an active interest in its history and spends money so generously on matters which have no direct relation to current production and profits. One could sum up these disadvantages by saying, with all possible tact and gratitude, that there is a certain lack of objectivity in the way the history of Surahammar is presented and a marked tendency to avoid certain topics. Three points in particular are likely to strike either an historian or an archaeologist who has the opportunity, as the present author has had, to study Surahammar as an outside observer. The first is that, for all the care which the company has devoted to its preservation, the old forge is curiously and disturbingly dead. It has been preserved in a fossilised condition, with everything safe, dusted and labelled, but entirely still. Nothing moves, everything is very quiet, the air is so full of reverence for the past and the dead that one longs to shout or sing in order to break the oppressive silence. An enormous effort of the imagination is required to recreate the forge as it was a hundred years ago, with the great hammers thudding rhythmically up and down, shaking the building several times a minute, the reducing rolls clanging, the whole place full of heat, sweat and haze and of the noise of teams of men welding the parts of the railway wagon wheels together by hammering the red-hot metal one after another and chanting a strangely primitive song, the tune and words of which survive, as they worked. No effort has been made to stimulate an awareness of the atmosphere of the forge in its working days. The facts and the machines and the lay figures of workmen in absurdly neat and clean working smocks are left to speak for themselves. They would greatly benefit from a little friendly assistance.

This, it may be said, is a museological or museographical problem, not an industrial archaeology problem, and so in a sense it is. But, and this is disadvantage number two, it is closely linked to a philosophical problem. In presenting the history of a factory or a company, one has the choice of doing so through the eyes of the owners or through the eyes of the workers or, following the example of Dr Tylecote at Ridsdale, through the eyes of neither. One is perfectly free, if one wishes, to practise a professional fiction, by concentrating entirely on the technology and pretending for the moment that it had no concern or connexion with people at all. What Surahammar does, in its museum and its booklets, is to present history entirely through the eyes and attitudes of the management. It is a very neat and tidy history and, as one reads it and looks at the results one says, 'It could not possibly have been like this. This is a grotesque over-simplification of what happened. Where is the viewpoint, where are the reminiscences of the men who sweated? Why is there no hint that the history and archaeology of Surahammar is theirs, quite as much as the masters?'

This means – and here one comes to the third disadvantage – that there are certain kinds of archaeology at Surahammar, certain archaeological problems and opportunities, which have been totally disregarded, because of prejudice and of a determination to present a certain kind of company face to the world. Two in particular come to mind. Surahammar, that is, the town, the ex-bruk, the forge, the steelworks, has to be seen and studied as an historical entity. It so happens that the Company owns a small number of large, very beautiful houses close to the works, but on the rural edge of the town. These have always, since they were built in the late nineteenth century, been occupied by very senior members of the Surhammar management, the Chief Engineer and so on. The assumption has always been that this kind of person and their families would be well-to-do, cultured people, willing and able to lead the kind of lives for which such houses would provide a highly suitable stage. Until recently, this has been the case. The Swedish industrialist, especially in the prosperous and highly regarded iron and steel sector, has been a broadly educated, well-rounded person and, not unnaturally, he has tended to marry the same kind of woman. They have consequently lived in houses where there has been ample space for books and servants, where music could be played and listened to in comfort, and where one could enjoy a life-style which might best be described as ample and satisfying. But times and people change, and the new generation of

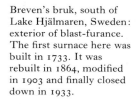

Breven's bruk, south of Lake Hjälmaren, Sweden: exterior of blast-furance. The first surnace here was built in 1733. It was rebuilt in 1864, modified in 1903 and finally closed down in 1933.

technocrats at Surahammar have other ideas about what constitutes a desirable life-style. The traditional kind of managerial house no longer fits managerial people and one consequently has, recently created, something for which the term 'management archaeology' is appropriate. But nowhere in any of the Company's recent publications is there even the suggestion that such houses exist, even though one, the grandest of all, has been converted into a private hotel for VIP visitors.

Few of the workers' houses belonging to the old bruk at Surahammar still exist. They, too, have not been found to be in accordance with today's living fashions, but they have been pulled down and replaced with discretion and virtually nothing is said about them in any official brochure aimed at the general public. Yet the modern steelworks employs a large proportion of the people who live in Surahammar, and, from this point of view, today's company town is only yesterday's bruk writ large.

Two major points emerge from this brief discussion of the Suraham-mar situation. The first is that, in nearly all instances of conservation, one gives up one thing in order to gain another. In conservation, as in anything else, perfection is an unattainable dream. The old forge has been saved as a symbol, and at the price of much else. And the second is that, to be of real value, industrial archaeology must be fully objective – whether the bias comes from Swedish conservatism or Czech com-

Plan of buildings existing at Breven in 1973:

1 Charcoal furnace
2 Ore roasting kiln
3 Charcoal store
4 Inspector's house
5 Carpenter's workshop
6 Stores
7 Former workshop, afterwards stores
8 Office
9 Workshop
10 Former inn, afterwards dwelling house
11 Manor house
12 Former cow-house, afterwards stores
13 Museum
14 Church
15 Workers' houses
16 Wash-house
17 Power-station
18 Wood-stores

munism is immaterial – and it must take a broad view of what constitutes the site. The factory has to be studied, recorded and documented in its total environment, however lacking in cohesion that environment may at first sight appear to be.

Surahammar is, from an archaeological point of view, a 'difficult' site, in the sense that one can understand the significance of one item in the works or the town only by being aware of all the others. Since this involves a consciousness of what belongs to several different periods and to at least three social classes, the task must inevitably seem to be both daunting and untidy, however rewarding the results might be. One sees this very clearly by comparing Surahammar with the bruks which have survived in something like their old form. A number of them, all established for the purpose of smelting iron with charcoal, and all in the county of Örebro, have been recently described in a single volume[3] by a group of industrial archaeologists, led by Sweden's most distinguished practitioner in this field, Dr Marie Nisser. Although the twelve iron-smelting communities with which this book is concerned contain structures and remnants of structures built over a period of 200 years and in one or two instances even longer, they all belong to the age of relatively small-scale production and, as was inevitable with the use of charcoal as a fuel, they are all in rural, forested areas, so that each site holds together within natural, clearly defined boundaries. They are, one could reasonably claim, 'easy sites', presenting none of the kind of problems which worry the public relations department of a large modern industrial concern. Politically and socially, they are 'safe' places.

Buffon's forges, Côte d'Or

Industrial archaeologists are, as yet, not thick on the ground in France, although industrial historians, digging deep into company archives and Government reports are plentiful enough. Bernard Rignault, of the pioneering Museum of Man and Industry at Le Creusot is exceptional, in his dual devotion to the archaeology and history. His work on the eighteenth-century forges at Buffon[4] is an example of industrial archaeology at its most thorough and rewarding.

Georges-Louis Leclerc de Buffon, the naturalist, had wide interests. In the course of experiments with iron-smelting, carried out during the 1760s at Aisy-sur-Armançon, he succeeded in producing iron of excellent quality from the very low-grade ore found in Burgundy. It was, he wrote, 'as good as, if not better than what is obtained from Sweden or Spain', and he decided to begin production on his own account, 'as

[3]   *Hyttor i Örebro lan* edited by Marie Nisser, and with contributions from Torbjörn Almquist, Jan Lisinski and Lena Simonsson. Jernkontorets Berghistoriska Utskott, 1974.

[4]   'Les forges de Buffon', *Mémoires de la Commission des Antiquités du département de la Côte d'Or*, Vol. XXVII, 1970–1, pp. 209–25.

soon as I have enough wood'. In 1768 he received the necessary permission from the Government and proceeded immediately to set up a
complete ironworking unit – furnace, forge and slitting and rolling mill
– on his estate near the town of Montbard. The village closest to the
ironworks had the same name as himself, Buffon, which causes occasional
confusion when one is going through the records. There was a plentiful
supply of water to drive the machinery and money was not spared to
make the works as up-to-date as possible in every way.

The taxation imposed on iron, very foolishly, by the State proved a
considerable handicap, because customers tended to put price before
quality. But Buffon persevered and in 1778 his works produced 400 tons
of iron, sold partly as forged bars and partly as finished material of all
kinds, ranging from flat sheets to specialised castings. For the owner,
however, the site was essentially a full-scale laboratory, where he could
carry out continuous experiments. In 1777 ill-health compelled him to
hand over day-to-day control to a manager, who swindled him and
eventually absconded with a large part of the working capital. After
Buffon's death, the works closed for a while, but resumed production
early in the nineteenth century and continued active until 1885, when it
was converted into a cement works. After 30 years, cement production
at Buffon came to an end and the whole complex of buildings was
abandoned. Much of it was in a ruinous condition when Bernard
Rignault began to survey it during the late Sixties, exactly two centuries
after iron-making was first established on the site. The two plans
reproduced here, one showing what existed in 1768 and the other what

Plan of Buffon's Forge, as
it was in 1768.

A Main entrance
B Main courtyard
C Vegetable garden
D Small garden
E Ramp
F Water channel

1 Covered area
2 Workmen's sleeping quarters
3 Cartsheds and stables
4 Harness room and groom's
  quarters
5 Iron store
6 Pigeon loft
7 Orangery
8 Clerk's lodging
9 Manager's lodging
10 Chapel
11 Administration
12 Staircase to furnace
13 Charcoal store
14 Ore shed
15 Furnace
16 Refinery
17 Slitting mill
18 Hammer mill
19 Covered area

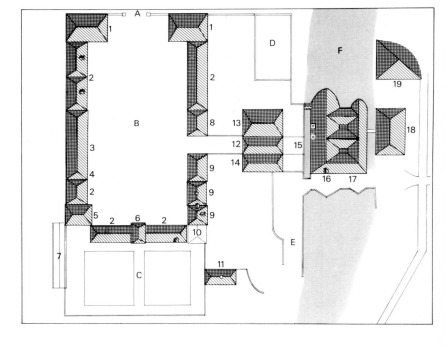

remained 200 years later, are an interesting documentation of decay and neglect.

The plans make it clear that the whole working and living complex was planned with great care, in order to have an industrial unit which was both efficient and architecturally pleasing. Housing and ancillary buildings were grouped around a central courtyard, with the main entrance to the works at one end of it, and the furnace, forges and other working elements placed a short distance away, close to the mill-race which had been constructed to drive the waterwheels. The workers' cottages were of the local peasant type and an enormous vegetable garden was laid out behind the closed end of the courtyard. There was a large stable and carriage-house, with a blacksmith's shop adjoining. The courtyard buildings also contained a bakery. The chapel, orangery and bath-house did not form part of the original buildings, but were added during Buffon's lifetime.

Bernard Rignault's paper is to a large extent a catalogue of disasters. Having established exactly what was on the site when Buffon's work had been completed, he proceeds to draw up, from various sources, a demolition report and to place on the map anything which still survives. A great deal was pulled down during the nineteenth century, including one of the lodging blocks. Some of the housing, however, has recently been restored and converted into holiday accommodation ('habitations secondaires'). Only the furnace survives, unaltered and in its entirety. It was classified as an Historic Monument in 1943 and is therefore protected against further decay and depredations.

Plan of the Forge in 1968.

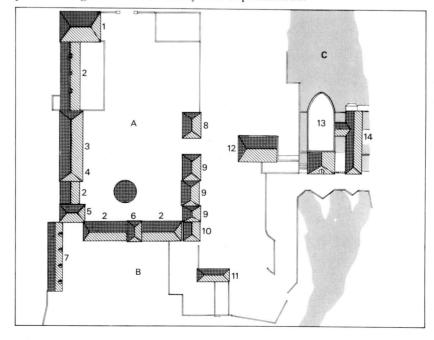

A Main courtyard
B Garden
C Water channel

1 Covered area
2 Workmen's sleeping quarters
3 Cartsheds and stables
4 Harness room and groom's
   quarters
5 Iron store
6 Pigeon loft
7 Orangery
8 Clerk's lodging
9 Manager's lodging
10 Chapel
11 Administration
12 Covered multi-purpose area
13 Refinery
14 Slitting mill

In studying this very interesting and important site, Dr Rignault has been constantly asking himself two questions: 'How did it all happen?' and 'What did it look like and feel like when everything was in full operation?' The second kind of musing and investigation produced a drawing, reproduced here, showing a group of buildings which is bound to make one admire both Buffon and the period in which he lived. 'If only,' one feels, 'industry could have always been like this, seemly, disciplined, in pleasant surroundings, on a human scale.' The advantages of having one controlling, planning mind at work and of laying out the whole site at the same time are very apparent. This is that very rare phenomenon, an industrial unit created from the beginning as part of the landscape, co-operating, not quarrelling with its surroundings. An eighteenth-century landowner, as Dr Rignault shows, created a pleasant building almost by instinct. But only a sensitive and properly balanced archaeologist will observe this and have the ability to communicate it. A mere historian of technology would miss the whole point of Buffon's ironworks. Its essentially civilising function would get lost among the thud of hammers and the plashing of waterwheels.

Reconstructing an industry or a factory from its physical remains is a skilled business, demanding an exceptional degree of enterprise, organisation and, above all, imagination on the part of the researcher. By no means everyone has the qualities required, but it is the pedestrian, unimaginative nature of so many industrial archaeology reports which has done more than anything else to give the subject a bad name, and to bring fully justified accusations of superficiality and 'antiquarianism'. No apology is therefore needed for including here another and very fine example of the art and skill of reconstruction, or for considering a further ironworking site.

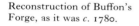

Reconstruction of Buffon's Forge, as it was *c.* 1780.

*The reconstruction of the sixteenth-century Paget ironworks at
Cannock Chase, Staffordshire*

In 1964 the Lichfield and South Staffordshire Archaeological and
Historical Societies published in its annual volume of *Transactions*[5] a
long paper by George R. Morton which aimed at reconstructing, 'by
material remains and documentary evidence' the Paget Ironworks,
which had been based on blast-furnaces at Teddesley and on the Rising
Brook, near Hednesford and which operated from 1561 until the mid-
eighteenth century.

The iron industry in Britain was being transformed by the introduction of the blast furnace at the time when the Paget Ironworks was
established. Mr Morton begins his paper with a brief and lucid
explanation of what the change involved, a wise and kindly move, since
he was writing in this instance for readers whose main interest was in
archaeology, not technology.

Previously, malleable bar was made direct from the iron
ore in a two stage process, and since production rates were
low – in the order of two cwt. of finished bar per day per
furnace – and the yield only about $12\frac{1}{2}\%$ from ore to bar,
requirements in terms of water-power were also low.

The new pattern comprised a blast furnace, producing

[5] Vol. XXIV, 1964–5, pp. 20–38. Mr Morton, now unfortunately dead, was at that time
Principal Lecturer in Metallurgy at Wolverhampton College of Technology.

Paget Ironworks:
reconstruction of works in
progress in the Finery,
Forge and Chafery.

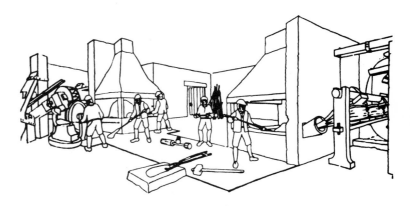

A. Water Wheel
B. Bellows, breach end entering tuyere
C. Cam on wheel axle
D. Beam of return mechanism for bellows
E. The finery hearth
F. The finer working the heat
G. A loupe with tongs fitted
H. Half-blooms awaiting reheating for drawing into bar
I. The chafery fire, (note beehive shape)
J. The beehive 'muffle'
K. Heated ancony end ready for the hammer
L. The hammer-man at work

high carbon pig iron, the blast for which was provided by
two pairs of leathern bellows driven by a single
water-wheel, followed by decarburizing the brittle pig
iron in a finery hearth, reheating in the chafery fire,
hammering to bar, and possibly slitting in the form of rod.
Each of these later processes, i.e. finery, chafery and
hammering, required individual water-wheels, and so the
water requirements were very much greater than for the
blast furnace alone. In consequence the industry adopted a
non-integrated pattern in which the blast furnace became
established in regions of relatively low water supply, whilst
the forges usually migrated further down stream where a
much greater water supply could be obtained.

Paget was constructed and operated on this new basis. Two grades of
pig-iron were used in the forge, one very malleable, the other, extensively
used for the manufacture of nails. An exact analysis of similar ore from
the same area is included in the article. Plenty of timber for charcoal-
making was also available within a short distance of the furnace –
Cannock Chase was heavily wooded at that time – and the inventory
of the furnace for 1570–1, preserved in the William Salt Library at
Stafford, allows one to estimate how much wood and charcoal the Paget
ironworks would have needed to keep in stock. Morton reckons that, to
supply each furnace, 1.125 acres were stacked with cordwood and that,
converted to charcoal, this would have kept a sixteenth-century blast
furnace supplied for 140 days. It is a great deal of wood, and from figures
like these one can easily understand why the local timber reserves were
exhausted so rapidly and how essential it was to find a way of using coal
as a replacement for charcoal.

For convenience of loading, the charcoal blast furnace was usually
built against the side of a hill. The furnace, square-sectioned, was about
20 feet high. Ore and charcoal were transported across a bridge and put
in at the top and the molten products, pig iron and slag, tapped off at the
bottom. The buildings serving the furnace therefore had to be on two
levels. The ore and charcoal were stored in covered buildings at the
high level, the casting house and the blower house were on the lower
level. The approximate dimensions of all these buildings can be worked
out from the quantities of material given in the inventory. Before carrying out any archaeological work, one could therefore expect the area of
the charcoal store to be about 193 sq. yds., the ore store 94 sq. yds. and
the casting house would have been about 20 feet square.

There was no record or trace of the waterwheel or the bellows, but
details relating to the Royal Ironworks in the Forest of Dean, which
were comparable to Cannock, suggest a wheel of 22 feet in diameter and

a bellows 18 to 20 feet long. The temperature inside the furnace would have required some kind of refractory lining and excavation of a slag heap confirmed the belief that sandstone blocks were used for this purpose.

By studying the dates on which payments were made to different categories of workmen, George Morton was able to reconstruct exactly what went on at the Furnace during each month of 1576–8. During the period 15 February to 23 March 1576, for instance, 'the furnace was allowed to cool, the hearth and side-walls of the bosh removed by the filler, the necessary repairs made to the stack and the hearth and side-walls completely re-built. During this period the founder was responsible for the supervision of the reline and usually set the hearth in person.' One even knows the name of the men who carried out these tasks – John Symons, the founder; Redman, the filler; Gryfflyn, the mason, and so on.

What has been done so far is to construct a model based on two kinds of evidence, the surviving accounts of the ironworks and the knowledge of the buildings, equipment and procedures at other sites for which different or supplementary information is available. The archaeological work served to check, confirm or modify these preliminary conclusions. Once the sites of the furnaces and forge-buildings had been precisely identified, by studying old maps and by following the evidence of place and field names like Furnace Coppice, Cynder Field, Slitting Mill, and Forge Farm, it became possible to discover foundations, slag and other remains. Mr Morton's article is consequently full of such passages as:

Here a large spoil heap of waste charcoal intermixed with slag globules and the rake-out of furnace fires still exists, and the area once occupied by the furnace pool can be traced.

and

The site of Teddesley furnace (SJ 947144) provided somewhat of a problem, since Yates[6] shows no pool in the area. However, a search among the early maps held at the William Salt Library revealed a 'Cynder Field' in the vicinity of Hazel Mill. The site was traced at Bangley Farm near Newtown, on the road from Pothal Pool to Penkridge, and the existence of the furnace appeared to be well known by the farmer and his sons. Here the dam of the furnace pool remains in good order, and although the pool is drained, its extent can still be seen. In an excavation by several members of the Society,[7] the hearth and ground level of part of the furnace were traced, and several useful pieces of the structure found. In particular, mail bricks used in the structure of the stack,

---

6   *Yates' Map of Staffordshire*, 1775.
7   The Lichfield and South Staffordshire Archaeological and Historical Society.

and showing the effects of the working temperature, assisted in developing the reconstruction of that part of the furnace. In addition, an interesting portion of the junction of the sandstone blocks of the bosh and the mail bricks of the stack confirmed the angle of the bosh previously found on the Cannock site.

Three aspects of George Morton's article deserve particular attention. The first is that it appears in the annual publication of a reputable local archaeological society, which is an indication that the work is considered worthy of attention by archaeologists whose main interests are almost certainly not industrial at all. It is felt, in other words, to belong, because of the methods employed, to the general corpus of

Yates' Map of Staffordshire, 1775, showing area containing Paget Ironworks.

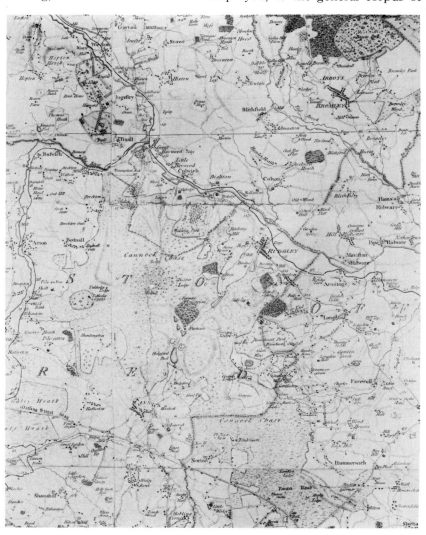

archaeological investigation. In the second place, a man who earns his living by teaching metallurgy is interested in the past as well as the present of his subject and takes pleasure in applying his scientific and technical knowledge to historical problems relating to the iron industry. And, thirdly, that he is as much at home with archives and printed records as he is with the study and analysis of foundry relics. This combination of interests is a very fruitful one, particularly when it also includes a strong measure of natural curiosity. Whether, or in what way, George Morton would consider himself a professional industrial archaeologist is difficult to say.

One begins to understand the real value of this multi-angle approach only when one is in contact with the work of people who take a narrower or more partial view of what industrial or technological history is about. Three examples, all good of their kind, will illustrate this. The Nordic Museum in Stockholm have published a very useful and imaginative volume called, in English, *Memories of where I used to work*.[8] In this a number of old industrial workers recalled conditions in ship-yards, factories, foundries and workshops many years ago. The result was a vivid and convincing picture of what life was like for a manual worker before Sweden attained her present level of prosperity and concern for social welfare. But the workplaces themselves are left vague and unsubstantial. We are given no clue as to whether the editor has visited them, to see what conditions are like today, if the enterprise still exists, if it has grown or shrunk, how the veterans' reminiscences look in perspective. 1953, of course, was before the days of industrial archaeology, a fact of which one has constantly to remind oneself when speaking of books written in the recent past. There is no doubt at all that the entrance of industrial archaeology on to the historical scene has changed the writing of industrial, technical and social history in a number of significant ways. One can feel its presence, even when there is no direct mention of it, and even the most conservative and staid of historians are at least beginning to show signs of guilt if they confine themselves to books and documents and make no reference at all to the physical remains of the past.

If, of course, the factory or whatever the subject of the study may be, has continued in operation until very recently or, even better, if it is still functioning and still concerned with the same type of product, the archaeology is difficult to avoid, although it may not be recognised as such. In these cases, it is possible for the title of a report to be misleading. The Hungarian publication, *Technikatörténeti Szemle* is, as its title suggests, concerned with the history of technology. Its 1964 edition[9] included an article by István Latinák on a scythe-factory at Szentgott-

---

[8] *Verkstadsminnen* edited by Mats Rehnberg, Stockholm, 1953.
[9] Edited by Ottó Vizy, Budapest, 1964.

hard. The subtitle, in English, 'A flourishing enterprise in nineteenth-century Hungary', would probably suggest to most people that the factory began and ended its career in the nineteenth century, whereas in fact it continued until well after the Second World War and much of the old plant is now preserved for its historic interest. What has happened in this case is that the author has decided, perfectly understandably, to put his emphasis on the period when the factory's importance and prosperity were at their peak, the days when a large part of the hay and the corn in Central Europe and the Balkans was still cut with scythes. This has led to a comprehensive account of the technology in use at the time and of the economic basis of the factory's activity. The fact that its operations continued much later and that there is still much to be seen on the site is added half apologetically as an afterthought. This treatment of the archaeology as a not particularly important postscript to a serious economic or technical paper is very characteristic of the 1960s, when scholars were not yet sure of the propriety and safety of paying attention to industrial remains, but were equally frightened of not being considered progressive, practical men.

This gradual edging towards industrial archaeology, feeling one's academic way very gingerly in case the route should prove unreasonably dangerous, was noticeable to a greater or lesser extent in all countries. One sees it especially clearly when one looks back through a series of annual volumes, such as *Daedalus* in Sweden, or *Volund* in Norway, and watches industrial archaeology creeping in a little more year after year, from the mid-Sixties onwards. Gunnar Thuesen's long, authoritative article, 'Iron-founding in Norway up to 1850', published in *Volund* in 1963, has little more than a photograph, with the date 1949, to remind the reader that the famous Fritzøe Verk did not disappear during the nineteenth century.

Eighteenth-century engraving, showing brass hollow-ware being produced by men working at the water-powered hammers.

The hammers, Fig. 5206: workman A is hammering flat sheets into basins C; workman D is producing hollow-ware; workman E is forging sheet into strip, to be used for wire-drawing. Fig. 5203 shows a hammer in its non-working position. By means of the strut K it is raised high enough to prevent it being tripped by the logs.

One could describe this change of attitude in another way, by saying that the thoroughgoing, full-blooded, utterly confident industrial archaeologist starts with what he can see and touch and works outwards and backwards from it, whereas the person who is at heart an economic or technical historian adds in the archaeology to his writings and lectures, rather like illustrations of a book. It may be useful to conclude this section with an examination of a recent German work on the Stolberg brass industry, to see what is regarded as central by the author and what secondary or marginal. If the physical evidence is central, then we probably have a publication which belongs to industrial archaeology. If it is secondary, we are almost certainly confronted with something that deserves a different subject-label.

The title of this handsome[10] large-page brochure is, in English, *Technical Monuments : Monuments of the Stolberg Brass Industry*.[11] It is the second in a series to what are called 'technical monuments'. The term is somewhat misleading, since other titles in the series are *Working-Class Housing Estates* and *The Homes of Industrialists*. Almost two-thirds of the book about Stolberg brass there is composed of pictures,

[10] During the past five years or so, a number of German publications on technical and industrial history have been among the most attractive, not to say sumptuous in the world. A particularly high standard is reached by *Technische Kulturdenkmale*, produced regularly by the Research Group attached to the Open-Air Museum of Technology at Hagen.

[11] *Technische Denkmäler : Denkmäler der Stolberger Messingindustrie* Arbeitsheft 2, 2nd edn, Bonn: Landeskonservator Rheinland, 1974.

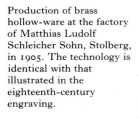

Production of brass hollow-ware at the factory of Matthias Ludolf Schleicher Sohn, Stolberg, in 1905. The technology is identical with that illustrated in the eighteenth-century engraving.

illustrating the buildings and processes of this important Westfalian industry from the late seventeenth to the early twentieth century. The range is excellent, extending from an extraordinary group of grave-stones in Finkenberg cemetery to plans of individual works, and from portraits of notabilities to factory interiors, with the workers busy at their machines. Merely by looking at these pages, one could not fail to realise that brass-founding and brass-fabricating had brought great prosperity to at least some of the local inhabitants during the past 300 years.

To a large extent, the illustrations are allowed to tell the story, and the text which traces the development of the industry from its medieval beginnings is relatively short. It is divided into seven sections – 'The importance of the industry'; 'Reasons for the establishment and growth of the industry'; 'The copper-works'; 'The owners'; 'The workers'; 'Raw materials'; 'Production and manufacturing'. An excellent gazetteer forms an eighth section. Very clearly written and with no waste of words, the information provided is designed, not to provide a detailed history of the brass industry, but to make proper sense of the material remains. There is consequently no doubt that, in this book, the archaeology is central and that it is presented as archaeology, not as architectural history.

In the seventeenth and early eighteenth centuries the Stolberg brass industry was the most important in the world; largely for political reasons, it declined very much during the eighteenth century, but recovered in the second half of the nineteenth, after the adoption of modern mass-production methods. Most of the works were built during the seventeenth century, always to a courtyard pattern, with all the windows facing inwards, in order to make it easier, in those dangerous

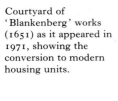

Courtyard of 'Blankenberg' works (1651) as it appeared in 1971, showing the conversion to modern housing units.

times, to defend the buildings against attack. In the early years of the eighteenth century, when the industry was still prosperous, many of the owners' houses were greatly improved and enlarged, with large gardens and orchards to make life more agreeable. Their wealth, at its peak, is illustrated by the fact that in 1720 Gotthard Schardinel, who owned 20 furnaces, had one tutor for each of his sons. A further clue to their social status and self-esteem is provided by their portraits, several of which are reproduced, which show them in a style usually reserved for the nobility. One important reason for their riches and for the rapid growth of the industry was that in Stolberg, unlike in Aachen, there were no guilds and no guild restrictions. Productivity could therefore be pushed much higher and prices could be kept lower and more competitive.

Most of the workers lived not in Stolberg, but in the surrounding district. They lived in what were in effect company barracks during the week and went home to their families as soon as they were paid on Saturdays. The working hours were long, 12 a day in summer and 11 in winter, and the discipline severe. The foreman was given a weekly quota for each hammer. He was fined for every pound made below the quota, while anything over the quota was set against losses due to care-less work and holidays.

The general picture, then is of a tough, driving body of employers and of a labour force which had to work very hard for its money. The book tries to link these features of the industry and the community to the buildings that survive, in order that the archaeology can be brought alive and made more intelligible. What remains is only a small fraction of what once existed. The courtyard factories, where they have not been demolished, have mostly been converted into housing and, without plans and old photographs to serve as a guide, it is not easy to understand what their original function was. Only three of the once numerous furnaces are still to be seen and only one of the old courtyard complexes still operates both as a factory and as the family home of the owner.

What the Landeskonservator's department has achieved in producing this report is a model for any government body, and, for that matter, a model for any industrial archaeologists anywhere. The aim is never lost sight of – to explain the significance of what can still be seen – and one can detect no bias in favour of or against particular social groups or interests and no anxiety to make a political point. This is not to say that every scrap of information which one would like to have is to be found between the covers of the book. Plans of some of the interiors, for instance, would have been very welcome and, in the files in Bonn, they may well exist, ready for anyone who wishes to consult them. One cannot expect every detail discovered during a survey to find its way into a published report.

5

Transport

In all countries, the number of what the Americans call train-buffs and we in Britain call rail-fans or railway enthusiasts is very considerable. These people, no matter what their age, are usually extraordinarily knowledgeable within certain limits. They are able to discourse learnedly and accurately about the minutiae of locomotive types, signalling systems, timetables and rail profiles, but they appear to know little and care less about such matters as wages, legislation, refreshment rooms, unemployment, fares and strikes. Much the same would be true of the following which exists for aeroplanes and cars. The interest, for most people, lies in the movement side of the industry. The vehicles themselves are what matter; the infrastructure – roads, airports, bridges, carparks, garages, town terminals, factories, ticket offices – is considered very dull by comparison. Yet it is, ironically, the dull stuff which, where transport is concerned, provides the archaeologist with most of his raw material. One might almost say the railway archaeologist subsists on the rail-fan's left-overs; where they do have raw material in common, they are almost certain to regard it in quite different ways. To the railway enthusiast and the railway archaeologist a station, for example, is not at all the same thing. One will find highly significant what the other is likely to dismiss as trivial, and the old railway man who is used to talking to enthusiasts may well find the archaeologist's questions very strange.

What we are faced with is a failure, so far, to come to any agreement as to the constituents of railway culture or automobile culture or aeroplane culture. The archaeologist must of necessity be concerned with the culture which this or that site represents. To him, there is no difference, in this respect, between an old filling station, an old car showroom, an old car ferry or an old car manufacturer's catalogue. They all belong to a past stage, or several past stages, of automobile culture and they all have a contribution to make to an understanding of how such a culture has developed. One says 'automobile culture' for convenience, although the term is not, of course, strictly accurate. Purists might prefer to talk of 'automobile sub-culture' or of a 'culture based on the automobile', and we shall not quarrel with them. The point at issue is what is relevant and what is not, and one has to insist, whether a particular breed of fans likes it or not, that to the archaeologist every kind of physical evidence, prestigious or modest in the extreme, which helps the historian to get his bearings and to make well-founded assessments is relevant and important.

This does not mean, of course, that enthusiasm is a bar to being a good archaeologist or a good historian. On the contrary, the more intense one's interest, the more likely one is to have the curiosity and the stamina to follow a clue to the end. No-one has ever written better about railways than Robin Atthill, who has spent most of his life in Somerset, and who mourned the passing of the Somerset and Dorset as if it had been a close relative, which indeed it was. But this is a man who is quite exceptional among railway enthusiasts or, as he himself prefers to be called, railway lovers, someone who combines a poetic feeling for the old days of railways with a passion for exact scholarship. So, in Mr Atthill's book on the Somerset and Dorset,[1] we have exemplary railway archaeology:

The branch line from Edington was seven miles fifteen chains long, but a forty-eight chain extension diverged just north of Bridgwater station to serve the cattle dock, and curved right round in a semi-circle to reach the east bank of the Parrett. Its course can still be traced by sundry concrete posts of LSW or Southern vintage in tell-tale stretches of abandoned fencing – through a timber yard, past the site of Barham's brickyard, to certain rotting timbers in the mud-banks of the river. These are all that survive to mark the site of the Somerset and Dorset wharf, where freight was unloaded from ship until the time of the first world war, under the supervision of the wharf master whose red-brick dwellinghouse still stands a little inshore.

Combined with a delightful talent for communicating the essence, the special flavour, of this strange and always unremunerative railway:

At Evercreech Junction there would be a coal fire burning in the waiting room, and later in the year bowls of primroses on the table. Presently a faint susurration of steam would suggest that the branch-line train was ready to start; at Edington Junction its approach might even be heralded by the ringing of a station bell belonging to the Somerset Central Railway. For the Somerset and Dorset had nothing whatever to do with the diesel era. It was somehow fitting that on the very day that the closure was announced, scenes from the film version of R. L.

[1] *The Somerset and Dorset Railway* David and Charles, 1967.

Stevenson's comedy *The Wrong Box* were being shot on location at Bath Green Park.

One has to accept that railway enthusiasts or aeroplane enthusiasts or canal enthusiasts or car enthusiasts are not quite like their fellow men. What, from an archaeological point of view, one is always hoping for is that some part of this peculiar dedication – the word is hardly too strong – might be diverted away from steam locomotives and vintage Bentleys and towards more prosaic but equally vital items, such as the furnishing, decoration and lighting of railway waiting rooms and the 1930 petrol pump surviving in the haulier's yard. One is longing, in other words, for more people with the temperament and the energy to follow Robin Atthill's example of temporarily deserting the engine sheds, the platforms and the tunnels in order to plot the line the railway once took through the timber yard and past Barham's brickyard to the wharf master's little red-brick house. One wants, in plain terms, a good supply of railway-educated people who are willing to walk about with their eyes and notebooks open over territory where railways once ran and run no longer. And people of this kind are far from easy to find.

As a way of emphasising the broad definition which is required for such terms as 'the railway industry' or 'the automobile industry', the examples discussed below are taken from very different sections of these industries. Some are concerned with the construction of vehicles and rolling stock, some with the routes and the passenger handling facilities and some with what we might call the amenities of the industry. Manufacturing is given priority, in order to begin the list with something as far away from the fans' usual pastures as possible.

The Rogers Locomotive Company, Paterson, New Jersey
From 1973 to 1975, Paterson was the scene of two important research projects, the Historic American Engineering Record's Architectural Survey and Research Project and the Great Falls Development Salvage Archaeology Project. The work was made more urgent by the construction of a storm drain to serve two major highways, New Jersey Route 20 and Interstate Route 80, the line of which ran straight through Paterson Historic District. In October 1974 archaeologists, historians and architects from both research teams presented papers on their work at an Industrial Archaeology Symposium, held in Paterson.[2] Among these reports was one by Brian Morrell, 'The Evolution of the Rogers Locomotive Company, Paterson, N.J.'.

During the nineteenth and early twentieth centuries, Paterson had three companies making locomotives – the Rogers Locomotive and Machine Company, the Grant Locomotive and Machine Company and

---

[2] The papers were published as a double issue of *Northeast Historical Archaeology*, Vol. 4, Nos. 1 and 2, Spring 1975.

the Danforth and Cooke Locomotive Companies. Of these, the Rogers locomotive works was the largest. The Rogers Works produced the first locomotive, the 'Sandusky' in 1837. By 1854 the company was making more than 100 a year and in the 1860s the Civil War brought increased prosperity. During the 1870s, the works was rebuilt. Brian Morrell describes this development in a commendably terse style which presents all the essential facts and tells the reader where to go for more. Here is an example of the method.

The many old buildings had several times been outgrown and added to as technology evolved. Low ceilings held

Extent and location of Historic District, Paterson, New Jersey.

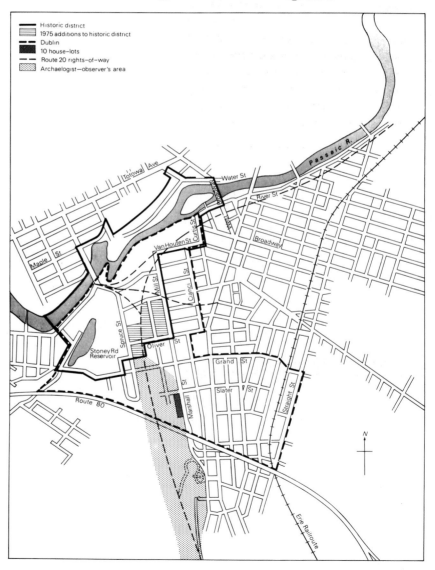

Route of storm-drain in
relation to features of the
Historic Industrial
District.

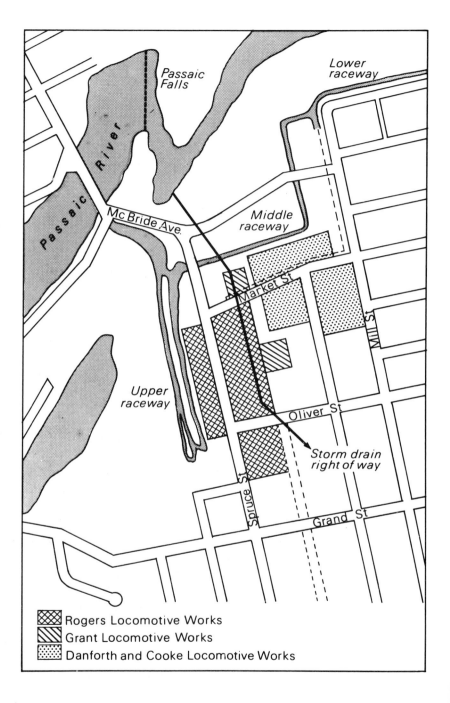

smoke in the rooms and afforded poor lighting (Clayton and Nelson 1882: 431–2). A grand-scale building campaign leveled all the old structures in the Spruce Street – Pine Street block. In 1871, the millwright shop on the corner of Spruce and Market Streets, the foundry, and the iron planing shop were demolished, and before the end of the year the large new erection shop was constructed on their site. This new structure, still standing, was 200 by 56 ft., with two stories and large attic for a machine shop (Clayton and Nelson 1882: 431–2).

After virtual closure during the recession of the mid-1870s – at one time only 20 out of a previous 1,648 employees remained – the works continued to expand for a number of years, with occasional fires and partial rebuilding, but 'during the 1890s, the Rogers Works slowly succumbed to an ever-evolving technology that made the shops and tools once more outdated and unfit to maintain a reasonable competition within the industry'. Between 1900 and 1905 it changed hands twice, but was never profitable, and in 1913 all locomotive building at the works came to an end. Some of the buildings were demolished fairly soon afterwards and by 1926 all the Rogers buildings had been sold off.

With the rise and fall of the Rogers company clear in his mind, the reader may feel at this point inclined to ask, 'So what? Plenty of other nineteenth century American companies failed to keep up with the times and eventually faded away. What is so special about this one that its remains should be preserved and venerated?' The answer is provided by a second paper in the Symposium Report, by Ralph J. Leo,[3] 'one of the major contributors to the design of the locomotive that became the standard for American railroads in the mid-19th century was the Rogers Locomotive and Machine Company'. This is not quite the same as saying that as an innovative engineer Thomas Rogers was on the same level as George Stephenson, but it does certainly mean that he was a great man in his time and that his factory at Paterson was a place of exceptional importance in the history of American technology.

When America began to build railways in the 1830s, the locomotives had to be imported from England, because there was little or no engineering knowledge to draw on and no means of producing and machining heavy castings or of rolling and fabricating large boiler plates. In 1833 the Paterson and Hudson River Railroad, which was then under construction, ordered a locomotive, the 'McNeill', from George Stephenson's workshops. Thomas Rogers, who had no previous experience of locomotives, was given the job of assembling it. It worked to the railway company's complete satisfaction and it served Rogers as

[3] 'An examination of the Technology that evolved from the Rogers Locomotive and Machine Company, Paterson, N.J.'

an apprenticeship to locomotive building. His own first locomotive, the 'Sandusky', contained a number of significant advances on Stephenson's design. Of these, the most important were making the driving wheels of cast iron, with hollow spokes and rim – a remarkable novelty at the time – and the counterbalancing of the driving wheels. Rogers also experimented successfully with a new position for the driving wheels to increase adhesion, and was one of the pioneers of the 4-4-0 coupled wheel design, which proved so well suited to American conditions.

The many other locomotive improvements to come from the Rogers Works included driving-wheel brakes, insulated cylinder jackets, feed-water heaters to increase fuel economy, and a boring-mill, which could bore a 16 by 24 inch cylinder in 8 hours.

With these facts as ammunition, the archaeologists began to negotiate with the State and Federal authorities to persuade them that what remained on the Rogers Works site was of great historic significance.

The general case for preservation is summed up in these words:

At present, above-ground remains of the Rogers Works include the erecting shop, the office, the frame-fitting shop, the storehouse, and the millwright and turning shop. All these buildings are occupied by textile manufacturers, except for the erecting shop. This historic structure, owned by Great Falls Development, Inc., awaits restoration and adaptive re-use suitable to the Historic District.

The Rogers buildings are generally in good repair. They should not be viewed as something obsolete or useful only as monuments to an industrial past. In fact, they are

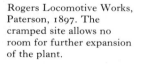

Rogers Locomotive Works, Paterson, 1897. The cramped site allows no room for further expansion of the plant.

stable, useful structures that can be monuments to a great future. If the historical value, beauty, and soundness of these and other surrounding buildings are recognised and utilised, the Historic District and the city can be re-vitalised.

The Historic District contains, of course, other industrial buildings than those formerly belonging to the Rogers Company, textiles being particularly well represented, but it was the former locomotive works that was in special danger from the notorious storm water drain and therefore the spearpoint of conservation activities. Americans are much concerned these days with the concept of 'historicity', a blend of historical and authenticity. An Historic Area must have its historicity proved and certified, and it is good to know that the result of the industrial archaeologists' efforts at Paterson has been 'the definite establishment of the historicity of the Historic District', together with 'the physical expansion of the District'.

The work carried out at Paterson in the early Seventies was urgent and its immediate purpose was obvious. It is interesting to speculate, however, if it would have taken place at all if the storm-water drain had not existed as a spur to action. Industrial archaeologists have to make choices between sites which appear to offer rewarding possibilities, and it is natural to give priority to something which still survives but may very well have been ignored by recent historians. The bibliography included in the 1975 Symposium Report shows that very little has been

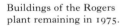
Buildings of the Rogers plant remaining in 1975.

written about Paterson in the present century, but danger has brought it into new and, as it happens, fully deserved prominence. The industrial archaeologists have been forced into a major public relations job on its behalf.

The last Bollman Truss

When the first great wave of railway-building was in progress in Britain, between 1830 and 1860, there was no shortage of stone, bricks, cement and skilled workmen to build the many bridges and viaducts required. America, with a chronic labour shortage, was not blessed in the same way, and its early railways for the most part had to be taken across rivers and ravines, of which there were a great many, on timber struc-

Savage, Maryland: map showing relation to Bollman Truss bridge to railway branch and spur and Savage Manufacturing Co. mill.

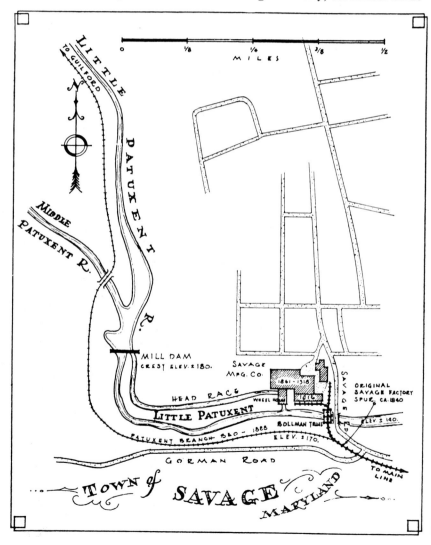

tures. These soon began to fall into disrepair and from about 1850 onwards pre-fabricated wrought-iron spans were increasingly used to replace earlier timber and stone bridges which had either become dangerous or had been washed away by floods. One of the best known and most successful designers of this type of bridge was the Baltimore engineer, Wendel Bollman. Hundreds of Bollman bridges were built, but very few survive. One, at Savage, Maryland, is in all probability the oldest non-stone railway bridge or viaduct in the United States. It stands close to a former cotton mill, which began operating in 1815, before the days of railways, and it was erected, largely for the benefit of the cotton mill, to carry the Savage branch of the Baltimore and Ohio main line from Washington to Baltimore.

Robert M. Vogel, an architect by training and head of the Department of Civil and Mechanical Engineering at the National Museum of History and Technology in Washington,[4] has a special interest in the history of American railways, more particularly in their technical development, and, by perseverance and close observation of the site, he has managed to solve a number of problems connected with the Bollman bridge at Savage[5] and, in the process, to discover a great deal of useful information both about Bollman's activities as an engineer and about the construction of bridges in the mid-nineteenth century.

It appears that the owners of the cotton mill took the first opportunity of having a spur connected to the new branch line, in order to bring their raw materials in and carry their finished goods out. This involved taking the track over the Little Patuxent River, a task which was performed by a wooden trestle bridge for a number of years. Before the Civil War, however, in the early 1850s, the textile company managed to get hold of a Bollman truss, to replace the timber structure. This gave good service until the 1880s, when the mill was extended, necessitating a re-alignment of the track and bridge. Another Bollman truss was bought second-hand and installed in the position where it can still be seen.

The Baltimore and Ohio, Mr Vogel's researches have revealed, was a firm believer in Bollman trusses. By the 1880s, it and its subsidiaries were using more than a hundred of them. Bollman's prestige was partly due to the destruction caused by the Civil War. During the years following the war, there was an urgent need for bridges, both for newly built

[4] Mr Vogel is largely responsible for the remarkable success of industrial archaeology in the United States. The Society for Industrial Archeology, established in 1972, was created on his initiative and, from the beginning, he has edited the Society's *Bulletin*, which combines news and project reports with an effectiveness not so far achieved anywhere else in the world.

[5] His evidence and conclusions are set out in 'Speculations on the history and original appearance of the last Bollman truss', *Industrial Archaeology*, Vol. 7, No. 4, November 1970.

lines and also to replace bridges destroyed or damaged during the fighting. The Bollman design – a nineteenth-century predecessor of the famous Bailey bridge – which could be fabricated, transported and erected quickly and easily, was ideal for the purpose. Some were made by Bollman's own bridge company at Canton, Baltimore, and some by the Baltimore and Ohio itself, at its works at Mount Clare, Baltimore. The Savage bridge, in Mr Vogel's opinion, was made at Mount Clare in 1869 and was first used somewhere between Baltimore and Ohio, the exact site being unknown. In 1887 it was taken down and moved to Savage.

The research leading to these conclusions was complicated and ingenious. Mr Vogel studied photographs of other Bollman bridges built during 1869–70 – the bridges themselves have disappeared long since – and found that on the decorative portal at each end they had six cast-iron strips screwed to the main casting. These were made to a standard pattern and carried these inscriptions in raised letters:

Top left	W. BOLLMAN, PATENTEE
Bottom left	BALTIMORE, MARYLAND
Top centre	BUILT BY B. & O. RR. CO.
Bottom centre	[The year of fabrication]
Top right	PATENTED 1852
Bottom right	RENEWED 1866 [This refers to the patent, not the bridge]

The plates on the Savage bridge have gone – the fixing screws rusted away and were never replaced – but a photograph of the south portal, taken in 1923, shows a portion of the top centre plate, containing the

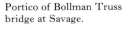
Portico of Bollman Truss bridge at Savage.

letters '. . .LT BY B. & O.' When the bridge itself was examined carefully, it was possible to see outlines of all six plates on both the north
and the south portal. On the evidence of photographs, the bridges built
before 1866 had no inscription plates, but all those dating from then
until 1870 have them. This narrowed the construction date down to a
period of five years. A memorandum was then tracked down in the
Baltimore and Ohio archives, giving the date of manufacture as 1869
and, given the support of the archaeological evidence, there seems no
reason to doubt this.

Mr Vogel wished to complete his excavations by finding out what
colour the bridge had originally been painted, so that, during the
restoration which was planned, this unique Bollman relic could be
presented to the world once again as it had looked a century earlier. No
descriptions of the bridge existed and there was nothing in the archives
about painting. There were, however, half a dozen wet-plate negatives
of various Baltimore and Ohio bridges, taken in the early 1870s. It is not
easy to deduce colours or shades from black and white photographs, but
there appeared to have been a consistent and symbolic scheme, with the
body of the bridge, that is, the compressive elements, painted to look
dark and heavy, and the tensile elements, the diagonals and counter-
stays, light and airy. Comparisons were possible between the bridge and
the shades, as seen in the pictures, of trees and cloth, and, when this
information was combined with knowledge of certain Victorian con-
ventions and with the probability that the B. & O. would have wanted a
striking livery, to show off its bridges to visiting engineers, it seemed
likely that the light colour in the photographs represented a deep ivory
and the dark colour a deep red. Such investigation as was possible by
scraping the ironwork of the bridge confirmed this view.

The Savage bridge is one of industrial archaeology's classic cases.
The bridge was very fortunate in the archaeologist who devoted his
attentions to it, that its history was pieced together by someone who
possessed both remarkable imagination and intuition and an exceptional
knowledge of nineteenth-century American engineering. This combination of qualities also happened to belong to someone who was in a
position of influence. The bridge owes its survival and its preservation
as a monument of great national importance to this kindly act of fate. If
the right man had not happened to be in the right place at the right time,
the last example of one of America's most significant nineteenth-century
engineering achievements would almost certainly have gone for scrap.

The Barentin viaduct, Le Havre to Paris railway
The first great railway in France, from Le Havre to Paris, was built by a
British engineer, British contractors, largely British labour and, to a
great extent, British finance. The French had no experience in such

matters and the British, as the world pioneers of railways, had a great deal. The principal contractor was Thomas Brassey, whose name had been a legend in England for his powers of organisation and his reliability. Work on the first section of the line, from Paris to Rouen, began in 1841 and the contract had to be completed in two years. Brassey shipped 5,000 experienced men over to France and, while the work was in progress, lived in Rouen with his French-speaking wife, whose services as an interpreter were invaluable.

The British navvies,[6] supplemented by a mixed assortment of Germans, Belgians, Italians, Dutchmen, Spaniards, and French, were as famous as Brassey himself. They ate enormously, drank heavily, and performed prodigies. The French came to watch them, for the sheer pleasure of seeing them work. 'Often,' said the engineer, Joseph Locke, 'have I heard the exclamation of French loungers around a group of navvies – "Mon Dieu, ces Anglais, comme ils travaillent".'

[6] For a full account of these formidable men and their achievements, see Terry Coleman, *The Railway Navvies* Hutchinson, 1965.

Map showing railway lines built by Thomas Brassey in France.

To begin with, all the specialised materials and equipment had to come from England, but within a short time Brassey set up factories in France for the purpose, using experienced British workers and managers. William Buddicom, the superintendent of Crewe railway works, was persuaded to construct and operate a works at Sotteville to make locomotives and rolling stock for the Paris–Rouen railway. It later supplied, very profitably, what was required for the other lines radiating from Paris.

The line to Rouen was somehow completed on time, despite an appallingly hard second winter, when continuous frost made most work impossible and caused great difficulties for the navvies, who were unable to earn enough to live at the standard to which they were accustomed. The second contract, from Rouen to Le Havre, was much more difficult, involving a great deal of tunnelling and the construction of a major viaduct at Barentin, 12 miles from Rouen. One of the major problems in this connexion was the great quantity of brickwork required. To carry this out, an army of bricklayers was recruited from all over Britain and shipped to France. They did what was required of them, but they were always complaining, and Brassey found them far more troublesome than his navvies ever were.

The line was nearing completion, when the Barentin viaduct collapsed, shortly after it had been finished. It consisted of 27 arches, 100 feet high, with a total length of 600 yards. There had been torrential rain for several days and the arches went down one after the other, until the whole viaduct was in ruins. A number of theories were advanced as to why the catastrophe had occurred – poor quality mortar, over-hasty construction and ballasting the viaduct before the mortar was dry were the most popular suggestions – but the collapse was never satisfactorily

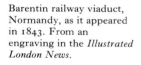

Barentin railway viaduct, Normandy, as it appeared in 1843. From an engraving in the *Illustrated London News*.

THE BARENTIN VIADUCT.

explained. Brassey rebuilt it at his own expense in six months and completed the contract three months ahead of schedule, in exchange for which the grateful railway company refunded him the costs of the rebuilding.

The Barentin viaduct has never been studied or written about specifically from an archaeological point of view, although, of necessity, it has figured prominently in biographies of Brassey and Locke, and in histories of the French railways.[7] There are therefore two relevant questions: first, should this archaeological neglect be remedied and, second, what would an archaeological investigation yield that is not already known? There are several ways in which these questions can be answered. The first is that, as every industrial archaeologist knows, or should know, nothing is quite the same in reality as it is in a book. No two people have quite the same kind of vision or pick out the same details as significant. In the case of a railway or a canal, the only way of appreciating its merits is to travel along it, not once but repeatedly. Anything constructed for transport purposes has to be felt and understood in its entirety, in order to grasp how well it does the job it was designed to do. To inspect individual tunnels or bridges is important, but what really matters is the route as a whole. This is what concerned the people who financed the line in the first place, who contracted to build it, and who travelled over it.

To comprehend Brassey's problems and to be in a position to assess his extraordinary achievements, especially the speed at which he worked, one must therefore travel to Le Havre from Paris by rail, a thing very few people do nowadays, and one must look out of the window all the way, noting the changes of terrain and trying to imagine what constructing the railway was like, for the navvies, the miners who drove the tunnels, the bricklayers and, not least, for the engineers and contractors themselves. Having done that, one is in the correct state of mind to consider a particular feature of the line. One cannot treat the Barentin viaduct in isolation, even though the events connected with it were more spectacular than for any other item in Brassey's contract. And yet, to travel over the viaduct in full knowledge of all the circumstances, is to put oneself in a very privileged position in relation to one's fellow passengers, who have no idea that they are being carried over such a momentous piece of railway archaeology. From the ground, one can increase one's respect for Brassey and his workmen in another way. The masonry appears very sound after more than 130 years of exposure to the weather and to regular battering from the trains crossing the

[7] The best modern account of Brassey's achievements is to be found in Charles Walker, *Thomas Brassey, Railway Builder* Frederick Muller, 1969. The only biography of Joseph Locke was published more than a century ago, J. Devey's *Life of Joseph Locke*, 1862.

valley. Only repointing has been required over the whole period. One important technical detail deserves consideration, however. If Barentin were to be built today, the bricks would certainly be laid in a strong mortar of sand and Portland cement. Brassey used a lime mortar, which was all that was available at the time, and which requires great care in the preparation and the mixing. This great viaduct is consequently a monument to lime mortar, and to the men who prepared it in such huge quantities quite as much as to the resilience of Brassey and Locke, after the shock of seeing their work lying as a heap of rubble on the floor of the valley. The archaeologist with a truly catholic and enquiring mind will, of course, see the little villages strung out along the line, not as mere villages, but as places where Brassey's navvies lodged and drank and fought, and where his bricklayers sulked and moaned, communicating with the natives as best they could.

Ideally, perhaps, one should be introduced to the archaeology and history of a railway by someone who has an intimate knowledge of both, and who will point out on the spot and while one has one's eyes trained on the feature in question details which one would be unlikely to notice for oneself. In Britain, the Newcomen Society, the Association for Industrial Archaeology and many of the local societies achieve this in the course of their excursions and visits. An article on the Easingwold Railway, for instance, published in the *Transactions* of the Newcomen Society,[8] may seem very lacking in archaeology when one reads it, but when one observes that it was 'read on 24 May 1968 at the derelict terminus of the Easingwold Railway during the Summer Meeting based on Harrogate', one's attitude to it immediately changes. It then becomes, not merely history, but history presented to a group of people who are standing, one hopes reverently and attentively, at the place where the history happened, soaking in the archaeology for themselves.

The Rideau Canal, Ontario
Although it is officially known as the Rideau Canal, the name is misleading, since for much of its length it is nothing more than a well-marked channel, along the Rideau River, through the lakes and down the Cataragui River into Lake Ontario. It was built 150 years ago by the Royal Engineers, under the direction of Colonel John By, to counter the threat of attack from the United States by providing an alternative safe route for the transport of troops and military stores from Montreal to Kingston. It formed part of a master plan, which included making the St Lawrence navigable throughout its length and providing a continuous waterway route from Lake Erie to Lake Ontario and from there to the St Lawrence and the sea. The Rideau link, which had involved a good deal of canalisation, was opened to traffic in 1834, by which time

8 Charles E. Lee, 'The Easingwold Railway', Vol. XL, 1967–8, pp. 175–8.

the threat of invasion from the United States had receded. It served little economic purpose – it had been financed and constructed for military reasons – and first canals and then railways on the American side of the frontier brought freight more quickly from the interior to the Atlantic ports. But it is one of the most peaceful and pleasant of the inland waterways of North America and understandably popular with holidaymakers.

Its history has been written by Robert Legget,[9] who has used a wide range of documentary sources, extending from the local histories compiled by Women's Institutes – the Tweedsmuir Books – to Colonel By's letters in the Public Archives of Canada, supplemented by many conversations with people with long personal and family memories of the waterway and by his own wanderings and exploration of its route. His method throughout is to describe what he sees, to imagine what it looked like when it was first built, to discuss the techniques used by the builders and the difficulties they faced, and to put everything into its general political and historical context – an enormous task, carried through by Mr Legget's great affection for the places he is writing about. Here, for instance, is part of his description of the dam and chain of locks at Jones' Falls, the result of personal observation of the site and archival research.

[9] *Rideau Waterway* Toronto, 1955; revised edition, 1972. A more condensed and slightly more sober version of the history of the Rideau is William D. Naftel's *The Rideau Waterway* Society for Industrial Archeology, Occasional Paper No. 3, Washington, 1973.

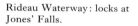
Rideau Waterway: locks at Jones' Falls.

The chain of three locks is in itself an unusually fine piece
of masonry construction, as can best be realised by
standing near a gate on one of the upper locks when boats
are locking through. The site was a natural one, but a good
deal of excavation had to be carried out for the building of
the lock masonry up what now looks like a natural
staircase. Something of what the site was like when the
locks were built can be imagined by looking closely at the
upper (fourth) lock, set in its narrow rock channel.
Considering all the rock work for locks and dam, the
importance of the blacksmith's shop at the time of
construction can well be imagined; it is still standing, an
old building to the south of the upper lock. Unfortunately
the old log blockhouse built here to protect the workers in
the first instance and then the works themselves, from the
long anticipated further attacks from the south, was
removed some years ago.

The immense quantities of stone required for the dam
and locks necessitated an unusually large labour force. A
construction camp was therefore the first major
undertaking, and accommodation for 200 men was
provided. When the work was in full swing, there were
forty masons employed, most of them in the two special
quarries which were opened up in the forests nearby; the
most suitable stone was found about six miles away,
between Elgin and Phillipsville. The great blocks of
carefully hewn stone were hauled by oxen to the edge of
the river, transferred to floating scows, and then towed by
small tugs to the site of the works. Apart from manpower,
there was, of course, for motive power on land only the
few oxen which had been brought into the forests for slow
haulage jobs. We know that the dreaded swamp fever was
especially severe in this construction camp at Jones Falls.
One of the old records tells us that at a critical period
during the summer of 1828 there was no one able to take
even a drink of water to his mates, since everyone in the
camp including the doctors had been attacked. Many men
died and were buried in a small graveyard set aside near
the great dam.

Mr Legget's book was published in 1955, in pre-industrial archaeology
days, when people were industrial archaeologists without knowing it,
and he never mentions the term once in the 222 pages of his book. But
his approach is as valid and useful now as it was 20 years ago, and it is
difficult to see how the book could have been any different if it had been

written today. In the Fifties it was still possible to say that 'remarkably little has been written about the Rideau Canal'. Robert Legget was able to enjoy all the satisfactions of the pioneer, at a time when it was not fashionable for serious historians and archaeologists to take this kind of subject in hand. He has the talent, not possessed by all archaeologists, of bringing the past alive, while keeping the story firmly anchored in what survives and can still be seen and pondered over. He is always on the watch for references to men who came from Ireland to make a better life for themselves, died of canal fever or blew themselves up, and lie buried in abandoned and overgrown little cemeteries, little girls who fell in locks while they were being constructed and drowned, and lock-keepers who worked sixty hours at a stretch, for a dollar a day. But perhaps the greatest virtue Robert Legget possesses as a writer about canals is his appreciation of the fact that a canal has to be thought of as a single unit. It cannot be understood by concentrating on a flight of locks here and a pumping station there, and one can get the feeling of it during its working days only by travelling along it, by boat or on foot, at the pace of the people who once took the barges from lock to lock. To do

Map showing Rideau Waterway, Ontario, and its links with the Ottawa River and St Lawrence.

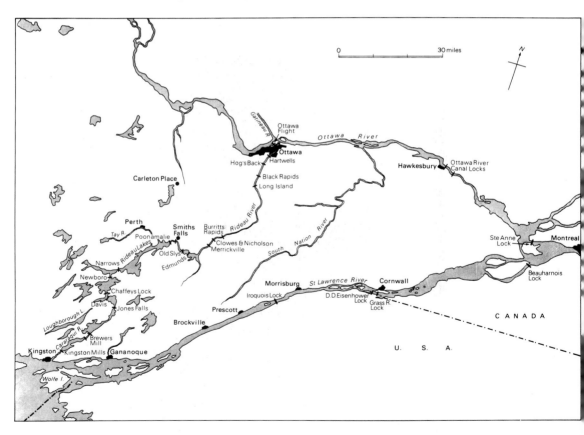

it proper justice, a canal demands a book. An article squeezes the life and point out of it.

The port of Antwerp

How does one deal with the archaeology of anything as complex as a major port?[10] The question was dealt with thoroughly and at length at a colloquium, held in Antwerp in 1974,[11] under the auspices of the University's Centre for Entrepreneurial History (Centrum voor Bedrijfsgeschiedenis). Industrial archaeology is a much 'newer' subject in Belgium than in Britain, and the organisers of the colloquium felt obliged to state, before getting down to business, what they understood by the term 'industrial archaeology'. 'For us,' they said, 'archaeology is an auxiliary science of history, which derives its methods for the greater part from archaeology.' It is essentially an interdisciplinary study; 'the engineer, the architect, the geographer, the industrial designer will each bring from his specialised interest a relevant and indispensable body of knowledge without which industrial archaeology cannot grow into a recognised branch of historical science'. It is and must be a basically humane science, aiming at 'establishing and explaining the relations between machines, technology and man'. It provides 'opportunities for understanding the conditions of life in the past and for gaining an insight into human behaviour'.

The colloquium therefore assembled a miscellaneous group of

[10]   The problem is just as difficult for an airport where, like Heathrow in London, or Kennedy, New York, the facilities have been added to and modified, bit by bit over a long period of time.

[11]   The proceedings were published as *Colloquium industriële archeologie van de Antwerpse haven*, as a special supplement, April 1975, to the *Tijdschrift der Stad Antwerpen*.

Map showing location of warehouses in Antwerp in 1874.

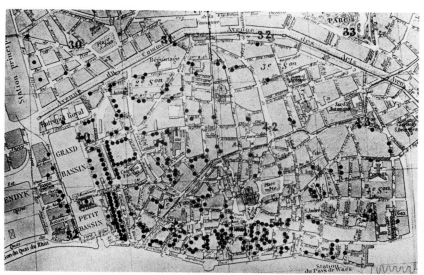

experts to see how this general aim might be realised in the case of the port of Antwerp. It worked out what it called 'a typology of source-material' (typologie van de bronnen). This seemed to fall into three groups:

harbour-construction (locks, docks, bridges, quays, railways, sheds);

technical harbour-equipment (motive power, cranes, special hoisting machinery, dredgers, ships);

Windlass in 1867 warehouse in Korte Brutstraat, Antwerp.

harbour enterprises (ship-building yards, ship-repairs, firms of ship-owners).

Each of these types of material requires three kinds of research:

Techniques – evolution, innovations, foreign influences.

Economic – place of the port in the national economy, links between economic and technical changes, influence of mechanisation on output and productivity.

Social – organisation and intensity of work, wages, standards of living, housing, urbanisation.

Cutting across and affecting all three types of research are what the colloquium termed 'cultural–historical considerations' (the phrase goes awkwardly into English). By this seems to have been meant political thinking and action, recruitment and training of workers, motivation and discipline, and the part to be played by the State in industrial and commercial affairs. Every investigation, the participants agreed, would be greatly helped by paying proper attention to oral tradition. The documents and the buildings by themselves do not provide all the information required, or with the right emphasis.

To see how this ambitious programme might work out, the colloquium listened to and discussed three specialised papers, one on warehouses, another on the growth of Antwerp as a world port, and the third on the hydraulic harbour equipment. These three papers could be roughly classified as constructional–architectural, economic, and engineering–technical. Taken together and individually, they give a very good idea of what a complete historical–archaeological survey of a large port is going to involve. They also provide a clue as to why such a survey has not yet been attempted anywhere in the world. The warehouse paper[12] may be taken as an example of the method suggested.

In preparing this survey, Mr Alfons Thijs decided for two reasons to take 1874 as his starting point. The Franco–Prussian war had caused an enormous increase in the demand for harbour facilities in Antwerp, which could be met only with the greatest difficulty. A document had accordingly been prepared, setting out exactly what storage capacity was available at the port. This document, dated 1874, shows that the great majority of the warehouses were to be found within the area of the demolished Spanish fortresses, an extremely congested part of the port, which made access by road very difficult. Many of the warehouses were centuries old, yet, when it came to building new ones, the Antwerp merchants, for some inexplicable reason, followed the traditional design. No thought seems to have been given either to convenience, or to the safety of the workers. New warehouses were

---

[12] Alfons Thijs, 'Pakhuizen te Antwerpen in 1874: een balans na honderd jaar'.

built without stairs, so that goods had to be carried, in all weathers, up a ladder placed against the front of the building.

A century later, as Mr Thijs discovered, 13 per cent of the warehouses in use in 1874 were still to be seen. They have been surveyed, measured and recorded, any old machinery and equipment being particularly noted, and they provide a remarkable illustration of the re-thinking which has taken place in this field during a hundred years, and especially during the last fifty. One could fairly say – and this was the theme of the colloquium – that the connexion between the growth of the traffic at the port and the evolution of its harbour equipment gives any archaeological and historical study its necessary cohesion and discipline. Each of the three special studies presented to the colloquium made this abundantly clear, and one awaits the major work which is now under way with very great interest, both for itself and as a model for similar studies elsewhere. An archaeology-based survey of the ports of London, New York or Copenhagen, to take only three obvious examples, would be very rewarding.

Lighthouse at St Paul Island, Nova Scotia

The oddly named Canadian Government department, Indian and Northern Affairs, produces an admirable archaeological series, under the general title, *Canadian Historic Sites : Occasional Papers in Archaeology and History*. One of these papers[13] – it is really a 100-page book – by Edward F. Bush, is devoted to lighthouses. After a general introduction, dealing with the technical development and administration of lighthouses in Canada, there is a region-by-region description of the more important sites, with an account of how and why they came to be established, what changes have occurred since the early days, and what their present condition and appearance is. The list is unfortunately not complete, but in its present form Mr Bush's survey provides a very good idea of the way in which Canada has attempted to solve the problem of providing navigational marks for shipping, not only along the sea-coast but on the equally dangerous Great Lakes as well.

The details of what was done at St Paul Island, a bleak place off the North Cape in the Cabot Strait, will serve to illustrate how Edward Bush has set about his task. In the days of sail, St Paul Island and Scatarie Island, off Cape Breton Island, were the sites most in need of lighthouses. The dangerous currents, fog and sudden squalls made these areas 'a mariners' nightmare'. Writing in 1833, a Nova Scotia lighthouse commissioner spoke of 'the melancholy view of the numerous wrecks with which the shore is strewed'. He went on to say that 'the whole coast is covered with pieces of the wrecks of ships and in some coves there is an accumulation of shipwreck nearly sufficient to build smaller

[13] *The Canadian Lighthouse* Occasional Papers, No. 9, 1975.

ones. The number of graves bore strong testimony also that some guide
or land mark was wanting in the quarter to guide and direct the
approach of strangers to this boisterous shore.'

In 1839, after much discussion and bureaucratic delays, two lighthouses were built on St Paul Island, the proceedings having been
somewhat speeded up by the loss, in 1834, of the immigrant ship
'Sibylle', which went down off St Paul Island with all its 323 passengers.
Since at that time the Island was outside the jurisdiction of any of the

St Paul Island, Nova
Scotia: south-west point,
showing nature of site and
1914 iron-tower
lighthouse.

Atlantic colonies, the Imperial authority took control of the situation, 'as in some degree of National concern'. The cost was shared between the colonies concerned and the Canadian government. The Novia Scotia Commissioners took charge of the construction of 'two good and sufficient lighthouses with bells and guns'. The establishment was also to include a life-saving station of six men 'with boats and full provisions'. There was disagreement on the materials to be used, but eventually the choice fell on wood. Construction was difficult, since there was no harbour and everything had to be unloaded on the beach. It was, not surprisingly, difficult to find men willing to work in such an exposed and unpleasant place.

The lanterns were of iron, with plate glass windows, but by 1889 these had been replaced by 12-foot iron lanterns of a different pattern, which allowed 'new pressure lamps sent to the island two years ago' to be installed, producing a much better light.

The lighthouse at the southern end of St Paul Island, together with the adjoining keeper's house, was destroyed by fire in 1914, to be replaced by the present short cast-iron tower and a petrol vapour light producing 35,000 candlepower. Its companion at the northern end of the island was still standing, in its original wooden form, in the early 1960s, but

Map showing St Paul Island in relation to other lighthouses on Canada's Atlantic coast.

has now been replaced by a concrete tower with an aluminium lantern.

Two important points come immediately to mind after reading Mr Bush's entry for the St Paul lighthouses. The first is that very few, if any of his readers are likely to visit the island to have a look for themselves. Mr Bush is therefore likely to remain, for most people, the sole source of information, and one is left in doubt as to whether he has ever been to St Paul Island himself, although he may well have been. The second point concerns the nature of the archaeology in this case, since neither of the original structures still stands. On this it is easier to give a fairly confident answer. The archaeology is the site, the ghosts surrounding it and the wrecks in the sea around. These sites, one could say, have a three-stage archaeology. Stage One was a piece of rock with nothing on it, in a highly menacing area. Stage Two was the same piece of rock with a wooden tower and a light. Stage Three had either an iron tower or a concrete tower. But these few square yards of rock have been part of the archaeology of lighthouses continuously since 1836, when the decision was taken to build on them. From that time onwards, rocks with or without towers have met the prime requirement of an archaeological site, that it shall tell us more about human culture and experience than we would otherwise know.

6

Textiles, clothing, footwear

Textiles pioneered the Industrial Revolution. The first true factories,[1] that is, establishments which provided workers with the powered machinery which they could not afford to buy for themselves, were set up early in the eighteenth century for spinning silk. They were English, and the starting date is now fairly generally agreed to have been 1702, when Thomas Cotchett opened a three-storeyed water-powered spinning mill in Derby, by the side of the river Derwent. This modest building, only 62 feet long and 28 wide, of which the slender remains are now incorporated into a technical museum, has a good claim to be called the world's first factory and to have begun the process of industrialisation which, for better or worse, has transformed society. Factories took a considerable time to establish themselves, however. Even in England, where conditions were especially favourable, they did not appear in large numbers until after the middle of the eighteenth century, when a series of inventions had made spinning and weaving mechanised operations, instead of handicrafts.

The archaeology of the textile industries is both rich and continuous, extending from the early eighteenth century into our own times. It covers spinning and weaving mills, for silk, woollen and synthetic fibres; all branches of clothing manufacturing; and the housing built by textile firms for their workers. It is in every way international. Artisans, managers, machine-builders and entrepreneurs have moved from country to country, looking for better opportunities and carrying new ideas across national boundaries. Machinery made in Bolton, England, finds its way, second hand, to Hungary and then, still full of useful life, to Tunisia. A family of indigo-dye experts transfer themselves from Saxony to Budapest. A man who has learnt new spinning methods from Samuel Arkwright in Derbyshire, England, takes his knowledge, illegally, to New England. Textile workers from Gloucestershire, England, made desperate by the depression in the woollen industry there, emigrate to South Africa in the 1830s and set up a mill of the Gloucestershire type there.

[1] Andrew Ure's definition, contained in his book, *The Philosophy of Manufacturing* (1835) has stood the test of time. A factory, he said, is a place which provides an opportunity for 'the combined operation of many orders of work-people, adult and young, in tending with assiduous skill a system of productive machines continuously impelled by a central power'. (p. 13)

During the past 25 years, considerable research has been undertaken on both sides of the Atlantic into identifying and studying eighteenth- and early nineteenth-century textile mills and particularly to investigating their methods of construction. The textile manufacturers were pioneers of new building techniques and materials, as they were of new machines and new ways of setting people to work. The major problem which had to be faced by the owners of any multi-storeyed factory was fire. Wooden floors soon became soaked with oil and were therefore highly inflammable and, at a time when fire insurance was still in its infancy, the risk to a manufacturer's investment was sufficient to bankrupt him. Strenuous efforts were therefore made to develop

Ratingen: remains of Europe's oldest mechanised textile mill, 1783.

buildings which were, as far as possible, fireproof, with as little wood in them as possible.

Such buildings were expensive, but they were built to last and one of the most interesting features of eighteenth- and nineteenth-century textile mills is their astonishing stamina. They can, of course, be demolished, and many have suffered this fate, but, of those which have survived, a considerable number have passed from one industry to another after their textile days had come to an end. In some instances one is faced with an industrial palimpsest, in which layer after layer of industrial use has to be stripped off in order to discover the original textile factory underneath.

Redundant textile factories have been a feature of industrial life in all Western countries for many years. Electric motors have made the multi-storeyed factory, built for a concentration of steam power, unnecessary and in many countries – the United States is a good example – textiles have left their traditional areas altogether and moved to areas where living and working conditions are more pleasant and where there are fewer labour problems. It is possible that this is only the first stage, so far as the old industrial countries are concerned, on the way out of textile manufacturing altogether. There are those well qualified to judge who believe that within 30 years, possibly less, most of the world's textile factories will be found in the developing countries. If this turns out to be true, the amount of textile archaeology left behind, in the way of buildings and machinery, will be formidable.

To some extent, the same development has been taking place in the clothing and footwear industries. A great deal of ready-to-wear clothing and of shoes and sandals is now exported from such places as Taiwan, Hong Kong and Cyprus to the high-wage Western countries and it is impossible to say at the moment how far this process is likely to go. If it continues on an increasing scale, there will be a considerable rise in the quantity of shoe and clothing archaeology in Britain, Germany, the United States and all the other countries which apparently can no longer afford to manufacture these essential commodities for themselves.

An industry does not, of course, live by its buildings alone and one of the most difficult tasks facing the archaeologist who has no more than a shell of a former textile factory to work from is to recreate, at least for his own satisfaction and education, the atmosphere and, above all, the noise of the mill in its working days. Most types and periods of textile machinery are represented in museum collections somewhere and there is no difficulty in discovering how these machines worked. But a machine in a museum is not at all the same as a machine in a factory. Somehow one needs to discover, for example, how congested the mill was in its operational days; how much working and walking space there was round each machine; how careful the weaver or spinner had to be to avoid becoming entangled in a complex of machinery, pulleys and belt-drives which constituted his day-to-day working environment; what the noise level was like; how the mill was heated, if at all; how it was ventilated, and what the temperature of the workrooms could be reckoned to have been in, say, mid-July and mid-January. One is also likely to do better archaeological work if one knows something about the make-up of the labour force, i.e. about the relative number of men, women and children, and if one has some basic facts about the accident, sickness and mortality rates among the workers. If one does not at least try to get this information, one is a mere architectural or technical historian, not an industrial archaeologist.

The early American textile mills

One of America's leading industrial archaeologists, Dr Theodore Sande, has recently been making a comparative study[2] of one important group of mills, in Rhode Island. Concentrating on the period from 1790 until the Civil War, he has asked himself, 'What technological, economic and social forces do these buildings express, bearing in mind that we are not dealing with the work of professional architects or gifted amateurs pre-occupied with or guided by fundamentally stylistic and formalistic concerns, but with pragmatically-motivated millwrights and business-minded entrepreneurs, seeking practical answers to crucial technical and economic questions'.

In 1793, Almy, Brown and Slater built a spinning mill at Pawtucket Falls, on the Blackstone River. It was 47 feet long, 29 feet wide and 2 storeys high and it was the first successful textile factory in North America. Between then and 1860, a large number of textile mills were set up in Rhode Island. Dr Sande has identified 286, divided according to the decade during which they began operating as follows: 1790–1800, 9; 1801–10, 44; 1811–20, 68; 1821–30, 41; 1831–40, 57; 1841–50, 36; 1851–60, 31.

Examining the dimensions of these mills, one finds that, over the period studied, that not only does the plan-size increase, but the ratio of width to length also increases. 'Thus, not only do textile factories become wider and longer, they become progressively narrower, or more attenuated, in proportion as well.' In general, height tends to remain relatively uniform throughout the period. Rhode Island mills were usually three or four storeys. Outside the State, many textile mills built before 1810 were much larger and often built of stone, something that was not seen in Rhode Island before 1807. Does this mean, asks Dr Sande, that the Rhode Islanders were backward compared with their

[2]   The results are published in *Old-Time New England*, the Bulletin of the Society for the Preservation of New England Antiquities, Vol. LXVI, Nos. 1–2, Summer–Fall 1975.

neighbours? He thinks this was not the case at all. They were more cautious, building larger and more solid mills only when the increase in the size of the market justified such a step.

But there was another reason, and one has to be grateful to Dr Sande for discovering it. 'Factory size,' he points out, 'is related to power available.' The early mills were water-powered, because there was no alternative. Before the coming of railways, steam engines could only be used on coastal sites, where there was easy access to coal supplies. So 'textile mills, especially those built in the outlying rural portions of the state, away from the large rivers, were limited in size in the early decades by the amount of waterpower they could obtain'. Having generated the power, it had to be transmitted to the machines, and the Rhode Island

The New England cathedral, industrial model: Lippitt Mill (1810), West Warwick, Rhode Island.

textile factories did this in a peculiar way. They used horizontal line shafting, hung from the underside of the ceiling beams. To begin with, the shafting was made of square-sectioned timber, to which the cast-iron pulley wheels locked tightly. The shafting rotated at only 50 r.p.m., because a lot of energy was lost through friction, and for this reason both the belts to the individual machines and the shafting itself was kept as short as possible. Consequently, the Rhode Island mills were restricted in length, compared with the British, and had much lower ceilings.

The continued use of wood, with an eventual mutation to wood-frame and stone, instead of brick as elsewhere, had, in Dr Sande's view, a great deal to do with the type of business organisation to be found in the area. Throughout the first half of the nineteenth century, Rhode Island preferred partnerships, while the rest of New England developed a corporative system for its industries. The second built for a more distant future than the first.

A co-partnership is apt to see itself in terms of the anticipated lifespans of the partners, and to build solidly within these mortal limits, perhaps allowing a slight margin for expansion. A corporation, however, is more likely to see itself extending well beyond the lifetime of the founder, reaching far into the future. Specific long-range changes are not predictable, but the *concept* of change is implicit and the corporation tends to seek the most flexible type of construction to accommodate it. Stone walls are not easily altered, brick walls are. Bricks are modular, repetitive units, and brick walls may be similarly breached, in most instances, for additions.

The New England mills as a whole, unlike the British, did not favour fire-proof structural flooring, using iron beams and brick arches. It was too expensive for them, and there was plenty of good timber available. What was eventually adopted, with the support of the fire insurance companies, was a system of slow-burning timbers, with beams 14 by 12 ins., and under-flooring planks 3 inches thick, with an upper floor an inch thick on top of that.

Given these structural requirements, the building might have had a variety of styles. What in fact developed was something derived, not from the eighteenth-century American house nor from 'pre-industrial utilitarian structures of residential scale, such as grist and fulling mills', but from churches and town halls. There was, believes Dr Sande – and his evidence is very convincing – 'an almost conscious attempt to give the early textile factory a splendid civic presence'. This represented a tension within the manufacturers themselves; they were anxious to live in the past and the present at the same time. The external appearance of the factory satisfied the first need, the new technology inside the second. The owners of these new mills were, to use Emerson's words, finding 'beauty and holiness in new and necessary facts, in the field and roadside, in the shop and mill'. The design of the new manufacturing temples expresses, Dr Sande believes, this attitude of mind.

The industrial cathedral was built in nineteenth century New England. The ecclesiastical analogy is present both in the stylistic transference observed and in the factory's visual dominance over the nineteenth century town as the church had provided the focal point for the eighteenth century village. The factory displaced the church, becoming the place where the American worker celebrated his unique sectarianism, freely choosing to sacrifice himself to mechanised processes in an effort to gain financial independence and improved social status.

Whether this process should be called the secularisation of religion or

The New England cathedral, industrial model: Rodman Mill (1843), Rocky Brook, Rhode Island.

the spiritualisation of industry is a matter for argument. What is certain, however, is that Dr Sande's approach to industrial architecture is a very fruitful one and an excellent example of the need for industrial archaeologists to ask 'Why?' instead of contenting themselves, as they all too often do, with 'What?' and 'Where?'

The Bradshaw Woollen Mill, Bathurst, East Cape

During the summer of 1966, Mr Lyall Engels, an architect in practice at Grahamstown, South Africa, wrote to me about an early nineteenth-century woollen mill at Bathurst.[3] His firm had recently surveyed the

[3] See Kenneth Hudson, 'A Gloucestershire Mill in South Africa', *Industrial Archaeology*, Vol. 4, No. 3, 1967, pp. 226–31.

The New England cathedral, religious model: St John's Cathedral (1810), Providence, Rhode Island.

mill, as a preliminary step in the restoration to be financed by the Simon van der Stel Foundation. The Foundation exists to help with the rehabilitation and preservation of all types of historic monument. Mr Engels enclosed a short article[4] on the history of the mill. This records that in 1820,

> Samuel Bradshaw, a weaver from Gloucestershire, and 34 years of age, landed on the beach below Fort Frederick from the transport, 'Kennersley Castle' on 30th April, as leaders of the Gloucestershire party of British settlers. . . . Among the settlers there were a number of trained weavers, and Samuel Bradshaw examined the possibility of establishing a mill for processing wool. . . . His intention was first to produce blankets.

Mr Engels was anxious to discover more about Samuel Bradshaw and to obtain details of the type of machinery with which Bradshaw was familiar and which he would therefore have installed in his new mill at Bathurst. The intention of the Foundation was to buy or make equipment which would give as accurate an impression as possible of the mill as it was in its working days.

With the assistance of Mr Brian Smith, of the Gloucestershire Records Office, and Dr T. A. Ryder, the Vicar of Cam, it was discovered that Samuel Bradshaw was baptised at Cam in 1784, making him 36, not 34 in 1820. Dr Ryder noted that, as a result of the decline of the local cloth trade between 1820 and 1830, many people emigrated from the area, mostly to America. 'If,' he added, 'Bradshaw was a

4   In *Proceedings* of the Lower Albany Historical Society, No. 2, January 1959.

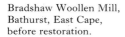

Bradshaw Woollen Mill, Bathurst, East Cape, before restoration.

weaver, it might have been that he worked in one of the mills at Dursley, and not the one in Cam, as that one did not close, whereas those in Dursley did.'

On that matter of the machinery, Kenneth Ponting, the authority on the West of England cloth industry, and himself a cloth manufacturer, pointed out that in 1820 the woollen trade in the West of England was in a state of transition. The yarn-making and the finishing were being done in the factory, the weaving in the homes. 'If,' he said, 'one wishes to put together a typical West of England mill of this period, it is without much doubt a scrubbing[5] and fulling mill at which one should aim.' The chances of being able to buy scrubbing or fulling machinery of this period he put at nil. Replicas would have to be made of models in museums.

At that point one can conveniently return to the mill itself, which is certainly South Africa's oldest item of textile archaeology and in all probability marks the beginning of the woollen industry in South Africa. From research carried out locally, it had become clear that Bradshaw's mill had not conformed to the Gloucestershire pattern indicated by Kenneth Ponting. The work was not subdivided between home and factory, as it would have been in Cam or Dursley; everything happened under one roof. Spinning jennies and looms were imported

[5] Scrubbing was the name given to the process whereby the wool was passed through a carding machine to be opened and mixed.

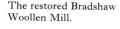

The restored Bradshaw Woollen Mill.

from England, and production started in 1826. The mill met an urgent need. There were plenty of sheep, but an acute shortage of woven material and many settlers were compelled to wear sheepskin clothing. To meet the demand, Bradshaw had to add the manufacture of cloth to that of blankets.

Business was excellent until 1834, when the settlers started leaving Bathurst because of trouble with the Xhosas. The mill was set on fire and badly damaged by a Xhosa raiding party in 1835. It was repaired, a third storey added and the machinery replaced. The market for its products had, however, declined, since many settlers did not return to Bathurst, preferring the attractions of Grahamstown, which had become the business and political centre of the Eastern Cape. Bradshaw's descendants eventually had to close the mill and by the end of the century it had become derelict. It remained in this condition for more than 60 years until it was bought by the Simon van der Stel Foundation and restored as a museum and monument to the 1820 settlers. One is now faced with the strange situation, whereby the only functioning Gloucestershire woollen mill of the period is in rural South Africa.

The first two floors of the mill are stone-built, the third and later floor being of brick. The roofing is of imported Welsh slates. The drawings made by Mr Lyalls' firm in the Sixties show that it was 25 ft.

Interior of Bradshaw Woollen Mill before restoration.

3 ins. long and 17 ft. 10 ins. wide. It had a basement, two storeys and a loft. The height from ground level to the eaves was 21 feet. Water to drive the wheel was provided by the Bathurst River, a tributary of the Kowil. A weir was built up-stream, and the impounded water led down through a contour furrow to a point at which it could be discharged into the wooden plume and down to the 18 ft. undershot waterwheel. Down-stream, there was a stone trough for scouring the wool. Evidence of all these arrangements is still to be seen.

Bradshaw's mill tells so many stories that it is difficult to select any one line of research as being the most fruitful. The site can be studied as an interesting example of the spread of technology and material culture from one continent to another, of the courage shown by the settlers in adapting themselves to a completely strange and at times very hostile environment, the extent to which the nineteenth-century colonies were dependent on imported equipment and materials from the Mother Country, of the very small scale of a factory which was quite adequate to meet local needs or of the solidity of the building, which has stood up to fire and to three-quarters of a century of neglect without collapsing. Fortunately, its small size and remote location have helped it to survive and to be preserved and presented in a meaningful way. Had it been twice the size, the money to put it back into shape and equip it might very well not have been forthcoming.

Two mills at Laconia, New Hampshire

These two mills, the Belknap-Sulloway Mill (1823) and the nearby Busiel Mill (1873) are both very handsome structures, in the centre of the town. They can serve very well as illustrations of the ingenuity that is often displayed in the United States nowadays in preserving and making use of old mills whose textile manufacturing days are long past. The conservation as such is not the most important part of the story. What matters a great deal more is the fact that, as a result of the joint efforts of industrial archaeologists and architectural historians, it was possible to educate both officialdom and the general, tax-paying public to the point at which agreement could be reached that the mills were worth saving and that, restored and cared for, they could be an ornament to the town, rather than a blot on it. The process, as the Americans have discovered to their own and the world's benefit during the past ten years, is cumulative. Once an old industrial building has been rescued and, as the current phrase has it, recycled, in one town, it becomes a little easier to achieve the same kind of success elsewhere. It is because the two mills at Laconia gave rise to a major controversy, which was eventually brought to a solution satisfactory to all parties, that it seems justifiable to discuss in some detail what took place. It was a situation which put industrial archaeology to a very beneficial test. If the mills were as good and as important as the archaeologists said they were, then there ought to be a way of getting the message across to the influential people who had the ultimate power to decide whether they should be saved or destroyed. If these people were not convinced, then it was always possible that the mills had been oversold, and that the public had been faced with something very close to a confidence trick. There is, after all, such a thing as the conspiracy of the professions, against which the public is right to defend itself and there is, alas, no reason to suppose that organised industrial archaeologists are necessarily any more moral or scrupulous than organised doctors or lawyers, when it comes to defending their vested interests. Industrial archaeologists, after all, have made so many manifestly extravagant and occasionally absurd claims on behalf of old buildings that their credibility has, in some quarters, become rather seriously weakened. The Laconia incident, like a number of other recent classic cases, has compelled both the preservers and the demolishers to think out and present their case more clearly, and this can only be in the public interest.

Like all the New England textile towns, Laconia suffered severely from the textile industry's move to the Southern states, already under way in the 1930s and almost complete by the 1950s. An urban renewal scheme, involving extensive replanning, demolition and rebuilding, was

Map showing Laconia in relation to other former mill towns in New Hampshire, and especially to Harrisville, Manchester and Concord.

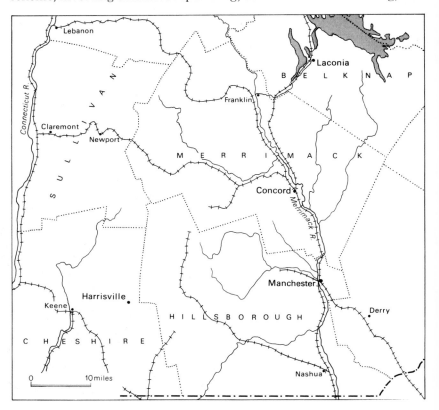

under way by 1961, and by that time it had been agreed that the two brickbuilt mills, which were prominent buildings in the centre of town, should be kept. There is no doubt that their 'civic' appearance, to which Dr Theodore Sande has drawn attention (p. 165 above) was largely responsible for the decision to give them a new lease of life. Whatever their historical merits, Belknap and Busiel would almost certainly not have survived if they had not possessed the central tower, which in the case of Belknap amounted almost to a steeple, and if their general appearance had not reminded local residents and the town authorities of the town halls and court buildings which could be found all over New England. One could say that the pastiche, neo-Colonial style of so many new public buildings caused Americans to think well of these two mills which had been built to serve a strictly utilitarian purpose but which enshrined the architectural conservatism respected by a great many Americans, especially, perhaps, those with money and not very much education. It was the style of 'class' and respectability, with no Left-wing taint about it. In this case, and it was by no means unique, ordinary

Mill Plaza, Laconia, New Hampshire: a successful American rehabilitation and conversion project. The picture shows Belknap Mill (1823).

citizens came to appreciate industrial archaeology through their hearts more than their heads, which is no bad thing.

There were, naturally, a variety of suggestions as to what should be done with the mills. One idea called for Busiel to become the new City Hall and for Belknap to be converted into an educational and cultural centre. A hard core of citizens, however, could see no point in saving old industrial buildings, and in 1970, when the town administration changed, the Council was persuaded that the empty mills, which by now were looking unkempt, were 'unsafe', a word much used in all countries by developers who are anxious to tear down the old and replace it by something new and more profitable. The decision was taken to build a new City Hall and to demolish the mills.[6] At this point local preservationists got together to form the Save the Mills Society. Experts were brought in to give evidence that both mills were of great historic importance and structurally sound, and a publicity campaign and fund-raising appeal got under way. Busiel soon ceased to be a problem, because a local law firm was looking for new accommodation after hearing that their existing premises were to be demolished. They felt that the mill would suit them very well, but they did not need all the space, so they formed a company, One Mill Plaza Inc., to rehabilitate the building and turn it into professional offices. The adaptation was a great success. People were anxious to take space in what soon became regarded as a prestigious location – the ways of fashion are very strange – and the rents are now among the highest in the area. 13,300 sq. ft. were made available for letting, the rehabilitation having cost $28 a square foot, compared with an estimated $35–40 for new construction of the same quality. Industrial archaeology had turned out to be not only a civic and patriotic duty, but good business at the same time.

It should be pointed out that the One Mill Plaza Inc. was formed in the midst of a furious public controversy. The mills' enemies had made two, fortunately unsuccessful, attempts to burn the buildings down, and there had been much official manoeuvring to get rid of them by fair means or foul. At that time the owners were the Laconia Housing and Redevelopment Authority (LHRA), which was not opposed to the destruction of the mills. Many members of the business community, including a number of the most vocal, wanted to see a car park on the site.

The Save the Mills Society, seeing that LHRA was likely to allow this to happen, applied for an injunction to the Belknap County Superior Court to prevent LHRA and the

---

6   The story of how the mills were saved and converted to new uses is well told by Walter C. Kidney in *Working Places : the Adaptive Re-use of Industrial Buildings*, a book sponsored by the Society for Industrial Archaeology and published by Ober Park Associates, Pittsburgh, 1976.

city from destroying any part of either mill. The court responded by getting all three parties together for a compromise, which became that the mills would be granted a reprieve of a few months for a viable re-use and a stipulated sum of money to implement the plans to be produced.[7]

This is the politics of industrial archaeology and it is no less important than the research and reporting aspects of the subject. The Americans, with a strong tradition of local democracy and citizens' movements, have been much more realistic than most other countries about this, understanding that a fondness and respect for old buildings has to be matched with hard cash, and that, if industrial monuments are to survive, ways have to be found of re-integrating them into the main stream of the national life. The physical remains of two major nineteenth century industries, textiles and railways, have presented the preservationist movement with its most severe test and its greatest opportunities. The list of both mills and railway stations which have been successfully and imaginatively converted to other uses during the past ten years is very impressive, and has proved a considerable inspiration and example to the rest of the world, which had tended, understandably, to be defeatist in the matter of finding new uses for old industrial buildings, however much noise and protestations might be made during campaigns.

[7]   Ibid. p. 31.

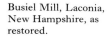

Busiel Mill, Laconia, New Hampshire, as restored.

The Clark shoe-making complex, Street

Clarks have been established in the small Somerset town of Street for over 150 years. They have grown prodigiously during this period, not only in Street, and Street is in every sense of the word a company town. This firm, the largest independent shoe-making concern in Britain, has Quaker origins, although the present family management has an allegiance to Quakerism which might best be described as nominal and traditional. Like most family businesses, however, Clarks are keenly interested in their history and in their place in the community. They have sponsored company histories, paid for a wide range of public buildings in the town, and established a very good museum on the premises. But they have as yet to be touched by any enthusiasm for industrial archaeology, and the purpose of the next few pages is to relate the industrial archaeology of Street – which, whether the firm realises it or not, is exceptionally rich, varied and instructive – to the attempts which Clarks have made, at considerable expense, to present their history to the world. The gap between what has been done and what might be done indicates what can be termed the town's industrial archaeology potential. Such a gap is not, of course, peculiar either to Clarks or to Street. To speak only of the field of clothing and footwear, and of England, the archaeology of Burtons and other leading clothing manufacturers in Leeds has not yet been explored with anything like the thoroughness and imagination it deserves. Burtons is a particularly good example of the nature of the task facing industrial archaeologists in this curiously neglected field.

With the recent contraction of its manufacturing operations, Burtons' enormous Hudson Road Mills, built in the 1920s and 1930s, and still the largest clothing factory in the world, are a monument to the pre-war days in which there was a steady and growing market for made-to-measure suits and when overcoats could still be afforded and worn by all classes. It seems very possible that within the next ten years, possibly less, this great factory complex and the tailoring traditions which went with it will have passed into history. The time for research is obviously now, while the workers who built up the business in its great days are still alive and able to communicate their memories, and when the archaeology is still intact. There is, incidentally, no Burton museum and no Burton company history.

Clarks, however, have a museum, several company histories and, beyond argument, great archaeological potential. They also appear, at the moment, to be in no danger of contracting or closing. The conditions for industrial archaeologists would appear to be perfect.

A plaque on part of the Street factory reads:

This building was erected by Cyrus Clark in 1829 as an extension to his rug-making premises, which consisted of

his house and outbuildings. These in course of time have
given place to larger buildings, and this 1829 block is now
the oldest building surviving in its original external shape.

Since the 1820s, five generations of Clarks have extended and
adapted the buildings, set up additional factories in other towns in the
South-West, extended into shoe machine-building, component-making
and tanning, and developed a completely new range of technology. The
shoemaker in the old sense of a man who made a pair of shoes, has
disappeared, to be replaced by factory workers whose skill lies in making
pieces of shoes and assembling them, accurately and fast. The management, at one time wholly confined to members of the family, but now
more broadly based, is less paternalistic than it was 50 years ago, but the
town as a whole bears an unmistakable imprint of the tight and on the
whole benevolent control exercised over it by a succession of Clarks
over a long period, a period during which the Company owned most of
the land, employed most of the people and kept a close watch on their
private lives and conduct, and prevented other firms from establishing
themselves in the area. All this is represented and expressed in the
archaeology. There is, first, the evidence of the factory itself, solidly
built of stone to begin with and added to in the same general style until
the first phase of expansion came to an end at the beginning of the
present century. These manufacturing areas were used with little
radical change until the outbreak of the Second World War. Three
storeys high, low-ceilinged and with much of the machinery still driven
through shafting and belts, they belonged to the age of shoe-makers. The
post-war single-storey additions – they are really separate factories –
put up since 1945 were designed with modern assembly-line production
in mind. No shoes have been made in the old buildings for many years.
Partitioned and heated to today's standards, they now function more or
less conveniently as the Company's administrative base.

The second type of industrial archaeology to be found in Street
consists of housing, both the numerous residences of the Clark family
and the houses built by Clarks and rented to their workers from the
1880s onwards. There are several streets of them – the main ones are
indicated on the map – and, stone-built and with good gardens, they
have more of a middle-class than a working-class appearance. They are
certainly greatly superior to the council houses which Street has done
its best to absorb during the past 30 years. The members of the Clark
family, or at least those connected with the business, have always lived
in Street. They have bought, built, modernised and extended, and one
generation has handed over to the next. A substantial article or brochure
could be written about the Clark houses alone. It would, one hopes,
make the point that by continuing to live, if not exactly over the shop,
but at any rate within a short distance of their work, today's Clarks are

behaving in a very different manner from most of their fellow owners and managers in other parts of the country. The Clark homes are in Street, where the factory and the offices are; the Burtons soon acquired the habit of commuting from Harrogate to Leeds and many other industrialists make even longer journeys every day.

The third group of sites is made up of the public buildings – the Quaker meeting-house, the Bear Inn opposite the factory gates, bought up by Clarks in order to kill the licence and in this way to remove lunch-time and evening temptation from their thirsty workers, the Crispin Hall, Strode Technical College, the swimming bath and a number of others, symbols of the concern shown by each generation of the family

C. and J. Clark, Street: showcard of 1951, with the town-hall type factory on the left and the Bear Inn, opposite on the right.

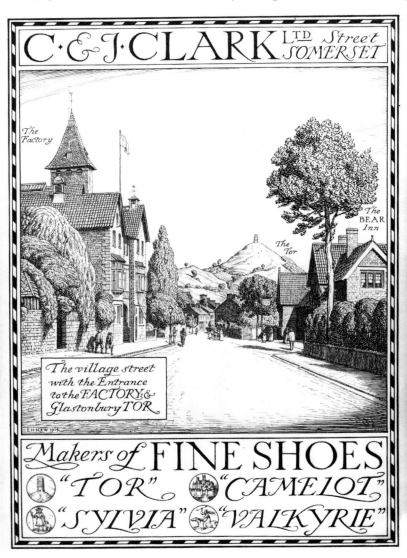

Plan of the shoe-making town of Street, Somerset, as it was in 1950.

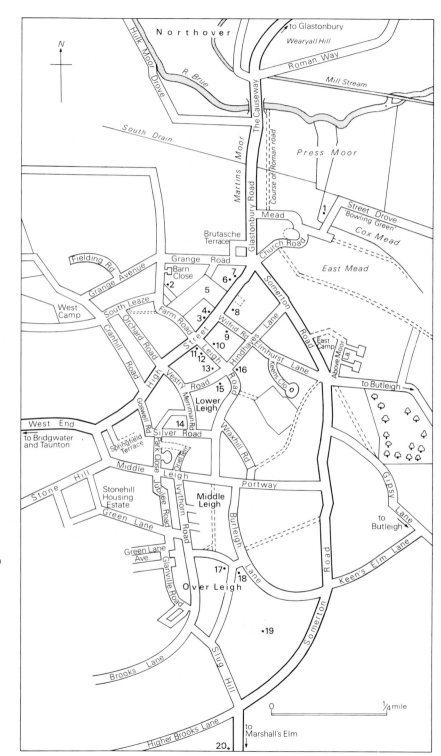

1 Avalon Leather Board Co. Ltd. (1877)
2 Street House (The Grange) on earlier farm site, late sixteenth century
3 The former Temperance Hall (1847)
4 Greenbank, enlarged 1866 and 1880
5 The factory (C. & J. Clark, Ltd.) 1825
6 Friends Meeting House, present building 1850 (Burial ground, 1658)
7 Goss House
8 The Bear Hotel (1894) on site of 'Jimmy Godfrey's' (additions, 1929)
9 Greenbank swimming pool (1937)
10 Street library (1924) designed with garden adjoining by S. Thompson Clothier
11 Strode School (1914), reconstructed and enlarged building opened 1927
12 Technical School (1899)
13 Crispin Hall (1885)
14 Merriman Park (1923)
15 Home Orchard, reconstructed 1932
16 Hindhayes (1807)
17 Overleigh House (1829), enlarged 1904, 1930
18 Whitenights, altered 1900, enlarged 1910
19 Leigh Holt House (1870)
20 Leigh Nook (built by William Reynolds on site of former farm)

to leave the town better than they found it and to provide an environment in which their workers might, in the broadest sense, improve themselves.

All this is very imperfectly represented in the museum, which presents the 150 years of the Company in a highly selective and very safe manner.[8] Opened in 1974, it succeeded a much smaller private museum which had been arranged in the old counting house of the factory and which existed 'to preserve examples of footwear made by the firm in the nineteenth and the twentieth century, although some specimens of footwear of earlier centuries have found their way into the collection from time to time'. When the decision was taken, in 1971, to establish a more ambitious museum, the original intention was that this should be a company facility, to be used by trainees, designers and visiting members of the shoe trade. As planning continued, however, it was seen that this in-house function could be included in a museum which would be attractive to the general public and the museum was finally designed in this form.

The exhibits are divided into four sections: 'Shoes from the Past'; 'Shoemaking in Street' – the historical background presented through documents; 'Shoemaking in Street' – shoes made by Clarks, showcards and other advertising material, the outworkers system; 'Shoemaking Machinery'. The displays end with the year 1950, but, although there is a good deal about the Clark family up to the early 1920s, all information of this kind then ceases abruptly, so that an uninstructed visitor might be excused for thinking that the family had been killed off in an epidemic or had, for some unexplained reason, sold the business and left the district. The official reason for the strange anonymity of the museum during the last 30 years covered by the collection is that no business should appear to exist for the self-glorification of those who own and run it, which is certainly in the Quaker style, but which leaves the visitor feeling puzzled and dissatisfied.

The museum deliberately tries to cut away anything connected with people who are still living, which, in a town largely dependent on the shoe industry, is a curious thing to do. Visitors are not encouraged to take an educational tour of Street after visiting the museum, although this could be done very easily. Maps of the town, similar to the one reproduced here, would be gladly bought by most of the people coming to see the museum, and a walk round the landmarks would add an extra element of reality to the collections in the museum. There are, so far as one can see, three main reasons why this idea has not so far been

---

[8] For a description of the museum and an account of its development, see Elaine Dyer, 'The Street Shoe Museum, Street, Somerset', *Museums Journal*, Vol. 74, No. 1, June 1974. The history of the Company is dealt with by Laurence H. Barber, in *Clarks of Street 1825 to 1950* privately published by Clarks in 1950, and by Kenneth Hudson, in *Towards Precision Shoemaking* David and Charles, 1968.

found acceptable in high places. The first is that it would be wrong to do anything which might lead to visitors looking over garden hedges or peeping into sitting rooms, although, since Street is unlikely ever to become the Costa Brava or the Tower of London, the risk would seem to be a little exaggerated. The second argument is that it is safer in every way that the general public should not know where directors of the Company live, to which one always answers that people determined on robbery, murder and kidnapping will get this information whether they are helped towards it or not, and it seems a trifle unfair, and indeed un-Quakerly to treat everyone as a potential criminal. And the third reason advanced against making the whole of Street a museum is that it would encourage people to think too much of the past, and to regard both the Company and the town as relics of a departed age.

To all this one is entitled to answer that the Company cannot have it both ways. If history and tradition are important, as the existence of the museum and the publication of official histories implies, then the living evidence of history is important. The history of Street has to be considered as a whole. One cannot admit that one aspect of its history is for public consumption and that another is strictly for family and friends. Anyone is entitled to keep unwanted visitors out of his house, but the exterior, as one sees it from the highway, is public property. This is a critical matter, and one which is certain to become increasingly discussed as industrial archaeology, like architectural history and conservation, comes to be thought of more and more in terms of areas and less and less as individual buildings existing in a vacuum. The awful suspicion arises, however, that although 'workers' housing', whatever that may be, has now become a reputable branch of industrial archaeology, owners' and managers' housing is, for various reasons, to be kept well out of the field of study. Once the industrial archaeologist accepts this, he has compromised very seriously both with his professional integrity and his intelligence.

The archaeology of nylon

E. I. du Pont de Nemours patented nylon in 1938 and in the first year of its commercial production American women bought 64 million pairs of stockings made from the new material. On the production side, therefore, the archaeology of nylon goes back only 40 years, yet in that time more than one generation of buildings and machinery has come and gone, legends and myths have accumulated, and techniques have been radically changed. Nylon, one can fairly say, has compressed almost as much change and social effect into its 40 years as wool and cotton into a hundred or more. The time is ripe to assess this and to see what the relevant archaeology has to tell us. Every country which makes nylon on a licence from du Pont will, of course, have its own national history of manufacturing and making up this fibre but, because of the circumstances of the war, the British experience is the longest and, in its early stages especially, the most interesting.

British Nylon Spinners, a joint ICI–Courtauld Company, was set up early in 1940 to operate the du Pont patents. The nylon polymer and the first extrusion machinery used in spinning it had to be imported from the United States and a small group of foremen was sent across the Atlantic from Britain to learn the new techniques. An old weaving shed in Lockhurst Lane, Coventry, was converted to produce Britain's first nylon yarn and for the whole of the war BNS was under contract to the Ministry of Aircraft Production to make ropes, cords and parachute fabrics. The opening of the plant was delayed by bombing damage, but on 23 January 1941 the first nylon yarn in Britain began to come off the machines.

After a second raid on Coventry, it was decided to spread the risk, and in 1942 a second production unit was established, in an old ICI Paints Division factory at Stowmarket, Suffolk. The Coventry and Stowmarket plants both continued operating until 1948. They represent the earliest nylon archaeology in Britain, and indeed in Europe, but both have unfortunately been demolished and are consequently not available as industrial monuments. On its 25th anniversary, however, the Company took the wise and, for an industrial concern, highly unusual step of collecting the reminiscences of people who had worked at Coventry and Stowmarket during the pioneering days.[9] One of them (Mr Les Pownall) had known the Coventry factory long before its nylon days. 'I remember', he said, 'that it all started in an old factory which once produced fire-engines and was used as a place where girls filled shells with explosive in the First World War. I worked in that factory making rayon warps when I was sixteen.' Another (Mr Bernard Moores) said, 'My most lasting memory is of the terrific amount of improvisation necessary, due to lack of proper equipment. An example was the cleaning of dirty spinning parts, blocks, pack parts, spinnerets and so on in buckets of nitric acid, boiled on a hotplate – much to the detriment of the room and the equipment there.'

[9] A selection of these memories were published in *Twenty-five years of British Nylon, 1940–1965*, issued by the Company in 1965.

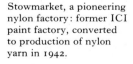

Stowmarket, a pioneering nylon factory: former ICI paint factory, converted to production of nylon yarn in 1942.

Everything was experimental, everything was
improvised. The original winding machine at Stowmarket
was a really memorable one. It was assembled from the
bits of two old 19th century machines of the sort then used
at Coventry. Its traverse is certainly worth mentioning.
The snag here was the reversal point. I tried the existing
weight at every point along the balance arm, but the shape
of the bobbins of yarn produced still varied from double to
single dumb-bells, from concave to convex. The cam
simply shunned contact at reversal point. I looked round
for some means of adding more weight to the arm and I
found an old bucket. One brick inside improved things,
but it was not quite right. A second brick – nearly perfect.
Then another half-brick – just right. Perfect reversal of the
traverse. The rest was easy and winding began.
Throughout the war the winding machine depended on
that dirty old bucket, covered in mortar, with two and a
half bricks inside (Mr Archie Jones).

This is the history of technology as it was experienced by the men
personally concerned. It is not the kind of history which finds its way
into academic accounts of new techniques and processes, but it is
convincingly real and without it one is bound to have a very distorted,
over-tidy, ridiculously over-scientific view of how progress occurred.
One only has to use a little imagination to realise that things must always

British Nylon Spinners,
Gloucester. Former
Bristol Siddeley aero-
engine factory in process
of conversion to a nylon
spinning plant, 1959.

have been like this. The first attempts to make spinning jennies and power-looms work must have been disastrous, but, at that time, nobody thought it worthwhile to collect such information from the people who had struggled to persuade the new machines to do what they were supposed to do.

The problems were not and never are merely technical. Hundreds of workers had to be taught to produce a material whose properties were completely strange to them on a type of machinery they had never seen before. And once the yarn was available commercially, the textile manufacturers and other customers had to be persuaded to try it. In the case of nylon, quick sales results were essential, once the big new plants at Pontypool, Gloucester and Doncaster were operating. It was no good producing vast quantities of yarn if there were no customers for it. Once nylon was accepted, however, and the market for it seemed secure, it continued expanding until the Seventies. In recent years, however, there has been serious over-capacity in the industry, as country after country has tried to enjoy what appeared to be a never-ending bonanza, and this in turn has produced shut-downs and the creation of a stock of ex-nylon factories,[10] which then automatically become study-material for the industrial archaeologist. Some of these plants, however, have been of archaeological interest even when nylon was prospering. The British Nylon Spinners[11] factory at Gloucester, for instance, had formerly been occupied by Bristol Siddeley Engines Ltd., who had no need of it once the war was over and the need for aeroplanes had faded away. The same company's Doncaster factory was bought in 1953, when British Bemberg Ltd. went into voluntary liquidation because of the fall in demand for the particular type of rayon yarn made by their cuprammonium process. In such cases as these, the factory buildings represent one industry in decline and another on the upswing. Eventually, no doubt, nylon itself will cease to need the factories and some quite different form of technology will utilise the vacant space. 'Has this factory ever been used for anything else?' is always a stimulating question, which can provide valuable clues to industrial history.

But when one industry takes the place of another in a town much more is involved than merely substituting one set of machinery for another. A fundamental difference, from a management and human point of view, between the spinning of natural and synthetic yarn is that the factory producing synthetic fibre has to run continuously, seven days a week, 24 hours a day. Since, in Britain, women are not allowed to work on a night shift and since the three eight-hour shifts are, for social

---

[10] The Pontypool plant, for instance, built in stages between 1946 and 1955, is now only half the size it was at its peak. The rest has been sold off to other industrial firms.

[11] Courtaulds sold their share in BNS in 1964. The Company was then re-christened ICI Fibres.

and psychological reasons, worked in rotation, this means that women cannot be spinners in such a factory, although they were always employed on this kind of work in cotton, silk and woollen mills. Once an area has a plant of the Gloucester or Pontypool type as a major employer, the pattern of domestic life inevitably changes[12] and the adaptation can be painful. Equally, if and when this particular industry goes from the district, habits will have to change once again, if the new occupants of the factory have no need of a night shift. If these phenomena are not studied when they happen, or at least while the people who remember them are still alive, much valuable historical information will be lost for ever.

The buildings themselves change with the times and it is interesting to see how they represent the philosophy of the company and the current industrial thinking which existed at the time they were built or adapted. All the post-war factories of British Nylon Spinners were established during the post-war period of prosperity and hopefulness. There was nothing penny-pinching about them and they have unmistakable style. Nylon, in the Forties and Fifties, was a prestigious new material, and anything connected with it had to present an image of modernity, hygiene and high fashion. So the factories were surrounded with lawns, trees and shrubs on a scale which would hardly be possible nowadays; the reception area and the offices were furnished in the best airport manner, and the dining rooms and canteens could not have been

---

12 As the Personnel Officer at Gloucester once told me, 'Our main problem at Gloucester in the early years was Roger the lodger'.

Aerial view of ICI Fibres plant, Pontypool, 1965. The right-hand section has since been sold off, as world production capacity had outstripped demand.

bettered anywhere. These buildings, in their prime, said quite unmistakably, 'We are not wool or cotton. We are nylon.' The image, like the buildings, has faded a little over the years, but, for those who have the historical perspective which tells them the significant details to notice, the change from the bubbling optimism of 30 years ago to the backs-to-the-wall realism of today is unmistakably reflected in the premises. The archaeology of decline is as important and as rewarding as the archaeology of decay and disappearance.

7

Power

'Power' is understood here to mean anything other than human strength which is used to drive machinery. The source of such power may be a river or a lake, the wind, animals, steam-engines, internal combustion engines or electricity. All these forms of power can be studied either in isolation, as in a museum, or at the site where the power is applied or used. The second, for most people, has more meaning. There is something forlorn and pathetic about a steam-engine or a waterwheel which has no work to do. One feels that it is a good thing when such a piece of technology is preserved, in somewhere like London's Science Museum, but that it would create much more impact if the surviving power-plant were actually in the place where it originally belonged, performing the tasks for which it was designed or, if it no longer runs, presented in a manner which is likely to stimulate the historical imagination.

Communication, whether through objects or through print is an uncertain business. For every person who sees a windmill first and foremost as a piece of machinery for grinding corn, there is another to whom it is mainly a beautiful object in the landscape and another for whom it is a nostalgic reminder of an age when work was organised on a small scale and when each district provided for its own needs. Le Moulin Saint-Pierre, a two-storeyed stone-built tower mill at Fontvieille in Provence is a case in point. It was built in 1815 and it is preserved as a memorial to Alphonse Daudet, who used it as the setting for his *Lettres de Mon Moulin* (1869). One can now view it either as a literary shrine, which is a perfectly proper thing to do, or as a piece of well-restored industrial archaeology, an item of study material for molinologists.

The molinologist – who is a highly specialised kind of industrial archaeologist, concerned solely with windmills and watermills – will make careful drawings of the working parts of the mill and write notes on its condition. In doing this, he will use his own technical language.

The lantern wallower has eight wood rounds, rungs or staves, 0.257 m. long between their two iron-banded massive wood plates. The rounds are much worn at their centres where they bore against the brake-wheel's trundles. The wrought iron quant, of 0.06 m. square section, has, some 0.6 m. below the wallower, the date, 1777, deeply and very clearly incised in it between five small, identical, symmetrically arranged impressions in the iron. They are exactly 0.014 m. in diameter and carry the initials 'IB'. The quant has an enlarged rectangular foot socketing into the top of the very massive two-armed fixed rynd.[1]

[1] *Transactions of the Second International Symposium on Molinology*, Brede, 1969, p. 285.

Danish smockmill.

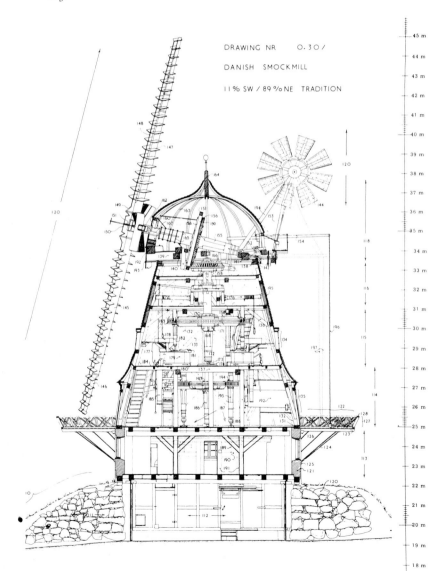

An equally single-minded steam-engine enthusiast might well express himself in the same kind of professional fashion. Posterity could be grateful for such minutely recorded documentation, but to confine oneself to this kind of detail is only one of several possible approaches. One can, for instance, very usefully place Le Moulin Saint-Pierre in its historical context. It was built in 1815, but it represents a type which was becoming obsolete in England a century earlier. English windmills, unlike French, underwent great technical changes during the eighteenth century, mainly in order to increase their produc-

Anders Jespersen, record page.

field survey of d water mills: if this sheet found with plottings, please return to: anders jespersen, 49 skolebakken, virum, denmark.

tivity. The reason was economic and it tells us much about the difference between French and English society at the time. The urban population in Britain was growing fast – it was almost stationary in France – and the new city communities had to buy their corn and flour from a distance and have it transported to them. Many mills therefore ceased to cater only for their local communities. The miller bought corn and sold flour and meal to the towns. In previous centuries he had served only the people in the immediate neighbourhood. He had no need of either a large mill or large storage building, since he dealt only with each farmer's grain as it was brought to him.

The windmills which were being built in England in 1815 were much bigger than the one at Fontvieille, with two, three and occasionally even four or five pairs of stones to grind the corn. These merchant-mills demanded much more capital, employed more men and provided a much more substantial income for their owners, as one can often see from the size and construction of the house by the side of the mill. The mills necessarily had large storage bins and what was inside them represented a considerable investment on the part of the miller, as indeed did the machinery, which was designed by some of the best engineering brains in the country, not accustomed to producing peasant-style work. Daudet's mill, on the other hand, has only one pair of stones and no storage bins at all. It was built to meet the needs of its own district and continued to do so until the outbreak of the First World War, an indication of the very slow progress of urbanisation in France. It was built simply by a miller who had little capital and who knew that his annual income from it was unlikely to be anything but modest. The machinery is made almost entirely of wood, and, as the date on it shows, the quant is a re-used piece. Local materials, stone and wood, were used to ensure a low first cost.

The example of the mill at Fontvieille has been chosen to illustrate four important points which need to be kept constantly in mind in connexion with the archaeology of power:

The technical description of machinery is not a task for amateurs. Only a person with extensive historical knowledge of its design and functioning is in a position to appreciate its significance, to make comparisons, regional, national and international, with other examples of a similar type and to draw attention to innovations and improvements.

To remain at the stage of description is to limit oneself to technical history. An interest in discovering why a particular technical change was made and what its social and economic effects were is just as important as the ability to identify such changes.

The source of power has to be closely and constantly related to the task the power was required to perform and to the way in which this fitted into the life of the community. A large early nineteenth-century corn mill, for instance, required a considerable number of men to operate and service it and to transport the material it required and the material it produced. A big mill was a major source of local employment and it provides valuable clues to the social history of the area within which it was placed.

The death of a piece of machinery is as important as its life. In order to deal adequately with what survives of a watermill or the building which once housed a steam-engine, one has to know when and why it eventually ceased working, what took its place and how easily the district accommodated itself to the change.

The industrial archaeology of power, as the following case studies should make clear, does not begin and end with check-lists and descriptions of mills, steam-engines and early electric power stations. With each change of scale and each replacement of one form of power by another, a new breed of worker is required, one type of employment goes and another takes its place, one feature of the landscape gives way to another. 'This,' says the industrial archaeologist, 'is how this particular piece of archaeology both caused and reflected change.'

Ryhope Pumping Station, near Sunderland

In 1972 the British Broadcasting Corporation made a television film about Ryhope. Behind the opening sequence showing the towering interior of the building, cathedral organ music of the most noble Victorian kind was played. It was entirely appropriate. The visitor is very likely to feel that he is inside some great religious building as he stands in the aisle – the ecclesiastic word comes naturally – and looks up over the engine screen to the gallery and towering roof above him. The atmosphere is that of a temple dedicated to the God of Steam, and any description or study of Ryhope which shows itself insensitive to this has failed. Both the head and the heart are required if the place is to be properly appreciated.

The point is well made in the leaflet prepared for pilgrims and tourists by the Ryhope Engines Trust. Claiming Ryhope, with considerable justice, as 'the finest single industrial monument in the North East', it is, it says, 'a distinctive example of the industrial architecture of mid-Victorian times and the engines show the high standards of mechanical engineering design and construction of that age. Visual appeal had not then been sacrificed entirely to function and there is finely restrained ornamentation on the chimney and ventilator outside and on the parallel linkages, valve chests and valve gears inside the building.'

Before considering the evidence for this, one might usefully make a general point. The 'monument' is the building complete with its engines. If the two were to be separated, the effect would be lost. The empty building would still remain an excellent example of Victorian industrial architecture and the engines, preserved in a museum, would still be superb pieces of engineering. But, apart from one another, they would no longer have the same power to impress. Each needs the other, if Ryhope is to be understood, in the fullest sense of the word. One could make a comparison, perhaps, with the Parthenon and what are now called, somewhat impertinently, the Elgin marbles, the vast sculpted frieze from the Parthenon removed from Athens by Lord Elgin and now installed in the sunless British Museum. Both are remarkable individually, but if they were brought together again, as one hopes they may be before too long, the collective impact would be much greater.

Ryhope Pumping Station is a classic instance of merit being rewarded. There was every reason why it should have been preserved and very few reasons why it should not. It was in nobody's way, the owners, the Sunderland and South Shields Water Company, were anxious to see it saved for posterity, and it was in excellent condition. Both the architectural and the technical historians praised it highly, using phrases like 'the finest pair of compound beam engines in Great Britain', there was a body of enthusiastic volunteers to look after it, and there was every reason to suppose that the public would be delighted to come and see it, especially if the huge beam engines could be seen working under steam from time to time.

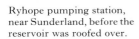

Ryhope pumping station, near Sunderland, before the reservoir was roofed over.

Dr Stafford Linsley, of the University of Newcastle upon Tyne, was instrumental in getting the Trust established and, as the recognised authority on Ryhope, he was the appropriate person to write the kind of study which put the site in its historical context.[2] It is instructive to observe how, as one of Britain's very few academics concerned full-time with industrial archaeology, he set about the task. He fortunately decided to present Ryhope not simply as a fine piece of engineering, but as a part of the general strategy of the Sunderland and South Shields Water Company, hoping and reckoning that what he wrote would be read by many people with very little knowledge of the area and its special problems, and probably not much either of the techniques of water-pumping. He began, so to speak, at square one.

The local demand for water, he pointed out, was increasing rapidly throughout the nineteenth century, both for domestic and industrial requirements. Various sources – rivers, springs, surface reservoirs and wells – were developed in an attempt to meet the demand. In 1788 the South Shields Water Company was formed, by Act of Parliament, for the purpose of 'supplying with Water the Town of South Shields and parts adjacent, and the Shipping resorting to the said Town'. Bishopwearmouth Water Company followed suit in 1824 and Sunderland in 1852. By this time, the sinking of new, deep coal-mines in the area had shown that there were abundant supplies of excellent water within the thick beds of magnesian limestone above the coal measures. To pump and distribute the water more efficiently, the three water companies were amalgamated in 1852 and the new company embarked on a programme of building large steam pumping stations, a policy which continued well into the twentieth century, in combination with the construction of dams and reservoirs.

The necessary land at Ryhope was bought in 1864, and the celebrated water engineer, Thomas Hawksley, who had undertaken a good deal of previous work for the Board, was commissioned to design the pumping station. It was a considerable undertaking. 'The overall requirements,' Dr Linsley tells us, 'were for two wells to be sunk, six boilers and two large compound rotative beam engines to be manufactured and assembled, the engine house, boiler house, smithy and chimney to be erected, two cooling ponds and one large reservoir to be excavated and constructed, main delivery pipes to be laid and suitable dwellings to be built for station personnel.' Work began late in 1865 and the station was working satisfactorily by early 1870, a remarkable achievement, in view of the depth of the wells and the careful planning required to make sure that each interlocking stage of the operation was completed to time. This was particularly necessary in the case of the pumping machinery.

2   S. M. Linsley, *Ryhope Pumping Station : a History and Description* Ryhope Engines Trust, 1973.

The main pumping engines had to be installed and working by the time, early in 1868, that the wells had been sunk to a depth of 230 feet, since beyond that the temporary pumps could not be expected to clear the water rushing into the shaft. The work was so well done that Ryhope gave no major trouble at all during the hundred years of its working life.[3]

The two engines, built by R. and W. Hawthorn of Newcastle have remained practically as they were when first installed. For those with a special interest in such matters, Dr Linsley provides a full ration of technical information. He points out at the same time that one has to think of the engines and the engine-house together. 'The structure of the beam engine house is integral with the engines which it contains. Not only do the foundations of the building have to serve as foundations for most of the engine components, as well as provide support for the well heads, but also the massive rocking beams must be supported at some twenty-two feet above ground level. The engine house and the beam engines must always be considered as an integrated unit.' It is this, more than any other single consideration which makes it essential to

Ryhope: view of interior, showing part of pumping-engines.

[3] The Station closed in July 1967.

preserve beam engines on their original site, if they are to be preserved at all. A badly built engine house was an absurdity. It had to be a carefully designed, solid construction if the engine was to work properly and for a long time, a point which can only be made effectively by providing the opportunity for studying the engine and its house at the same time.

But why, asks Dr Linsley, is the engine house at Ryhope much better than, strictly speaking, it need have been? Why did the architect go beyond what was functionally necessary? This question is often asked in connexion with Victorian industrial structures and the answer is always the same: because the people responsible for the building, the owners, were anxious to be thought well of, both by God and their fellow-citizens. The 'respectability' of industry and of themselves as

Ryhope: photograph taken during construction, showing method of raising the engine beams.

industrialists was very important to them. Water boards, for some reason worth detailed exploration, seemed to have a particularly strong desire to please. 'In many instances', Dr Linsley points out, 'these undertakings made considerable efforts to produce industrial structures which could not offend the most sensitive mid-19th century observer. It is a tribute to engineers like Thomas Hawksley, who was responsible for many such installations all over England, that today we retain an admiration for the "waterworks" style and standard of architecture which produced such structures as those at Ryhope.'

At these pumping stations, planning was total. Houses, reservoirs, cooling ponds, boiler houses, were located and interrelated on the site in such a way as to produce an integrated effect. With its gardens, lawns and trees, Ryhope, especially from the air, suggests a gentleman's mansion in its park, rather than anything as mundane as a water-pumping station. Only one thing seems to have been forgotten, that the trees would grow. In the course of time, falling leaves became such a considerable nuisance that, in 1956 the large reservoir, with its hand-some scalloped stone surround, was roofed in, so that all one now sees is a large lawn.

Dr Linsley has also investigated with much care the working procedures at Ryhope, using as his source material the Company's minute-books and regulations, as well as conversations with men who worked at the station. Shift-working was always necessary. The day shift required an engineman, a fireman, a coal trimmer who doubled up as boiler cleaner, and an engine cleaner. For the night shift there was only an engineman and a fireman. 'Floating' enginemen and firemen, going from station to station, were employed, to allow the regular men to have days off. Normally, each engine was run for a week and rested for a week, in order that cleaning and maintenance could be carried out. Each week, the Company sent its shaftmen down the shaft to inspect the pumps and carry out any maintenance on them that might be needed. They were, and still are, lowered down in a steel tub or 'kibble'. Ryhope has two such kibbles on display.

When the station closed, it passed under the control of a specially formed Trust, which had four aims – to maintain the boilers and engines in working order; to convert the coal store into a small museum of water-pumping and water supply; to rebuild the smithy and workshop; and to open the premises to the public. All these objectives have been achieved very satisfactorily. What should be particularly noted is the level at which Ryhope has been presented to the public. Dr Linsley's *History and Description* illustrates this very well. The average visitor is assumed to be interested, curious, with some basic historical and technical knowledge, and willing to add to his list of Things Worth Knowing. The risk has been deliberately taken of pitching the level too high, rather than too low, in the belief that it is more dangerous to bore visitors than to puzzle them. Broadly speaking, Dr Linsley and his colleagues have taken the view that 'what interests us ought to interest you if we try hard enough to communicate our enthusiasm'. If that makes them, in academic eyes, popularisers rather than scholars, no harm is done, especially since, in order to be a successful populariser, one has to be a good scholar first, partly to be sure that the subject is worth popularising at all, but even more in order to know what the important points are.

Watermills

Industrial archaeology can be regarded, according to who one is and what one's aims happen to be, as a means of adding to or modifying the existing body of knowledge, as a way of educating oneself, or as an agreeable hobby. One cannot say that any one of these is 'better' than another, and in any case they overlap. One can educate oneself in an informal way through one's hobby and there is no contradiction between making a contribution to scholarship and enjoying oneself. All three aims are entirely valid and all are necessary, if the subject is to have the broad political and educational base which is needed for it to thrive. It is useful, therefore, to examine in some detail an attempt made ten years ago in Denmark to provide the general public with reliable, attractive information about watermills. This took the form of a very well-produced 64-page booklet,[4] sponsored and published by one of the major oil companies and written by two leading authorities in this field.

Watermills, the reader is told, are part of the Danish tradition. At one time there were more than 3,000 of them; now there are barely 60 in working order. The purpose of the booklet is quite honestly stated – to persuade as many people as possible, through their new-found interest, to become members of the Danish Friends of Mills Association (Danske Møllers Venner), a pressure group which is closely associated with the Mill Board at the National Museum (Nationalmuseets Møllendvalg) and which pleads the cause of wind and watermills on all useful occasions. Clearly, the more Friends it has and, as a consequence, the more funds it has at its disposal, the more effectively the Mill Board can fulfil its central purpose of saving mills from destruction and of restoring them to use. This carefully thought out and well edited little book explains, in an intelligent fashion, where the surviving mills are, what their history and special technical features are, and what kind of condition they are in. The appeal is partly to local people living in the same part of the country as the mills described in a particular section and partly, no doubt, to visitors and holidaymakers who could well fancy a change from

[4] Bernhard Linder, *Vaerd at køre efter Vandmøller*, with technical advice by Anders Jespersen. Copenhagen: BP Olie-Kompagniet A/S, 1967.

Map showing distribution
of watermills on the island
of Fyn.

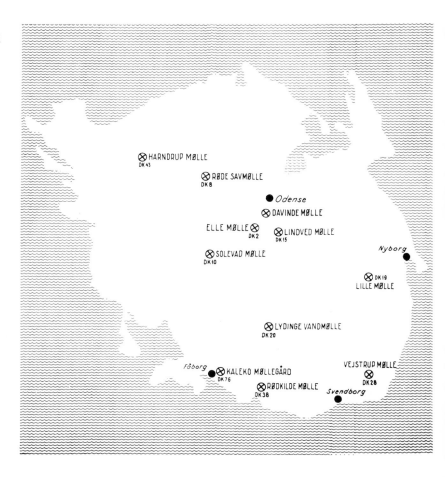

Lille Mølle, Fyn,
Denmark: transmission of
water-power to milling
machinery.

churches, castles and museums.

Three pages of the section devoted to Fyn will illustrate the method. On the first page, reproduced here, is a map showing the position of the eleven surviving watermills on the island. The second and third pages are devoted entirely to a single mill, Lille Mølle. There is a photograph of part of the exterior, with the two waterwheels; a map giving the exact position of the mill; a photograph of the interior, showing how the power is transmitted from the wheel to the machinery; and a diagram making this last point quite clear.

As one moves from page to page, one gets a good idea of the types and sizes of mill and of their main technical features. One is shown pictures and diagrams of the machinery, the different ways of getting water to the wheel, examples of undershot and overshot wheels, construction of the mill buildings, millers' accounts, living accommodation and repairs being carried out to parts of the wooden machinery. Anyone who reads this introduction to mills and mill-craft with reasonable care will finish up by being molinologically literate, able to realise what one is looking at when confronted with a watermill and, one hopes, anxious to learn more. It is an efficient, attractive beginner's course and great skill and much knowledge have gone into its planning and making. Most important of all its virtues is the fact that it never allows the reader to

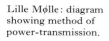

Lille Mølle: diagram showing method of power-transmission.

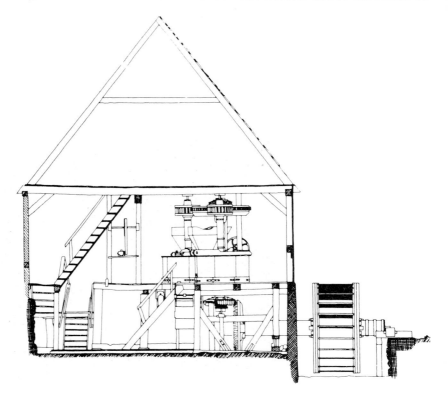

Map showing location of
Lille Mølle.

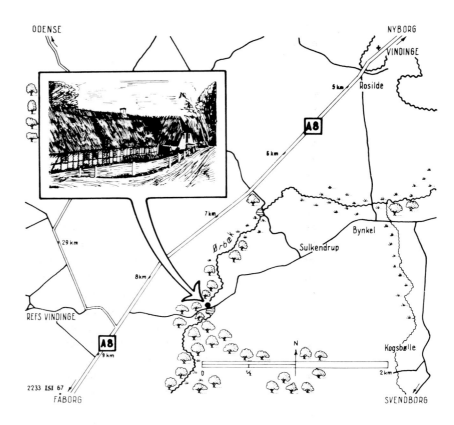

Lille Mølle: exterior of
mill.

forget that he is being introduced, not to beautiful buildings in which he might well feel inclined to live, but to working units, which are sited where they are in order to take advantage of a supply of free power. They are mills seen through the eyes of an engineer, not of a travel agency, and for this reason the book avoids any flavour of sentimentality or prettiness. One is not surprised to learn that it has been very successful and reprinted several times. It is the kind of publication that would be useful elsewhere. Ironworking in Sweden, covered bridges in the United States, ornamental cast-iron work in Czechoslovakia, salt-mining in Germany and Austria, are just a few of the subjects which would lend themselves very well to this fruitful combination of map, technology, environment, history and materials.

There is a further point of some importance. Just as the most ordinary small French children speaking French so fluently are likely to seem unnaturally clever to an English person who knows little of the language, so very basic information about the industrial archaeology of a country other than one's own often appears more profound and even more scholarly than it really is. If one, as a foreigner, knows little or nothing about Denmark or Danish watermills, a relatively elementary book acquires the charm and interest of an exotic, without the author having any intention of making it so. In many cases, the level of information provided about another country is more difficult to assess.

Three approaches to electricity works

'What' – the question is rhetorical but probable – 'have we got in the Rhineland in the way of old, interesting electricity works? Let us find them, describe them, photograph them and discover everything we can about their architectural, technical and economic history. Then let us make a digest of all our information and put it in another volume of our series on Technical Monuments in the Rheinland.' The Landeskonservator Rheinland is not very likely, perhaps, to have made his wishes known in quite these terms, but the results are certainly interesting and, to anyone not familiar with German style and prowess in this field, perhaps a trifle surprising.

Four power stations were considered of sufficient archaeological interest to qualify for the name, 'technical monument' and for inclusion in Working Paper 20.[5] They were the hydraulic installations at Raffelberg (1925) and Heimbrach (1904) and the municipal electricity works at Viersen (1905) and Krefel (1900) and they each qualified in the Report for entries of between 50 and 150 words. The amount of technical information provided is minimal, although there are references to books and articles where such details might conceivably be forthcoming; the

[5]   Axel Föhl *Technische Denkmale im Rheinland : Arbeitsheft 20* Bonn: Landeskonservator Rheinland, 1976.

emphasis is on the appearance of the buildings. The Krefel item is typical:

The generating station in the Hansastrasse in Krefel was built in 1900. Like that in Viersen, it is an excellent example of the distinction which we normally made at that time between the façade, which was intended to be impressive and to tell the world what it was looking at, and the sides and back of the building, which said nothing about its purpose. The crest and inscription on the Hansastrasse façade announced proudly why the building was there and what went on inside.

Façade of municipal electricity works (1905), Viersen, Rheinland, with stone lettering proudly proclaiming the purpose of the building.

Mülheim, Ruhr: Raffelberg hydraulic power-station (1925), using a fall of water produced by damming the Ruhr.

This is certainly true, and the accompanying photographs make the point even better than the text, but the reader in search of facts about the equipment, capacity and service-area of the station will go away hungry. The Landeskonservator's department, however, is primarily concerned with the appearance of the region it controls. The significance of an historic monument, from this point of view, is what it looks like, rather than what it is and does. In fairness to the authorities concerned with this excellent survey, however, it should be observed, with gratitude, that those who compiled it had a catholic taste and keen sense of what was important. The range of buildings listed and described is far wider than anything one would have found in a government publication 50 years earlier, if indeed such a publication had been thought desirable, which is unlikely. It is interesting to see, in the introductory chapter to the report, that much mention is made of the work published by industrial archaeologists in Britain, which is clearly and rightly regarded as the country from which the new thinking sprang. The influence of industrial archaeology, as a creed, on this book is very marked, whether or not one finds the technical details that one yearns for.

The Bristol Industrial Archaeological Society decided to deal very differently with the history of the city's electricity supply. The results of its researches were published in two parts. Part 1[6] covered the technical

6   George Watkins, 'Bristol Electricity Supply', *BIAS Journal*, Vol. 3, 1970, pp. 22–5.

Map of Bristol Municipal Electric Light Company's system in 1896. The line of the mains is indicated by the thick black line.

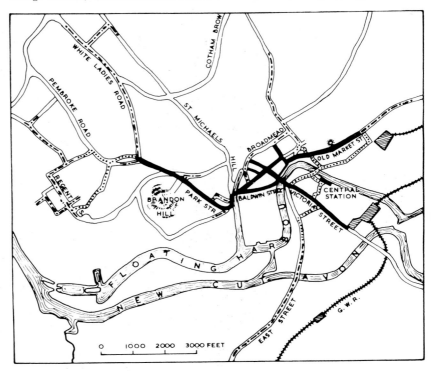

side of the story and Part 2[7] was more concerned with the personalities and the politics. Taken together, these two articles represent the only attempt known to me anywhere in the world to present a complete, objective, up-do-date account of how a local electricity undertaking grew up from its first beginnings and to relate this to what can still be seen on the various sites. It is a model of how the job should be done. One should perhaps add, for the benefit of those who are not familiar with the way a British society of this type operates, that the two people concerned have an intimate personal knowledge of the area they are describing, and that they carried out the work in their spare time.

The author of the first paper, George Watkins, is an international authority on the steam engine, and he became interested in electric power stations in the first instance mainly because of the steam engines used to drive the generators. Mr Watkins has always possessed a remarkable gift for presenting the details of a steam engine in a way that makes perfect sense to the layman[8] and this gift is much in evidence in this particular report. For the Bristol power station, unlike those mentioned above in the Rhineland, we know exactly where the power came from. At Temple Back (1894), for instance, 'the engines were all Willans compound type, with four alternators, two of 88 and two of 210 kw each, together with four small two-crank sets of 50 kw each', and at Avonbank

7   D. G. Tucker 'The Beginnings of Electricity Supply in Bristol', *BIAS Journal*, Vol. 5, 1972, pp. 11–18.

8   See especially his 'Steam Power – an Illustrated Guide', in *Industrial Archaeology*, Vol. 4, No. 2, May 1967, pp. 81–110.

Interior of Temple Back power-station, Bristol, as it was in 1894.

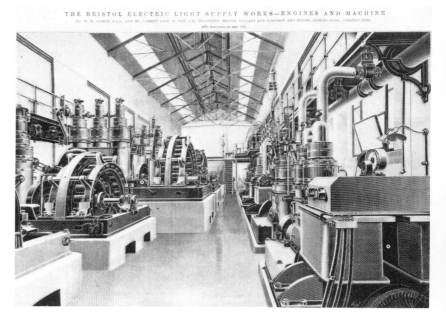

THE BRISTOL ELECTRIC LIGHT SUPPLY WORKS—ENGINES AND MACHINE

(1906) 'following the fine service of the Willans engines at Temple Back, two three-crank triple expansion sets each of 1000 h.p. (745 kw – 2000 volt – 93 cycles – 224 r.p.m.) were installed, together with two small sets for house service'.

As the article points out, Bristol can be regarded as a microcosm. The history of its electricity supply system represents the evolution of the power station, so that by studying one place in detail one can get a good idea of what was happening over the country as a whole. In Bristol, as elsewhere, the City Fathers proceeded with great caution. The city obtained a provisional Lighting Order in 1883, only a year after the passing of the Electric Lighting Act, but, wisely in Mr Watkins' opinion, did nothing about it for a number of years, preferring the experiments and mistakes to be made elsewhere. 'However, by 1890 the success of public supply of electricity was proved and reliable plant available, and Messrs. Preece and Kapp, as engineer and electrical consultants, were instructed to prepare a scheme, and a site at Temple Back, near the point of maximum load, with good access to fuel and water, was chosen.' The scheme was very well designed, 'since each street was served by two power circuits, so that if one failed the street was not left unlighted, whilst it allowed alternate street lights to be switched off after midnight when lower illumination was acceptable.'

Temple Back was extended several times and in 1900 it began to provide a supply for power purposes, as well as lighting. By then, however, it had become evident that this station could not meet the growing demand for electricity in the city, and 'the Avonbank site at St. Philips was chosen, this having the advantages of a colliery on one side, a canal on another and a Great Western branch railway at the back'. By 1925, Avonbank, too, had been outgrown and so had the old chaotic system of voltages and frequencies which varied from town to town. The 1926 Electricity Act laid down that the standard current was to be 3 phase-50 cycles. This made it possible to link up local systems and to produce current more cheaply from large, strategically sited stations. Loans to standardise equipment were available, and Bristol took full advantage of them.

The third Bristol power station, and the last before nationalisation, was at Portishead. It began working in 1928 and had two sets each capable of generating 20,000 kw, compared with Avonbank's largest set of 7,000 kw. The second stage at Portishead, Portishead 'B', belongs to the period of national ownership. Bristol provides exceptional archaeological opportunities for studying the development of the electricity supply industry since all its power stations survive. Temple Back is now used as a store and most of Avonbank has been converted into administrative offices, although it continues as a centre for distributing current.

Professor D. G. Tucker's researches into the supply of electricity in

Bristol, as indicated above, have been concerned mainly with what he himself calls 'the more human context'. Professor Tucker's investigations show that the consultant engineer, W. H. Preece, F.R.S., later Sir William Preece, emerges as a particularly interesting figure. He was Engineer-in-Chief to the Post Office from 1877 to 1897, but he somehow managed to combine this with private practice. This attracted the attention of Parliament. The Postmaster-General was asked 'whether he is aware that Mr. W. H. Preece, the Chief Electrical Engineer at the Post Office, is in the habit of taking private practice in electrical work; and whether, in view of the fact that he is a Civil Servant in receipt of an annual salary, this is in accordance with the Rules of the Civil Service?'[9] The Postmaster-General diplomatically replied that Mr Preece was an outstanding expert in his field and that the country had need of his services. However, 'his case is altogether exceptional and cannot form a precedent'.

The Bristol Corporation Committee papers reveal that Mr Preece gave excellent advice. He told them in the first place that it would be better for them to run the system themselves, rather than let a private undertaking do it. There were three reasons for the Corporation keeping control. They could borrow money more cheaply, they could supply electricity at a lower price and 'the profits derived from private lighting would subsidise the costs of public lighting', so keeping the rates down. He warned his clients that they must expect trouble from the Gas Company, which was unlikely to welcome competition. They should, however, stand firm, because 'my view is that the electric light is the light of the future, but I do not anticipate that it will do the least harm to gas, for the future of gas is the supply of fuel and heat', a remarkably prophetic statement.

Bristol evidently chose its advisers wisely. In addition to Preece, they had Gisbert Kapp, one of the best-known electrical engineers in Europe at the end of the nineteenth century. A Viennese, he set up in practice as a consulting engineer in Britain, after spending two years with Cromptons at Chelmsford. He became the first Professor of Electrical Engineering at Birmingham, and like Preece, served as President of the Society of Electrical Engineers. 'Thus,' comments Professor Tucker, 'the Bristol undertaking had the services of two of the best-known and most successful electrical engineers and it is therefore not surprising that technically the undertaking was very good.'

In 1892 the Corporation appointed its first Resident Electrical Engineer. With the name of H. Faraday Proctor he could hardly have failed to get the job. He was in his twenties and his salary on appointment was £260 a year. He became highly regarded by the Corporation and by 1902 he was receiving £700, an excellent salary for those days. Mr

[9] 20 May 1892. Question by Mr Labouchère.

Proctor did not retire until 1930 and it is a great pity that nobody collected his memories, which spanned almost the whole of the pioneering period, from the first power stations to the coming of the National Grid.

During the early years there were several other power stations in Bristol. Some, like those at Wills' tobacco factory and Fry's chocolate and cocoa factory, were privately run, but one, at Avonmouth Docks, belonged to the Corporation itself and was given permission in 1900 to supply current to the Petroleum Company, which had its premises near the docks. The situation regarding the Bristol Tramway Company was more complicated and led to a lot of bad feeling between the Company and the Corporation. In 1894, when there had been horse-drawn trams in Bristol for 20 years, the Tramway Company was given permission to build an electrified extension from St George to Kingswood. It was a great success, and the Corporation was asked to sanction the electrification of the whole of the system. The Corporation said it would agree only if the necessary power was obtained from its own power station. When this demand was turned down, the Corporation announced its intention of taking over the tramways, if necessary by compulsory purchase. Nothing came of the idea, however, and in 1898 the Tramway Company began the construction of its own central power station, next door to the Corporation's premises at Temple Back.

Trams vanished from Bristol streets before the Second World War, but the original power station in Beaconsfield Road, St George, still exists, as a lorry depot. Many of the iron standards which once supported the overhead wires supplying electricity to the trams have survived, having been thriftily converted into lamp standards.

The joint efforts of Mr Watkins and Professor Tucker have produced a picture of the development of Bristol's electricity supply which was not previously available. It has been compiled by working through a wide range of printed and documentary material, by talking to people

The Central Electric Lighting Station, Temple Back, as it appears today. The imposing building in the background is the Tramway Central Power Station.

who earned their living with the Company, and by a careful study of the power stations and their environment. Reading the two articles as a single unit, one can see how much would have been lost if any one of the elements in them had been missing. The personalities, the arguments in Corporation committees, the quarrels with the Gas Company, the tenders to supply equipment, the threats of legal and Parliamentary action are as relevant and important as the buildings, the steam engines and the coal supplies. This, if one must find a term for it, is multi-dimensional industrial archaeology.

The power-supply at the Tooele copper and lead smelter, Utah

It will have been observed by traditionalists that the present section of the book is concerned quite as much with the age of electricity as with the age of steam or the age of watermills, windmills and horse-wheels. This is partly in order to redress what seems an undesirable balance in industrial archaeology so far – there has been too much about power before the 1880s and too little about power after that date – and partly to emphasise the point which has been touched on several times in previous sections, that the business of the industrial archaeologist is to study power where it was used, not in museum-isolation.

Possibly the most notable instance of this type of study, in which power has been looked at in its immediate industtial context, is the paper by T. Allan Comp[10] arising from the survey carried out by the Historic American Engineering Record at the great Tooele Copper and Lead Smelter near Salt Lake City, Utah during 1971 and 1972.

In 1908 an important court decision in Utah compelled the proprietors of smelters to stop polluting the atmosphere. All but one of the

[10] 'The Tooele Copper and Lead Smelter', *IA : the Journal of the Society for Industrial Archaeology*, Vol. 1, No. 1, Summer 1975, pp. 29–46. Dr Comp is now the Historian for the Historic American Engineering Record. In this paper he is particularly concerned to show how the Company coped with pollution problems.

The Tooele Smelter, Salt Lake City, Utah.

existing smelters thereupon closed and any new smelter had to consider the needs of the community in which it was situated. Tooele, built between 1910 and 1915, was the second copper smelter and the first lead smelter to be constructed after the Utah court ruling. It continued operating until 1972, when rising maintenance costs forced its closure. The HAER survey was made at the eleventh hour, since most of the buildings were demolished during the following year. It is interesting to notice that the survey team consisted of four architectural students, a student metallurgist, two student engineers and one historian, Dr Comp.

Tooele was what was known as a custom smelter, that is, it treated ores from a variety of companies and sites. There were, in fact, two smelters on the same site, one for copper and one for lead. They were built and operated by the International Smelting and Refining Company, a division of the Anaconda Copper Company. Much of the construction material and smelter equipment was bought second-hand from the old smelting companies which had shut down and it was reckoned that 85 per cent of the first cost of the plant was saved in this way. Tooele cannibalised its neighbours. Archaeology was built into it.

The machinery and processing techniques at the plant were noted with great care by the HAER team and Dr Comp gives a summarised description here in his paper. The centre of the whole operation was the power house, meticulously recorded by both plans and text and described briefly by Dr Comp in these terms:

Power requirements for such a diverse operation as the Tooele Smelter called for a major power plant installation. Housed in a handsome brick structure 240 feet long and 52 feet wide, the plant provided AC and DC

Layout inside the Tooele power-station, virtually unchanged since 1915.

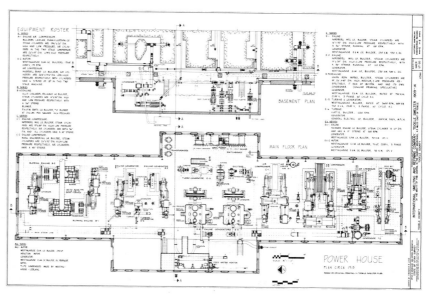

electrical power and air compressed at $2\frac{1}{2}$, 15, and 90
pounds per square inch. Two vertical, triple-expansion,
Union Iron Works marine engines dominated the center
of the building and powered alternating current
generators for lighting and electric motors throughout the
smelter. Two Nordberg-Corliss steam engines and a
Curtis turbine supplied power for the direct current
generators used to power the electric railway haulage
system and the motors in the numerous overhead cranes.
Air compressed to $2\frac{1}{2}$ psi for the lead blast furnace came
from two Roots blowers, powered by Corliss engines from
the Allis-Chalmers Reliance works. Two large steam
engines, one a 350 hp Nordberg, the other a 600 hp Rarig,
supplied 15 pound air to the copper and lead converters.
To supply air at 90 psi to the sampling mill, blacksmith
shop, and for pneumatic tools, the smelter installed a large
Westinghouse electric motor and a Laidlaw-Dunn-Gordon
steam engine. The power house, which additionally
contained a wide variety of smaller pumps, exciters,
motors, and its own shop, remained largely unmodified
throughout its 60-year history. The old marine engines
were torn out in 1924 and one of the Reliance
compressor units blew up in 1970, but the power house,
like the rest of the Tooele Smelter, achieved longevity that
proved its sound engineering.

Any one of the items included in this catalogue could have been
moved to a museum and displayed there. They were, in fact, mostly

Schematic drawing of
Tooele power-station.

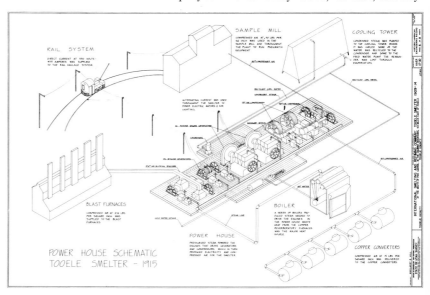

sold off to other concerns, to begin a new life elsewhere. But, so far as Tooele was concerned, they had meaning and purpose only so long as they formed part of the total power complex and had a job to do. The HAER team had the good fortune to be able to see them working and to record them for posterity, in that form. This is the study of power in its context, an industrial archaeologist's dream which is not, unfortunately, always attainable, but, equally unfortunately, often missed or neglected when it is.

8

Chemicals and related industries

Of all branches of industry, that concerned with chemicals and plastics is the least rewarding for the industrial archaeologist. The industrial historian, relying mainly on documentary sources and to some extent on personal reminiscences, has no special difficulty in finding the evidence he requires; but, in every country, the archaeological material is poor in the extreme. The point is made somewhat more tactfully by W. A. Campbell, who teaches chemistry at the University of Newcastle upon Tyne and who is the author of a volume[1] devoted to the chemical industry in a well-known industrial archaeology series.

It must be conceded that the chemical industry does not readily furnish material for the industrial archaeologist. Obsolete chemical plant has never inspired the same sentiments as veteran motor-cars or locomotives, and, where detailed accounts have survived, the end of a once-prosperous works is too often summed up in the final phrase 'sold for scrap'. A works at Jarrow-on-Tyne was sold to a dry dock firm only on condition that the site was previously cleared, and this situation might well be typical. The waste heaps, too, have not been matters for local pride: the communities which engaged in costly litigation over loss of amenity were not likely to spend more money on the conservation of monuments of pollution.

This amounts to saying that the chemical industry has done horrible things to the environment and that those areas which have suffered most are, understandably, anxious to remove the traces of devastation at the first possible opportunity. It is significant that Professor Owen Ashmore, the author of a standard work on the industrial archaeology of north-west England[2] should find so little archaeology worth mentioning, in an area which was making sulphuric acid in the eighteenth century and which was involved in the production of alkali on a very big scale during the whole of the nineteenth century. Widnes, Runcorn and

[1]   *The Chemical Industry* Longman, 1971.
[2]   *The Industrial Archaeology of Lancashire* David and Charles, 1969.

Northwich all had a large investment in chemicals. 'Widnes,' says
Professor Ashmore, 'is the chemical town par excellence, with seven
chemical works built between 1847 and 1855. The town did not really
exist before this date.' But it has all gone. Until 1939, St Helens,
Widnes, Warrington and Runcorn were proverbial for their polluted air
and hideous waste-tips. Forty years later, a visitor to these places might
well wonder what all the fuss had been about. The tips had nearly all
vanished, the poisonous smoke is no longer there, and trees, flowers and
grass grow as vigorously in South Lancashire now as in any other part
of the north-west. The Gazetteer at the end of Professor Ashmore's
book contains no item under the heading 'Chemicals' for Warrington,
none for Widnes, and none for Runcorn. For St Helens, the best that
can be discovered is a single entry:

Alkali industry. Only small traces of this former industry
remain. New Double Lock Alkali Works is the site of
works started by Muspratt and Gamble, 1828. Chemical
waste heaps are in Jackson's Road.

The other major English centre of the chemical industry in Victorian
times, Tyneside, has little more to offer, although at the peak of its
prosperity it gave employment to at least 10,000 people.[3] The industry
had been established here in the seventeenth century, to make alkali for
the local glass manufacturers. It moved on to make sulphuric acid and
soda. There is no shortage of information about the history of these
industries; what is lacking is archaeological evidence. Put more precisely,
we can read about the horrors of a Leblanc soda factory, but we cannot
experience them for ourselves, or visit a works which once used this
process. We are required to content ourselves with such statements as:

A Leblanc soda factory would appear as a collection of long
low buildings to house the furnaces, overlooked by the
huge rectangular pile of the chambers and dominated by
the tall chimney from which clouds of acrid fumes would
issue at intervals of a few hours, and outside the walls,
gradually attaining an eminence of its own, the wasteheap,
an eyesore at all hours, and in wet weather an offence to
the nostrils.[4]

We read about these horrors, but we cannot see or smell them for
ourselves. The fate of Allhusen's Newcastle Chemical Works, which
covered 50 acres early in the present century and was the last of the
Tyneside alkali works to operate,[5] is typical. 'Some of the buildings were

---

[3] On the chemical industry in this area, see W. A. Campbell (ed.) *The Old Tyneside
Chemical Trade* University of Newcastle upon Tyne, 1964.
[4] Ibid. p. 18.
[5] It shut down in 1921.

demolished', we are told, 'and some taken over by small firms requiring sheds or garage space; one building is described in the 1926 inventory by the melancholy phrase "now used as poultry houses". The waste heap alone remained in all its former majesty, but now this is being dug out and sold to farmers for lime.'[6]

The work ranked among the most unpleasant that industry had to

[6] *The Old Tyneside Chemical Trade*, p. 41.

Bleach-packers at a Tyneside works, *c.* 1900. This was one of the most dangerous of all industrial occupations.

offer. This was especially true of bleach packing and lime dressing. Men engaged on these tasks wrapped their faces in a roll of flannel several yards long, leaving only the nostrils uncovered. No other form of protective clothing was available. Minor acid burns were frequent and men fell into the soda vats from time to time and were not uncommonly overcome by fumes.

The Leblanc process in its earliest form was extremely wasteful and only the acute shortage of alkali made it viable. All the sulphur, all the nitre and all the chlorine found its way either into the atmosphere or on to the waste heaps. This situation changed completely during the second half of the nineteenth century. The far more efficient Solvay process, which treated brine with carbon dioxide and ammonia, was developed in Belgium in 1872. It was introduced to Britain under licence in 1873 by Ludwig Mond. He and his partner, John Brunner, overcame the great technical difficulties involved in large-scale production of soda by this process and established the industry at Winnington, on Teesside, to take advantage of the salt deposits in the area. In 1890–1, the United Alkali Co. was formed to take over all the existing firms on Tyneside. All but two – Tennants and Allhusens – were shut down and demolished. United Alkali itself survived until 1926, when it joined Brunner-Mond, the British Dyestuffs Corporation and Nobel Industries to form Imperial Chemical Industries.

Against this background – and the situation in the United States and on the Continent was not dissimilar – one can begin to understand why there is so little physical evidence of the pre-1914 chemical industry. Chemical plants of the nineteenth-century vintage were destroying themselves continuously, with the corrosion of both buildings and equipment. Constant maintenance and replacement was essential. New processes made old works obsolete and industrialists found it more convenient and economical to build the next generation of chemical works, which needed more space, away from the traditional areas. A growing public indignation against the pollution caused by chemical factories compelled their owners to take measures to mitigate the nuisance, although such improvements were slow in coming and did not become really effective until after the Second World War. Broadly speaking, however, it was easier to cure the trouble by building a new factory than by trying to change the system at an old one, which provided an extra incentive to give up old plant. And, lastly, the formation of mammoth concerns in the chemical industry caused the disappearance of most of the old plants.

Where there is any significant archaeology of the chemical industry it is usually a freak, with very special circumstances to explain its survival, or it is to be found in a back-water, rather than in the main stream. In the following pages we shall examine three examples which can be placed in one or other of these two categories. In general, however, it had to be admitted that, however great the value of industrial archaeology may be in other fields, it has little to contribute to building up or correcting an historical model of the development of the chemical industry. One can understand, by visiting the sites of the old works, why they were located in these places and, by talking to former workers in the industry, one can get a better idea of what it was like to be employed in 'the chemicals', but, for the rest, one has to accept the evidence of the written record and leave it at that, and to one's imagination. The buildings have nearly all gone and one can hardly complain if the waste lands caused by a century and a half of totally irresponsible industrial exploitation are rehabilitated. To demand that a token square mile of dereliction should be preserved intact as a memento of the past and as a dreadful warning is an interesting idea, but, alas, not practicable. As soon as the poisonous fumes stop belching from the chimneys and nauseating waste no longer piles up on the tips, Nature takes over and a mellowing process begins. The worst environmental horrors of the Industrial Revolution cannot be preserved for posterity to see and smell, much as one might like to do so.

The St Rollux Chemical Works, Glasgow

The St Rollux works, established in 1799, closed in 1964 and almost immediately demolished, had, for a chemical plant, an exceptionally long career. It was studied by John R. Hume, of the University of Strathclyde, not long before it finally shut down, and his report[7] offers a number of suggestions as to how this kind of survey might be carried

[7] 'The St. Rollux Chemical Works, 1799–1964', *Industrial Archaeology*, Vol. 3, No. 3, 1966.

Site plan of St Rollux chemical works, Glasgow, in 1964.

1 Office block
2 Arch
3 Heat treatment plant
4 Acid tanks
5 Carboy loading bay
6 Peterson sulphuric acid plant
7 Workshop
8 Engine shed
9 Base of lead chamber sulphuric acid plant
10 Tunnel
11 Booking office of Glasgow and Garnkirk Railway

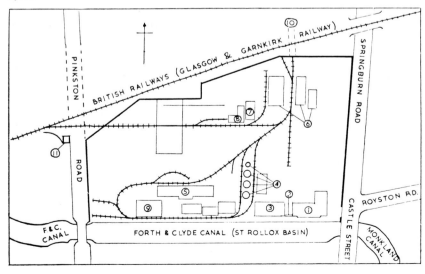

out in the future, more especially in those slower-moving parts of the world where old chemical works have, for one reason and another, contrived to defeat progress and to survive.

The works was founded when Charles Tennant moved from Hurlet, near Paisley, to a new site on the Glasgow branch of the Forth and Clyde Canal. Tennant built the works in order to manufacture bleaching powder, which he had just patented. Bleaching powder, made by passing chlorine over trays of slaked lime, was more convenient to use and transport than the bleaching liquor, made by allowing chlorine gas to run into a slurry of slaked lime, which Tennant had patented earlier. Tennant's new product provided textile manufacturers for the first time with a quick and easy to use bleaching agent. To make it, the factory needed sulphuric acid, salt, limestone and manganese dioxide. To begin with, the sulphuric acid was bought in, some of it from as far away as Halifax, but in 1803 St Rollux started making its own. At about the same time, Tennant began to make soda from the sodium sulphate left as waste during the manufacture of chlorine. The Leblanc process was introduced at St Rollux in 1818, and for the next 50 years soda was the principal product there. The enormous dump of waste from soda-making was still to be seen in the early 1960s. It has now been covered with soil and multi-storey flats built on the site.

After the formation of the United Alkali Company in 1890, the production of soda and bleaching powder came to an end at the St Rollux works and from then until 1926, when United Alkali in its turn was merged into the new Imperial Chemicals combine, little but sulphuric acid was made there, with a labour force of only a hundred men, compared with ten times that number at its peak.

Having completed this brief historical introduction, Mr Hume puts the key question, 'What was the value of this site to the industrial archaeologist?', deliberately using the past tense, since the works had just been demolished and he himself had surveyed it almost as a piece of rescue archaeology. He answered his own question in an interesting way. 'Although the early buildings had almost all disappeared, investigation of old maps showed that the area of the works had varied remarkably little with the passage of time, bounded as it was by two roads, a canal and a railway. This meant that a meaningful consideration could be made of the factors influencing the choice of this site for a new chemical works at the end of the eighteenth century.'

These factors Mr Hume lists as follows:

The raw materials – sulphuric acid from Prestonpans and Halifax, manganese dioxide from Devon, lime from Ireland and salt from the salt-pans along the estuary of the Forth – could all be brought in through the Forth and Clyde Canal.

Coal could be fetched from the Lanarkshire coalfield, via the Monkland Canal, without the need to pay double canal dues.

An adequate water supply.

A good supply of labour. Glasgow was only a quarter of a mile away.

The works was conveniently situated to supply the developing Glasgow cotton industry and the bleachfields in both Scotland and Ireland.

In addition to these advantages, Tennant benefitted from the large area of the site, which gave him plenty of room for tipping waste products, and from the fortunate fact that, since the works was situated to the north of Glasgow, the prevailing south-west wind carried the poisonous fumes away, rather than towards heavily populated areas, at least for most of the time. St Rollux was further helped, from 1831 onwards, by the opening of the Glasgow and Garnskirk Railway, which had its Glasgow terminus adjoining the works.

All the factors mentioned above were undoubtedly important, but, since they could have been identified and assessed by anyone with access to a good library and to maps going back to the 1790s, it is a little difficult to follow Mr Hume's argument that industrial archaeology can help to decide why Tennant established his new chemical works where he did. The real answer to his question, 'What was the value of this site to the industrial archaeologist?' is surely rather different and depends on whether the industrial archaeologist visited it before or after 1964, or at an even earlier date. If, for instance, he had been fortunate enough,

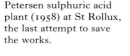

Petersen sulphuric acid plant (1958) at St Rollux, the last attempt to save the works.

as Mr Hume was not, to have been around in 1920, before the 455 foot chimney, the 'St Rollux stack', was felled, he might have marvelled at the grandeur of this great monument, built in 1842, which one observer described as being 'beyond the prose of street-walking mortals, the landmark of Glasgow as St. Paul's is of London'. This enormous steeple, he might have reflected, is on an industrial cathedral dedicated to the manufacture of bleaching powder and sulphuric acid, and that indeed would have taken him very close to the centre of what Victorian industry was all about, not forgetting, of course, that the main purpose of this prodigious height was to get at least some of the dreadful smoke well up into the air and away from the inhabitants of Glasgow and the surrounding countryside. The value of the site, in short, was its power to arouse wonder and sadness, to remind one that nothing is permanent, and that even the greatest chemical works in the world, which St Rollux at one time was, can be completely rubbed off the face of the earth in a matter of months. The capacity of industrial archaeology, especially the archaeology of the naked site, to arouse such feelings should not be underrated.

The oil refinery at Engelsberg, Sweden (1876)[8]

The petroleum industry is generally reckoned to have begun in 1859, when Edwin L. Drake succeeded in drilling a well at Oil Creek, near Titusville, Pennsylvania. At this time there were already in the United States about 50 plants where oil was distilled from bituminous coal and then chemically treated to make it suitable for lighting purposes. The same primitive type of refinery, which did little more than boil the oil, was used to begin with for crude oil, mainly to produce kerosene. Within a few years, however, larger and more specialised refineries were required to make a wider range of petroleum products and in much greater quantities. The old refineries, of which there were hundreds, were then closed and no example of this early type survives in the United States.

One is, however, still to be seen on an island near Engelsberg, in Central Sweden. It is intact and provides useful information about the methods used a century ago. The person responsible for building it was August Ålund, who had previously experimented with a refinery at Annelund. When this was struck by lightning and destroyed, he bought an island known as Bear Island (Barrön) on Lake Ämmänningen, built an oil factory on it and invited the public to take shares in his company, pointing out that he had discovered a method of distillation, using

---

[8] This account is based on an article by Per Ågren, 'Engelsberg's Oil Factory: an early petroleum refinery', in *Daedalus*, the Yearbook of the Technical Museum, Stockholm, 1967, pp. 9–30. Mr Ågren was formerly Technical Director of the Nynas Petroleum Refineries of the Axel Johnson Group, the present owners of the Engelsberg refinery.

steam, which allowed him to separate what he called the 'thin' (sträva) oils from the 'fat' (feta) oils. From the fat oils he could, he said, produce lubricants and greases which would fetch a higher price than the lighting oils. The capital was raised and the plant operated successfully from 1877 to 1902.

The factory is built of blast-furnace bricks, rendered on both sides with plaster. It had a wooden roof, covered with felt To begin with there were eight retorts, set in brickwork, but four more were added subsequently. These are made of rivetted boiler plate and each holds 300 gallons. A wood-burning furnace is provided for each retort. The condensing took place in a tin-coated copper cooler. There is a walled-steam boiler, with two walled-in superheaters. The equipment is completed by four iron tanks, each holding 500 gallons, and a filter press for solid paraffin.

Before the refinery began to operate, it was inspected by the

Map showing position of Engelsberg refinery, Sweden, in relation to the lakes and other inland waterways used for transporting crude petroleum and refined products.

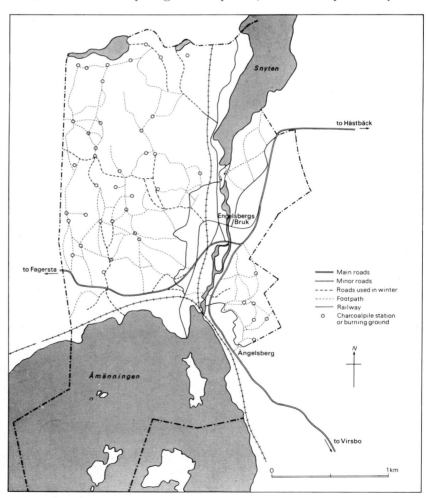

authorities. They had a number of objections to the arrangements. What particularly displeased and worried them was the fact that the fire-boxes of the retorts and the steam boiler had been put in the same room as the refining equipment and the tanks for the distilled products. To improve matters, they insisted that all the furnace openings and smoke channels should be insulated from the refinery proper by means of brick walls and fireproof ceilings. Airlocks were to be installed to separate the still room from the furnace room, and an earth bank was to be constructed to prevent any leaking oil from getting into the lake.

Distillation was not continuous. It was carried out in batches of between 210 and 260 gallons for each retort, the crude oil being let down from tanks on an upper floor. After distillation, the kerosene was chemically treated to improve its colour and smell, and blown through with air to remove any water. The oil that was to be used as a machine or cylinder lubricant was refined in what were known as bleaching vessels, suspended in two rows in the lake. The vats used for this purpose were made of iron plates, and the oil remained in them for three to four weeks, to improve the colour and to remove acids. This was particularly important in oil that was to be used for sewing machines and gun barrels, where the corrosion of the steel by acid would have caused serious problems.

Engelsberg: exterior of main building of refinery.

Records exist showing the percentage of the different kinds of product which were obtained from the crude oil. By volume, they were:

Kerosene	31.0%
Lubricating oil	17 5%
Lighting oil	12.5%
Gas oil	12.5%
Cart grease	6.0%
Pressed solid paraffin	6.0%
Light machine oil	1.1%
Losses	13.4%

The crude oil arrived in barrels and the finished products were distributed in barrels made at the factory. The customers were mostly mines and iron and steelworks, receiving their supplies either by rail or, more commonly, by means of the Strömsholm Canal.

By the close of the century, the refining of crude oil was becoming steadily less profitable, as a result of competition from imported refined oils. Refining ceased in 1902 and the company went into liquidation in 1907. It was bought by AB Oljefabriken, which carried on business trading in oil, but not refining it, until 1927, when it too went into liquidation. At that point it was bought by the well-known industrialist, Axel Johnson, who owned the ironworks at Engelsberg. The refinery was fortunate in its new owner. The Axel Johnson Group has expanded greatly during the past half century and, following the example of its founder, a man with a keen and active interest in the history of tech-

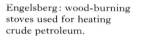

Engelsberg: wood-burning stoves used for heating crude petroleum.

nology, it has shown itself anxious to preserve historic material in its ownership. The refinery has been carefully maintained since Axel Johnson bought it and it is now classified and protected as a national monument.

One can see from this brief account that the preservation of this little refinery or 'oil factory' as the Swedes prefer to call it, was due to a remarkable chain of circumstances, hardly likely to be repeated elsewhere.

Two gunpowder mills

Black powder is a mixture of saltpetre, brimstone and charcoal. The technique for manufacturing it was gradually improved between the mid-thirteenth century, when it was first known, and the nineteenth. The various stages, as they operated in the latter period, have been usefully summarised in a flow diagram by Robert A. Howard, of the Hagley Museum, Wilmington, Delaware, in an article written for the American Society for Industrial Archaeology.[9] They relate to the complete process, as it was performed at the local Hagley Yard, but it can be taken as representative of the normal practice at the time, both in Europe and America.

In general, Mr Howard noted, two types of building have been used in the production of black powder. The first had three thick, solid masonry walls to channel any explosion in the desired direction, and was normal until the late nineteenth century. The second began to be found by the turn of the century. It had very light walls, often of timber, and was based on the new theory that the less masonry and rubble there was flying about in the air after an explosion the better.

Archaeological evidence of black powder making is to be found at two sites, one in England and the other in the United States. Both are preserved and safeguarded as historic monuments, but the nature and context of the restoration work carried out in each place has been very different. So, too, have the circumstances which have allowed the remains of these factories to survive. The two cases are presented here partly for their intrinsic interest and partly to show how very fortuitous such survivals are.

The British site lies on the outskirts of the Kentish town of Faversham, which can be claimed with some certainty to be the birthplace of the gunpowder industry in this country, not later than 1558. Its story, together with an account of the archaeological work carried out on the site, has been told by Arthur Percival.[10] The choice of Faversham as a

9   'Black Powder Manufacture', *I.A. : Journal of the Society for Industrial Archaeology*, Vol. 1, No. 1, Summer 1975, pp. 13–29.
10 'The Faversham Gunpowder Industry', *Faversham Papers*, No. 4, 1967. A revised version of this paper, with the same title, was published in *Industrial Archaeology*, Vol. 5, Nos. 1 and 2, February and May 1968.

Powder Sequence

Complete Process As Performed At Hagley Yard
From *c.* 1870 To 1921 To Produce Sporting Powder

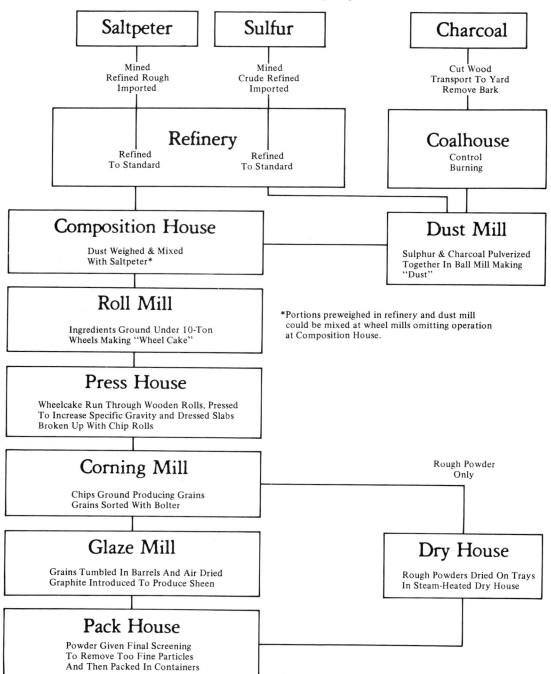

Saltpeter

Mined
Refined Rough
Imported

Sulfur

Mined
Crude Refined
Imported

Charcoal

Cut Wood
Transport To Yard
Remove Bark

Refinery

Refined
To Standard

Refined
To Standard

Coalhouse

Control
Burning

Composition House

Dust Weighed & Mixed
With Saltpeter*

Dust Mill

Sulphur & Charcoal Pulverized
Together In Ball Mill Making
"Dust"

Roll Mill

Ingredients Ground Under 10-Ton
Wheels Making "Wheel Cake"

*Portions preweighed in refinery and dust mill
could be mixed at wheel mills omitting operation
at Composition House.

Press House

Wheelcake Run Through Wooden Rolls, Pressed
To Increase Specific Gravity and Dressed Slabs
Broken Up With Chip Rolls

Corning Mill

Chips Ground Producing Grains
Grains Sorted With Bolter

Rough Powder
Only

Glaze Mill

Grains Tumbled In Barrels And Air Dried
Graphite Introduced To Produce Sheen

Dry House

Rough Powders Dried On Trays
In Steam-Heated Dry House

Pack House

Powder Given Final Screening
To Remove Too Fine Particles
And Then Packed In Containers

Diagram showing manufacturing units and technical processes at Hagley Mills, Delaware in the late nineteenth and early twentieth centuries.

centre was not accidental. To meet the needs of the Army and the Navy, the principal customers, the factory had to be in the south of England, where the main arsenals and dockyards were located, and it had to have easy access to sea or river transport. It was necessary, too, for it to be close to a seaport, since two of its raw materials, sulphur and saltpetre, were imported, the first from Italy and the second mainly from India. The third ingredient, charcoal, had to be made locally – it was bulky – and since two tons of wood were required to make one ton of gunpowder, it was best for the factory to be close to, if not in a well-wooded area. And, lastly, a reliable water supply was needed, to power the mills. Faversham fulfilled all these criteria.

The arrangement of the various works on the Faversham site is shown

Map showing sites of the gunpowder mills at Faversham, Kent.

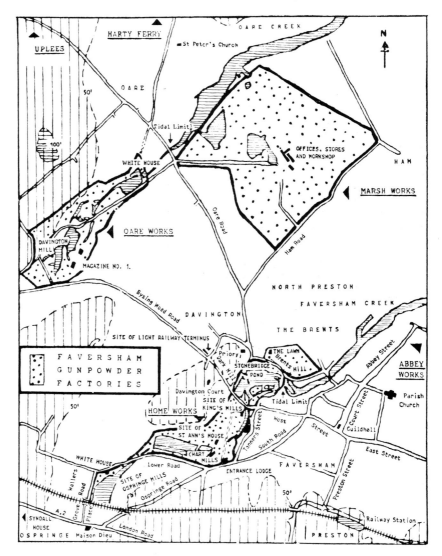

on the map. They were built at different times. The original works was established on what is now a housing estate, St Ann's. Over the years, this first works, the Home Works, gradually expanded, reaching its final form at the end of the eighteenth century. Towards the end of the sixteenth century another factory, usually known as the Oare Works, was established on the Oare Creek. Until 1760 both these works were privately owned and run, but in 1760 the Home Works was taken over by the Government and became the Royal Gunpowder Factory, under the control of the Board of Ordnance. A programme of expansion was put in hand and by 1774 the factory had a capacity of 364 tons a year. To produce this, there were 11 watermills and 5 horse-mills, for grinding, granulating and mixing the powder.

There were many accidents. A particularly bad one occurred in 1781, when three tons of powder exploded, destroying the corning mill and the dusting house and causing considerable damage to the town of Faversham itself. After this, two steps were taken. Work on the more dangerous processes was transferred to a new site, the Marsh Works, which was well clear of the town, safety precautions were intensified and a set of Works Regulations was drawn up. These, issued in 1786, were to serve as a basis for all later rule-books in the industry. They provide not only a guide to the risks incurred in making powder, but also to some of the equipment in use.

1. If any workman belonging to the Royal Mills wears his slippers out of those parts of the Works where they are intended to be used for safety, or wears his own shoes into any of the said works, any such workman is to be chequed a day's pay for the first offence and if they should so far forget their country as a second time to run the risque of blowing the works up through such negligence they are to be discharged and on no account to be entered again.

2. The respective officers will please to give the strictest orders for having the several works cleaned out whenever they require it, and the cleaning is not to be confined to the floors only but to every part of the machinery and buildings to prevent any accumulation of dust, which in a powder manufactory must be attended with the greatest danger.

3. The hinges of all doors and window shutters are to be kept well oiled, also the pulleys over which the window lines go and the grooves in which the sashes slide to be brushed and scraped as often as occasion requires to prevent any dangerous friction. The cogs, axles and other

parts of the machinery to be kept well soaped and oiled as has hitherto been the custom.

4. The pulleys belonging to the valves of the powder stoves must be carefully examined and if there is a possibility of the ropes rubbing against wood or if the sheaves of the pulleys are made of wood they must be altered, so that the ropes may rub against copper, and the sheaves be made of the same metal.

5. Whenever the powder tumbrils are required to come near a building in which powder is contained, brick rubbish must be laid on the ground after it has been very carefully examined that no flint or other stones remain therein.

6. Each of the corning houses are to be completed with canvas receivers in the dust troughs and a canvas curtain similar to that ordered for No. 1 corning house.

7. When barrels of gunpowder are lifted out of boats to be stored in the magazines or powder vessels, the strictest attention must be paid to have them brushed all over with a soft brush to prevent any grit hanging to them. The wheelbarrows on which they are to be carried, the hold of the vessel in which it is to be laid to be cleaned in the same manner.

8. All the wheelbarrows which are used to carry powder are to be fitted with copper hoops and gudgeons instead of iron.

9. The floors of the cooperage must be kept as clean from sand or gravel as the magazine and the coopers must work in their magazine slippers to prevent any grit adhering to the barrels or charge tubs, and before any of the articles are issued from the cooperage they must be well brushed and cleaned.

Two main types of precaution were taken against the effects of blast, should an explosion occur. One was to build tall, thick walls in strategic positions and the other, less well known, was to plant screens of trees. For this reason, the sites of many British gunpowder works are marked by a variety of fine trees. The Home Works at Faversham has at least twelve varieties. A number of these trees are now protected by Tree Preservation Orders and they certainly form part of the archaeology of the site.

In 1798 John Tickling, the Master Worker at the Faversham factory, made a series of sketches of the various processes which were in use there. They show a very close similarity between the mills at Faversham and those built by the du Ponts on the Brandywine River in the United States. The originals have unfortunately been lost, but the drawings were fortunately reproduced in a book published early in the present century.[11]

By the time of the Napoleonic Wars production at Faversham had been increased to nearly 600 tons a year and the works was employing a quarter of the male population in the town. After the end of the war, the demand for gunpowder dropped and the Government leased the Home Works to John Hall, who already owned the Oare Works. Hall subsequently bought both the Home and Marsh Works, bringing all three under the same ownership. A guncotton factory was built in 1846 at the Marsh Works. It was blown to pieces in the following year and from then on the works concentrated entirely on powder.

After the First World War and following the reorganisation of the British explosives industry, the Home Works was closed and the plant broken up and sold for scrap. One of the group of four mills known as

Chart Mills, Faversham, after restoration.

[11] E. A. Brayley Hodgetts, *The Rise and Progress of the British Explosives Industry* Whitaker, 1909.

Chart Mills was, however, deliberately left undisturbed. Oare and Marsh Works were shut down in 1934. A number of buildings associated with these two works survive, but the most important remains are those of the four incorporating mills, Chart Mills. One of these mills is almost complete. It has been restored and put into operating condition by the Faversham Society, with the help of grants from local councils, and it is now a popular tourist attraction.

It should be observed that the preservation and restoration of Chart Mills was due entirely to the initiative of a private society, which had very little money and which had to rely to a great extent on voluntary helpers to get the work done. A quite different situation existed in the case of the gunpowder mills – the famous Eleutherian Mills – on the Brandywine River, near Wilmington, Delaware. The Eleutherian Mills were named after the man who established them, Eleuthère Irénée du Pont, who came to America in 1799, partly as a result of the disturbances caused by the French Revolution. There was a great demand for gunpowder in the United States, much helped by the 1812 war, and within 20 years du Pont's factory had become the largest industrial enterprise in America. Du Pont, with widespread interests in the chemical and textile industries, are now one of the most important concerns in the United States. Fortunately for the Brandywine Mills, the du Pont family has continued to live in the area and owns large estates at Winterthur, not far away. The Swiss name, Winterthur, incidentally, recalls the place from which the du Ponts originally came.

Hagley Museum, Wilmington, Delaware: diorama showing Press House at black powder factory.

The du Ponts, both the family and the company, have spent a great deal of money on the conservation of the historical relics along the Brandywine. A major museum and an historical research centre have been established, in addition to the many restored buildings. These include the Brandywine Village Historic District, which has a number of houses dating from the late eighteenth and early nineteenth centuries, together with shops and flour mills; E. I. du Pont's stone and stucco mansion, built in 1803, is open to the public. Its furnishings reflect the changing tastes and interests of the family over a period of nearly 150 years. Close to the house is the original du Pont Company Office, built in 1837. It continued to serve this purpose until 1890 and it has been recently restored to show it as it was in about 1850. The President's Office in the building is furnished with original pieces. Lammot du Pont, the grandson of the founder, was the company's first professional chemist. He carried out his experiments in a small workshop about a mile away. This has been moved closer to the house and furnished with the kind of equipment that was usual in a mid nineteenth-century laboratory.

Pair of restored powder mills on Brandywine River, Delaware. The massive masonry construction long since outdated, reflects the mistaken beliefs current at the time that the stronger the building, the greater the degree of protection against explosion.

After the du Ponts moved from the house at the Eleutherian Mills in 1890, the garden, on which Eleuthère himself had lavished a great deal of attention, became overgrown and eventually disappeared from sight altogether. This, too, has been fully restored, following excavations which showed the position of the paths, well, gazebo, hot-houses and other items. The house and garden are an important part of the Brandy-wine archaeology, illustrating as they do that gunpowder, in the early nineteenth century, was a highly profitable commodity. But the kernel of the site, economically and visually, is formed by the series of stone-built mills set in pairs along the bank of the Brandywine. Some have been fully restored, some merely 'stabilised' and, taken in conjunction with other buildings on the site, and with the magnificent exhibits in the nearby museum, they present a picture of gunpowder manufacturing which is unequalled anywhere in the world.

There are probably three lessons to be learned from the examples of Chart Mills and the Brandywine complex. The first is that some on-site remains are essential if one is to get a feeling of this particular industry as it was during its working days. Its rural nature especially is difficult to appreciate unless one has some physical evidence of its presence, which can be looked at in its context. Secondly, the area has to be considered as a whole. The odd remains, haphazardly preserved and dotted about among gravel pits, modern housing estates and copses at Faversham are, in their way, just as instructive and nostalgic as the carefully and expensively tended relics at Wilmington. But, in both cases, the houses, the factory and the memories of the men who worked at this dangerous trade go together. They have to be regarded as an integrated whole. The third consideration applies equally well to every site mentioned in this book. The survival of Chart Mills and the Brandywine Mills has been due to providential, unique circumstances. If ICI had not decided to spare Chart Mills from the 1934 holocaust, if the du Pont Company had gone into liquidation instead of prospering, the physical, on-site documentation of gunpowder making would not only be greatly the poorer, it would be almost non-existent. The industrial archaeologist can only count his blessings.

CONCLUSIONS

The main concern of this book has been with aims and methods, with the contribution which industrial archaeology can make to the study of history. It is regrettable that the examples chosen for discussion have had to be taken from a relatively small number of countries, an indication of the fact that the usefulness of the archaeological approach to modern history is not yet as widely appreciated as it should be and one day will be. At the time of writing there are signs that industrial archaeology, after taking a long time to germinate, is at last beginning to strike roots and grow in a number of countries where the material available for study is both abundant and interesting. Australia, India, Japan, Italy and Brazil are cases in point. Other parts of the world, such as Spain, the Soviet Union and Argentina, have not yet progressed beyond the stage of expressing a polite but passive interest.

There appear to be two main reasons why the spread of industrial archaeology as a philosophy and as a body of techniques, has been so curiously uneven. The first is fear, often closely linked to a feeling of inferiority, and the second academic conservatism. In the preceding pages, an attempt has been made to deal, indirectly and by implication, with both these obstacles to taking a broader and more creative look at industrial history, and it seemed useful at this point to state one or two of the arguments more succinctly and emphatically.

Like any other branch of archaeology, industrial archaeology is necessarily rooted in a study of physical remains and in personal observation of actual sites. A person who refuses to go and see for himself and who carries out all his researches in an office or library is not an industrial archaeologist. 'Physical remains' is, however, a loose term. There is no reason why it should not include objects in a museum, and an industrial archaeologist would have to be puritanical and narrow-minded in the extreme, not to say foolish, to refuse to interest himself in museum material merely because it had been removed from its original site. There is, even so, an essential difference between looking at something where it belongs and has a function, and looking at the same object stripped of its environment and embalmed in a museum. The Chinese for a long time resisted the creation of museums for this reason. A piece of porcelain or a picture drew its life and, so to speak, its licence to exist from the room where it was originally placed. Transported to a museum and put in dead isolation in a showcase, it had little meaning any more. It had become a mere object. And so it is with an industrial site. London Bridge has been 'saved' by being taken to pieces, carried across the Atlantic and re-erected in a park in Nevada, but its significance has been completely lost in the process. From one point of view, one can welcome the 'preservation' of windmills, tanneries, blacksmiths' shops and the like in open-air museums but, torn from their roots, they are sad things and, more important, different things. They have changed their character. They may even undergo a double transformation. It is unfortunately not unknown for a museum to take an item of technical equipment and to display it as if it were a piece of sculpture, which is a subtle form of prostitution.

It is, of course, no more remarkable or eccentric to wish to study industrial sites than farm buildings or vernacular architecture. During the course of this book it has been repeatedly emphasised that there are certain thoughts, certain lines of enquiry, which are likely to present themselves to the mind and the imagination, when one observes this or that relic of the past in its context, when one can walk round it, peer into it, shine a light into dark places, stand inside it and generally get the feel of it. One cannot get the same results from a model or a photograph, even when these are supplemented by fragments of the old structure which has been destroyed. For those who find this difficult to believe, one can only ask if they would expect to experience the same sensation from looking at a model of St Peter's and St Peter's Square in Rome as from walking across the square and up the great steps and standing inside the basilica, looking up at the dome. There is no substitute for the thoughts and emotions which take place on the site, and this is as true of a cotton factory or country railway station as it is of a Palladian villa or a medieval castle.

As soon as one uses the word 'emotions' however, one begins to come under fire from those who have persuaded themselves that, to have any value, all scholarship must be ice-cold, with the head working flat out and the heart and senses put into a deep sleep. It is time that this attitude were castigated and seen for the nonsense it is. In order to understand the past and to talk and write sense about it, one has to feel the past. A great deal of bad and indeed useless historical writing has been inflicted on the public from a failure to realise this or, if it has been realised, from a lack of the courage required to put it into practice. How, for example, can one write about mortality rates in Victorian England without trying to understand what it was like to have child after child die from complaints which the doctors were powerless to cure, or to have one's family go down with cholera or typhoid because there was no proper drainage system and the water supply was a menace to health. To present statistics about population, birth rates, death rates, or epidemics outside the context of fatalism, trusting in God and helplessness which characterised the early part of Victoria's reign, and outside the new atmosphere of indignation, determination and knowledge which characterised public health measures 50 years later is to throw away the opportunity of bringing figures alive. Similarly, it is idiotic to think of technical developments in the field of textile machinery without at the same time trying to imagine oneself a woman several months pregnant working ten hours a day in a hot, dusty and appallingly noisy environment and having to be continuously careful, in a room not well lit and over-crowded with machinery, that her clothing and her hair did not get caught up in the machine or the driving belt, especially if she should happen to slip on the oily floor.

There is no point in saying that industrial accidents and the ten-hour working day are the preserve of one kind of historian, the factory build-ings and the machines of another, and the woman's thoughts as she worked of yet a third. This is academic specialisation gone mad. The industrial past means all three of these things, brought into the same focus and considered together. And at that point political considerations, inevitably and inescapably, begin to enter industrial archaeology. They do this in two ways, first, by allowing the researcher more or less free-dom to explore where he pleases and to bring his investigations to what he feels to be a logical and professionally satisfying conclusion and, second, by putting pressure on him, or by not putting pressure on him, to extract a meaning, a message, from his work which is acceptable to the fashion and political philosophy of the country in which he lives. One has to keep constantly in mind, when writing a book like this one, that there are relatively few countries of the world in which the indus-trial archaeologist is permitted to work freely. Windmills, watermills and, in general, anything constructed before 1850 are politically fairly safe. These things can be visited, written about and photographed without much fear of falling foul of the authorities. Anything later has to be approached with great circumspection. In most parts of the world now, any attempt to take pictures of railway installations of any kind, including stations, ports and harbours, bridges, aerodromes and air-craft, and factories of all kinds is not only severely and officially dis-couraged, but is likely to lead to the arrest of anyone found acting in this way, especially if he should happen to be a foreigner. Even among natives of the country concerned, the collection of the reminiscences of old workers is regarded as a highly suspect activity, ostensibly because 'it unsettles the old people', and very little of it goes on, except in the case of a dying craft, such as working on a handloom or in a water-driven forge, where it may be thought desirable, and politically innocuous, to have a record, sometimes on film, of how the work is actually carried out.

It is for this reason, more than any other, that industrial archaeology has blossomed in what is called, for good reason, the Free World, the Western-type democracy, and why it has been restricted elsewhere to that much less dangerous form of scholarship, the history of technology. The decision can always be justified, and is, by saying that the history of technology is 'scientific', whatever that may mean, while industrial archaeology is too vague a field to be worthy of serious academic attention. What is really meant, however, is that industrial archaeology, in the sense in which the present book has employed the term, is difficult to bring under tight administrative control, especially if groups of amateur enthusiasts are allowed to follow their fancy in exploring the working past of their own district. In order to save face and to keep up with the international academic Joneses, it may be decided to pretend, by adopting the term as a façade, that one is engaging in industrial archaeology, when in fact all that is being practised and offered is very old wine in new bottles. Anyone who doubts this should sit through such occasions as the Second International Congress on Industrial Monuments, held in 1975 in Bochum, in the German Federal Republic, and note the difference between the character and intention of the papers presented by the delegates from the Western and Eastern bloc countries.

There are therefore two causes of the obvious fact that the examples selected for discussion in this book have been drawn from a fairly small number of countries. One, as indicated above, is the political soil and climate favourable to the growth of industrial archaeology. Some improvement is noticeable here, but the process is regrettably slow. The other source of geographic imbalance is the overuse in Britain of the term 'Industrial Revolution' in connexion with industrial archaeology. This has brought about something akin to an inferiority complex on the part of countries whose industrial development has taken place during the twentieth century, rather than the eighteenth and nineteenth. If one insists that industrial archaeology is mainly concerned with the relics of the Industrial Revolution, one must not be surprised if areas of the world which were still mainly agricultural a century ago or 50 years ago feel themselves to be outside the club. Once it is made clear to them that each country has its own time scale of development, and that 'early industrialisation' does not mean the same in Romania, Brazil or Tanzania as it does in Britain, Belgium or the United States, the problem begins to solve itself. Each country, even in the Western world, has its own special kind of industrial remains and monuments, and the industrial archaeologist is just as interested in the early days of aeroplanes and nylon, which belong to the twentieth century, as with the beginnings of steam engines and electric power supply, which are much earlier. But, no matter what the date of an industrial site may be, the broad principles of investigation remain the same. One is always concerned with what can be seen on the site within its human, social and environmental context. Seen from this point of view, the links between industrial archaeology and geography are quite as strong as with industrial, economic or technical history. What must be emphasised with all possible force, more particularly for the benefit of those countries such as the Soviet Union which have not so far appeared to see a great deal of point or value in industrial archaeology, is that it is not a synonym for the history of technology and that it cannot be practised, as either an academic or an educational exercise, solely or mainly in museums and libraries. It is essentially a field study and a humane study, with everything that these two adjectives imply.

SELECT BIBLIOGRAPHY

A bibliography of industrial archaeology is not to be confused, as it usually is, with a bibliography of industrial and technological history. What is provided below is intended to illustrate the range and nature of books dealing specifically with industrial archaeology. That the bulk of them are British, German, Swedish and American is inevitable, since these are the countries where industrial archaeology has so far made its strongest appeal, where conditions have been most favourable and where most work has been done. Ten years from now, if present trends continue, France, Italy, the Netherlands, Australia and Japan will all, one hopes, be strongly represented.

Those in search of a list of books and articles which provide the necessary general background will find what they require by combining the excellent Further Reading sections of these books:

Armytage, W. H. G. *A Social History of Engineering* Massachusetts Institute of Technology, 1966

Ashton, T. S. *The Industrial Revolution 1760–1830* Oxford University Press, 1948

Habakkuk, H. J. *American and British Technology in the Nineteenth Century* Cambridge University Press, 1967

Kranzberg, Melvin and Pursell, Carroll W. (eds.) *Technology in Western Civilisation* 2 vols., Oxford University Press, 1967

Mathias, Peter *The First Industrial Nation: an Economic History of Britain, 1700–1914* Methuen, 1969

The information given in these bibliographies is not repeated here.

What might be called the bibliography of industrial archaeology proper falls into two parts, works concerned with the subject in general and works dealing with particular sites or regions. Books of both types inevitably become to some degree antiquated in their approach and method, and many of the sites which they describe or use for illustrative purposes have disappeared or been considerably changed in some way since they were originally published. The philosophy of industrial archaeology is only now beginning to crystallise out and this means that all the pioneering works, produced from the mid-Sixties onwards, have an old-fashioned flavour, which may well have a charm and appeal of its own, but which marks off the books in question as belonging to their period, when industrial archaeology was still in its first describing and collecting stage. Anything published before 1975 should therefore be used with caution and discrimination.

Industrial archaeology in general or on a worldwide basis

Hudson, Kenneth *The Archaeology of Industry* The Bodley Head, 1976
Pannell, J. P. M. *Illustrated History of Civil Engineering* Thames & Hudson, 1964
Pannell, J. P. M. *The Techniques of Industrial Archaeology* revised and edited by J. K. Major David and Charles, 1974

Particular sites or regions

EUROPE
General
Cantacuzino, Sherban *New Uses for Old Buildings* Watson-Guptill, 1975
Hudson, Kenneth *A Guide to the Industrial Archaeology of Europe* Adams and Dart, 1971
Jespersen, Anders (ed.) *Proceedings of the Second International Symposium on Molinology* Brede, Lyngby: Danske Møllers Venner, 1971

Belgium
University of Antwerp *Colloquium industriële archeologie van de Antwerpse haven* University of Antwerp, 1975
Wieser-Benedetti, Hans *Le Paysage de l'Industrie* Brussels: Editions des Archives de l'Architecture Moderne, 1975

Czechoslovakia
Majer, Jiří (ed.) *Studie z dějin hornictví* (Studies in the History of Mining) Annual vols., Prague: National Technical Museum, 1969 onwards

Denmark
Jespersen, Anders *Windmills on Bornholm, Denmark* Virum, Denmark: privately printed, 1958

France
Rolt, L. T. C. *From Sea to Sea: the Canal du Midi* Allen Lane, 1973

German Democratic Republic
Sillén, Gunnar *Industriminnen i DDR* Stockholm: Riksantikvarieämbelet, No. 15, 1970
Wächtler, Eberhard and Wagenbreth, Otfried *Technische Denkmale in der Deutschen Democratischen Republik* Berlin: Kulturbund der DDR, 1973

German Federal Republic
Borchers, Günther *Denkmäler der Stolberger Messingindustrie* Bonn: Landeskonservator Rheinland, 1971
Borchers, Günther *Arbeitersiedlungen* 1, Bonn: Landeskonservator Rheinland, 1975
Borchers, Günther *Arbeitersiedlungen* 2, Bonn: Landeskonservator Rheinland, 1975
Föhl, Axel *Technische Denkmale im Rheinland* Bonn: Landeskonservator Rheinland, 1976
Grunsking, Eberhard *Vier Siedlungen in Duisburg* Bonn: Landeskonservator Rheinland, 1975
Neumann, Eberhard G. *Industrie Architektur in Westfalen* Münster: Landeskonservator von Westfalen-Lippe, 1975
Schieck, Hans Friedrich and Schmidt, Norbert *Die Schwebebahn in Wuppertal* Bonn: Landeskonservator Rheinland, 1976

Slotta, Rainer *Technische Denkmäler in der Bundesrepublik Deutschland* Bochum: Bergbau Museum, 1975
Werner, Ernst *Die Eisenbahnbrücke über die Wupper beim Müngsten* Bonn: Kulturministerium Nordrhein-Westfalen, 1973

Great Britain

Atkinson, Frank (ed.) *Industrial Archaeology : Top Ten Sites in North-East England* F. Graham, 1971
Bracegirdle, Brian et al. *The Archaeology of the Industrial Revolution* Heinemann, 1973
Buchanan, R. A. *Industrial Archaeology in Britain* Penguin, 1972
Cossons, Neil *The BP Book of Industrial Archaeology* David & Charles, 1975
Cossons, Neil and Hudson, Kenneth *Industrial Archaeologist's Guide, 1971–73* David & Charles, 1971, 1973
Hague, Douglas B. and Christie, Rosemary *Lighthouses : their Architecture, History and Archaeology* Gomer Press, 1975
Hudson, Kenneth *Exploring Our Industrial Past* Hodder & Stoughton: Teach Yourself Books, 1975
Hudson, Kenneth *Industrial Archaeology : a New Introduction* John Baker, 1976
Hudson, Kenneth et al. Regional Industrial Series of Great Britain, David and Charles, 1966 onwards
Raistrick, Arthur *Industrial Archaeology : an Historical Survey* Eyre; Methuen, 1972
Rees, D. Morgan *Mines, Mills and Furnaces : Introduction to Industrial Archaeology in Wales* National Museum of Wales, 1969
Rolt, L. T. C. (general editor) Longman's Industrial Archaeology Series, 1971 onwards, with volumes on *Navigable Waterways*; *Iron and Steel*; *Roads and Vehicles*; *The Textile Industry*; *Civil Engineering*; *Railways*; *Mechanical Engineering*; *Railways*; *The Chemical Industry*; *Building Materials*; *Coal-Mining*
Wailes, Rex *Windmills in England* Architectural Press, 1948

Poland

Krygier, Eugeniusz et al. *Katalog Zabytków Budownictwa Przemysłowego w Polsce* (Catalogue of the Technical Monuments of Poland) 15 vols, Wroclaw, Warsaw and Kraków; Polish Academy of Sciences, 1959 onwards

Sweden

Holtze, Bengt et al. *Swedish Industrial Archaeology : Engelsberg Ironworks, a Pilot Project* Swedish Royal Academy of Letters, History and Antiquities, 1976
Nisser, Marie *Hyttor i Orebro län* Stockholm: Jernkontorets Berghistoriska Utskott, 1974
Nisser, Marie *Träkolshyttor : Orebro län* Stockholm: Från Bergslag och Bondebygd, 1971
Nisser, Marie and Sjunnesson, Helene *Massafabriker och Pappersbruk i Värmland och Dalsland* Stockholm: Svenska Pappers- och Cellulosaingeniörsföreningen, 1973

NORTH AMERICA

Abbott, Diane B. (ed.) *The Lower Peninsula of Michigan : an Inventory of Historic Engineering and Industrial Sites* Washington DC: Historic American Engineering Record, 1976

Armstrong, John B. *Factory under the Elms : a History of Harrisville, New Hampshire, 1774–1969* Cambridge, Massachusetts: Massachusetts Institute of Technology Press, 1969

Carter, William *Ghost Towns of the West* Menlo Park, California: Lane Magazine & Book Co., 1971

Comp, T. Alan (ed.) *New England : an Inventory of Engineering and Industrial Sites* Washington DC: Historic American Engineering Record, 1974

Glass, Brent D. (ed.) *North Carolina : an Inventory of Historic Engineering and Industrial Sites* North Carolina Division of Archives and History, and Historic American Engineering Record, 1974

Heisler, John P. *The Canals of Canada* Canadian Historic Sites, Occasional Papers in Archaeology and History, No. 8. National Historic Sites Service, National and Historic Parks Branch, Department of Indian Affairs and Northern Development, Ottawa, 1973

Holland, Francis Ross *America's Lighthouses* Brattleboro, Vermont: The Stephen Greene Press, 1972

Kidney, Walter C. *Working Places : the Adaptive Use of Industrial Buildings* Pittsburgh, Pennsylvania: Ober Park Associates, Inc., 1976

Legget, Robert *Rideau Waterway* University of Toronto Press 1955; revised edition, 1972

Molloy, Peter M. *The Lower Merrimack Valley : an Inventory of Historic Engineering and Industrial Sites* Historic American Engineering Record, and Merrimack Valley Textile Museum, 1975

Paul, R. W. *Mining Frontiers of the Far West, 1848–1880* Holt, Rinehart and Winston, 1963

Sande, Theodore Anton *Industrial Archeology : a New Look at the American Heritage* Brattleboro, Vermont: The Stephen Greene Press, 1976

Sande, Theodore Anton (ed.) *The New England Textile Mill Survey – Selections from the Historic American Buildings Survey* Washington DC: Historic American Buildings Survey, 1971

Stott, Peter H. *Long Island : an Inventory of Historic Engineering and Industrial Sites* Society for the Preservation of Long Island Antiquities, and Historic American Engineering Record, 1974

Thomas, Selmer (ed.) *Delaware : an Inventory of Historic Engineering and Industrial Sites* Eleutherian Mills-Hagley Foundation, and Historic American Engineering Record, 1974

Waite, Diana S. et al. *Historic Cohoes* Cohoes, New York: Model Cities Agency, 1971

Waite, John G. *Iron Architecture in New York City* Albany: New York State Historic Trust, and the Society for Industrial Archeology, 1972

Wolle, Muriel Sibell *The Bonanza Trail* Indiana University Press, 1952

SOUTH AFRICA

Walton, James *Water Mills, Windmills, and Horse-Mills of South Africa* Cape Town and Johannesburg: C. Struik, 1974

Periodicals containing articles on various aspects of industrial archaeology

Much of the information needed by industrial archaeologists is to be found in periodicals not directly devoted to the subject at all and in the journals of professional societies. *The Transactions of the Newcomen Society* have been published annually since 1920 and cover a wide range of technical subjects. In Britain *The Engineer* (1856 onwards) and *Engineering* (1966 onwards) contain valuable contemporary accounts of new engineering achievements and so do the *Journals* of the Institutions of Civil, Mechanical, Mining and Electrical Engineers. Comparable journals in other countries, especially France, Germany and the United States, are equally worth searching. *Technology and Culture* takes a world view, and follows a policy exactly indicated by its title.

In Britain, the *Architects' Journal* and the *Architectural Review* and in the United States *Historic Preservation*, the *Journal of the Society of Architectural Historians* and *Architectural Record* often publish articles and notes which come within the field of industrial archaeology.

The quarterly *Journal of Industrial Archaeology* provided, between 1963 and 1973, an unequalled opportunity for the publication of research. After a gap of three years, its place in Britain was taken by the *Industrial Archaeology Review*, which has three issues a year. It is supplemented by the more topical *Newsletter* of the Association for Industrial Archaeology.

In the United States, the excellent *Newsletter* of the Society for Industrial Archeology, based at the Smithsonian Institution, has been appearing regularly since 1972. The Society's *Journal* is published annually. Both the *Newsletter* and the *Journal* include material both from the United States and Canada.

The West German periodical *Technische Kulturdenkmale*, published four times a year by the Open-Air Museum at Hagen, sets a high standard of production and editing, and so does *Der Anschnitt*, which deals with mining history and is published by the Mining Museum in Bochum. *Der Anschnitt* has a very detailed and thorough international bibliography of books and articles concerned with the history of mining.

Since the mid-Fifties the periodical field has been greatly enriched by the appearance of the journals and bulletins of a number of newly-established societies with specialised interests. The *Bulletin of the Historical Metallurgy Group* is of this type and so, in America, is *Old Mill News* and the *Bulletin of the American Canal Society*. Many of the preservation societies, local and national, publish reports which include details of industrial sites and so, in Britain, do the county archaeological societies.

A complete annual bibliography of periodical articles which have a direct bearing on industrial archaeology is badly needed. Until it appears, information about current projects will remain frustratingly partial and haphazard. Meanwhile, it is comforting to realise that the *Newsletter* of the American Society for Industrial Archeology has, for the six years of its existence, missed very little of any consequence in the way of articles and books published in North America and finds room to include much foreign material as well.

INDEX

nd
8

1979

3/07